THE MONEY

THE MONEY

THE BATTLE FOR HOWARD HUGHES'S BILLIONS

James R. Phelan

Lewis Chester

RANDOM HOUSE
NEW YORK

LIBRARY OF CONGRESS CATALOGING-IN-PUBLICATION DATA
Phelan, James R.
The money: the battle for Howard Hughes's billions /
James R. Phelan and Lewis Chester
p. cm.
Includes bibliographical references and index.
ISBN 0-394-55637-2 (hardcover)
1. Hughes, Howard, 1905–1976—Estate. I. Chester, Lewis.
II. Title.
KF759.H83P46 1997
338.7'67'092—dc21 97-3985

Random House website address: http://www.randomhouse.com/
Printed in the United States of America on acid-free paper
2 4 6 8 9 7 5 3
First Edition

BOOK DESIGN BY JO ANNE METSCH

NOTE TO THE READER

BE ADVISED THAT this is not another biography of Howard Hughes, whose far-out life already has inspired a plentitude. This is a book about his money, which was his benefactor and most loyal friend for a half century. It propelled a shy Texas teenager out of obscurity into a remarkable variety of careers, into celebrity, and affixed the title "billionaire" to his name as if he had been so christened. It survived his passing and took on a life of its own as bizarre as that of its departed owner.

His money transformed Hughes into a hyperactive Hollywood director-producer at the improbable age of twenty-four and then, a few years later, into a neo-Lindbergh who broke every flying speed record in sight, including that for circling the earth. His money changed him from an ill-at-ease male wallflower into a world-class Lothario who pursued a throng of well-known Hollywood and social beauties. While so occupied, he designed and piloted, on its solitary flight of one mile, the largest plane ever built and also expanded a small domestic carrier into the giant international airline TWA. In his spare time, he put together the nation's pioneer aerospace and electronics defense plant, Hughes Aircraft. In his declining years, he invaded Las Vegas with an enormous bankroll, acquired overnight, and bought up seven casinos when no individual had ever owned even one.

To many, such an embarrassment of riches is an enviable American success story. But his death, on April 5, 1976, disclosed Hughes as a shocking American horror story. He had fled Las Vegas in 1970 into exile, where he wandered for six years in his own private asylum, the passive victim of such neglect that neither he nor his keepers dared expose him to public view. He died in midair on an emergency flight from Acapulco to a hospital in Houston, his long-forsaken birthplace. His body was indistinguishable from that of a penniless derelict, dehydrated, underfed, weighing only ninety-two pounds. He was ravaged by years of drug abuse, with broken needles embedded in his arms, and by a wide assortment of ailments despite the presence of four private doctors in his sixteen-man entourage.

His plight gave a cruel twist to the axiom that money cannot buy happiness. Hughes's money bought him an inordinate amount of misery. His money not only paid the lofty salaries, jet travel, and sumptuous quarters for his entourage—a tab of more than $2 million a year—it also financed an elaborate charade to conceal the reason for the group's existence. His retreat into solitude had begun gradually after injuries he suffered in a near fatal plane crash in 1946 got him hooked on painkillers. He was last photographed or interviewed in the early fifties and went into near total seclusion in 1960 with two male nurse-clerk-aides, who eventually expanded to six or seven. His disappearance was explained as the mere quirk of a genius seeking privacy to cope with weighty matters in his vast empire. In fact, his embrace of solitude was accompanied by a descent of his behavior into pathology. He spent much of his time huddled in blacked-out bedrooms, naked or in his shorts, ingesting a variety of drugs, avoiding all contact except with his aides, watching the same movies over and over, and obsessively seeking to ward off phantom hordes of germs with layers of Kleenex and medieval rituals.

His persistent invisibility encrusted him with rumor and folk-tales, including stories that he had been freeze-dried for revival in the future or that he had died and been replaced by a lookalike by those running his empire and intent on continuing to do so. After his death, this paranoia gave way to stories that he hadn't died but that someone else's corpse had been placed in his coffin. He had then slipped off on some momentous mission of his own, to reappear in due course like the phoenix.

The size of Hughes's fortune had for years been the subject of intense speculation, with estimates ranging from $165 million to $2 billion. (His wealth had its origins in a busy little two-story tool factory in which he was left a major interest worth $600,000 when orphaned at eighteen by his father's death.) *Fortune* magazine once ranked Hughes second to J. Paul Getty, an assessment that elicited scorn from the recluse. Such ratings were of necessity imprecise, particularly as applied to Hughes, who owned most of his enterprises outright, unlisted on any stock exchange. His net worth was also subject to plunges and swoops similar to those on a rollercoaster, mainly because of his secretive and eccentric way of doing business. At the time of his death, there were more than sixty lawsuits pending against Hughes and his empire. But even with these complications, the value of the assets controlled by Hughes was in the region of $6 billion, approximately three times the terminal wealth of J. Paul Getty.

Part of this fortune was located in his personal estate, which consisted of an impressive grab bag of lifelong acquisitions. It included his motion pictures, an airline and a swarm of private planes, seven Nevada gambling casinos, rich stretches of undeveloped land in Nevada, Arizona, and California, large commercial chunks of Las Vegas (including its premier shopping center and an airport), his cash, his helicopter company, his mining claims plus a bag of old casino chips he had neglected to cash in, and a heap of Christmas presents he had received long ago and never bothered to open. These holdings, after many adventures in probate, would yield a billion dollars.

The larger part of Hughes's wealth was located in the Hughes Aircraft Company, the maker of guided missiles, communications satellites, and sophisticated electronic gear, and grown fat on contracts from the Defense Department and the Central Intelligence Agency. Originally, Hughes owned this industrial mammoth outright the way an ordinary citizen owns a wristwatch or a ballpoint pen, but he deliberately allocated his stock to a custom-built Medical Institute for the purpose of dodging taxes. Hughes was the Medical Institute's one and only controlling trustee, a position he used to ensure that no more than a trickle of funds ever leaked into medical research. The vast profits made by Hughes Aircraft were either plowed back into the company or used to finance other Hughes operations. The value of Hughes Aircraft would eventually be determined in the marketplace by its sale to General Motors in 1984 for $5.2 billion.

A one-man fortune of $6.2 billion is hard to comprehend, but one bemused accountant took on the chore of illustrating it, employing a ruler and a map of the United States. "If you cashed $6.2 billion into hundred-dollar bills and taped them end to end," he said, "it would make a continuous green ribbon that would stretch from New York all the way across the continent to California—and then back east to a point in Pennsylvania."

By dying without leaving a discoverable will, without nominating a successor trustee to take over Hughes Aircraft, and without a legally established place of residence—another by-product of his zeal for tax evasion—Hughes guaranteed a chaotic future for his empire. More than a thousand people would hit the Hughes greenback trail, staking claims of heirship to his fortune. This fever of greed, fantasy, and legal contention was fueled not only by the magnitude of the money but by the sense that much of it was up for grabs.

There were those who lusted for The Money, fought for it, fantasized about it, lied for it, forged for it. One of the many fake wills that surfaced had such an ingenious scenario behind it that it was made into a popular movie, *Melvin and Howard,* which still surfaces on TV. Heirship claims clogged the judicial system with a horrendous tangle of litigation for more than a decade after Hughes's death. The throng included purported wives and mistresses, purported business partners, self-proclaimed children and self-described bastards, and any number of people asserting undying intimacy with the reclusive billionaire. Many fantasized that a remote perch, real or rumored, on the Hughes family tree would enrich them. Some had weird stories that turned out to be true, others had plausible tales that tended to fall apart. Nothing was wholly predictable, aside from the resolute hopefulness of the claimants. Among the more tenacious was a black man who maintained that the deeply bigoted billionaire was his father. He supported this with a photo of himself, clad in a dashiki, pointing out to the probate authorities that he was six feet four inches tall, "the same as my daddy."

Our narrative is about the winners and losers in this long and sometimes epic struggle, but it is the improbable character of Hughes himself that shapes all the events. To die without leaving a will is in no way typical of the very rich. Disposition of their wealth is an obligation that many view as mandatory and perform with quiet pleasure. Good friends are remembered, a favorite relative is rewarded for attentiveness and obedience, and rebels are punished retroactively for transgressions. J. Paul Getty revised his will twenty-one times, making seven revisions in his last three years, increasing or diminishing his benefactions as their recipients rose or fell in his favor.

Given the obsession with control Hughes exhibited throughout his life, it is indeed baffling that he should have died without a will disposing of The Money in meticulous conformity with his wishes. Although an extensive search after his death produced no valid testament, it cannot be said with certainty that he did not leave one because of the difficulty of proving a negative. The possibility that he did execute a valid will that someone subsequently destroyed cannot be completely ruled out.

One trait in his makeup could explain the absence of a will. Along with his addiction to control, he was plagued by an apparently contradictory aversion to making decisions. He was a notorious procrastinator who drove bankers, colleagues, and attorneys into choleric fury. When people prodded him to do something urgently, he would complain, "You're holding a gun to my head," and mulishly refuse to act.

During the last years of his life, Hughes received much prodding on the subject of his will from his aides, attorneys, doctors, and executives, all of whom were naturally keen to have some inkling of their prospects in the event of his demise. Hughes was not averse to a teasing pleasure in the subject matter. As it happened, he had already worked on a number of will drafts without ever appending a signature. He would even indicate to some of his more concerned aides that there was a valid handwritten will in existence and that they personally were in it. Since none of the aides who logged Hughes's every move managed to lay eyes on the document, however, this reassurance was treated with extreme caution.

One of Hughes's attendants, who worked closely with him for the last ten years of his life, thought that his final attitude to the whole will business could have been colored by exasperation with those trying to lay their hands on his fortune. "When Hughes faced death," he said, "I can just see him saying—'Screw them all.' "

There is another scenario. Hughes may have intended to leave a will, but, as with all his big decisions, he might have deferred its execution until the very last possible moment. But the last moment may have come sooner than expected. It certainly came in very peculiar circumstances, which would give rise to some talk of murder.

ACKNOWLEDGMENTS

THE MAIN SOURCE material for this book was provided by interviews with the principals in the story, and with many of the minor characters, conducted over a long period. Habits of secrecy did not expire with Howard Hughes, and a number of people would only communicate on background, nonattributable terms. But we are most grateful to all those who spoke to us on whatever basis.

Another prime source has been the mountain of paperwork that accumulated after Hughes's death in literally dozens of legal jurisdictions across the United States. One lawyer familiar with this terrain estimated that the full Hughes litigation record, if it could be assembled in one place, could not be read by one person in ten lifetimes. We have sought to examine the more important pieces with the help of archivists and well-disposed legal acquaintances. This help was particularly appreciated in Los Angeles, Houston, Las Vegas, and Wilmington, the busiest legal areas.

We are also indebted to many others for help, advice, encouragement, and support along a long trail. They include: Robert Maheu, former Hughes executive; Taylor Moore, attorney and researcher; William Miller, attorney for the Hughes estate; Arelo Sederberg, former public relations man for Hughes; the late Harold Rhoden, attorney for Noah Dietrich and proponent of the "Mormon will"; the late Herman Greenspun, publisher of the Las Vegas, Nevada, *Sun;* Wallace Turner of *The New York Times;* Gordon Margulis and Mell Stewart, personal assistants to Hughes in his terminal years; Alex Finer, Amelia Gammon, Carol Heaton, Mark Hosenball, Helen Jones, Dr. Neela Malviya, Pravin Malviya, Helen Martin, David May, Benedict Owen, Lyn Owen, Michael Powell, Charles Raw, John Shirley, and Tim Webb.

Finally, we would like to thank our editor, Bob Loomis, who kept us at it, in the nicest possible way.

CONTENTS

THE MONEY

1
—

AN ORDINARY
SORT OF DEATH

WHEN HOWARD HUGHES began to die in Acapulco, his keepers faced a crisis for which neither Hughes nor the people running his empire had programmed any solution. If they hospitalized him, outsiders would learn that the richest American was a grotesquely anorexic junkie. If he died in his Acapulco hideout, they would have to produce his pitiful corpse and account for how it got that way.

They had moved him from Freeport in the Bahamas to the fun-loving Mexican beach resort on February 10, 1976, and installed him in the pyramid-shaped Acapulco Princess Hotel in his last blackout bedroom. It was his seventh hideout in his six years of exile from the United States. This was in itself a disruptive move for such a sick man, but Hughes had been told that the drugs he craved could be more easily procured in Mexico. In fact, during the last two years of his life, Hughes's drugs had been routinely supplied by a pharmaceutical firm in New York City.

By the end of March he was in a dreadful condition. He virtually stopped eating and taking liquids. The weight of the six foot four inch billionaire dropped to less than ninety-three pounds. He had fallen out of bed on March 1, dislocating his shoulder and shearing an old tumor on his head. The shoulder remained out of its socket, and his scalp wound was patched over with tape. He had broken his hip in an earlier fall in London and had not walked for three years. There were multiple bedsores on his back because he insisted on sleeping in one position and a maze of needle tracks on his arms and groin where he shot himself up with drugs.

He was attended in this condition by four physicians, six highly paid personal aides, and five lower-level functionaries, at a cost of $2 million a year. The entourage had grown to this cumbersome size by accretion, the way the hulk of an old ship acquires barnacles. Whenever anyone, inadvertently or otherwise, had come face-to-face with Hughes in his bizarre state, the billionaire had added him to his staff at an exorbitant salary to forestall him from disclosing what he had seen. Hughes and his staff were thus hostages to each other; he provided their affluence, and they kept his secrets. Two of his doctors had a stronger grip on Hughes; they had been his covert source of codeine, which is opium-based, and Valium, restricted drugs obtainable only by prescription.

There were two other strange aspects to this entourage. Hughes had been a fabled womanizer in his day, but there were no women involved in his care, and, indeed, none had been allowed in his presence for many years. Another peculiarity was the predominance of Mormons. Hughes had never exhibited much interest in the Mormon faith, but he judged that its believers were cleaner and more dutiful than most. As such they had, originally at least, seemed like the best kind of companions for Hughes in his long quest for a germ-free existence.

He had retreated into near total seclusion in the late 1950s, with only two personal aides and one doctor. He had then stripped off his clothes and, for reasons never explained to anyone, spent most of the rest of his life in scrawny nakedness. This made concealing him an imperative, which he recognized and helped to orchestrate. In his long descent into madness, he had extensive periods of lucidity in which he clearly perceived his plight and the damage its disclosure would wreak on his image and empire.

As his condition worsened in Acapulco, his keepers reacted in the manner of people who face an ordeal that has no escape hatch. They denied there was any ordeal. They reminded themselves that Hughes had frequently starved himself in the past and then subsequently resumed eating. For a while they reassured themselves with the delusion that this would happen again. When this could no longer be sustained, the nightmare option of hospitalizing Hughes was bucked up the line to superiors in the Summa Corporation, which controlled Hughes's business empire.

In Summa's California headquarters there was a thorough debate on the list of possible locations where Hughes could be admitted to the hospital with maximum discretion. The shortlist included Los Angeles, Houston, Salt Lake City, London, and Bermuda, but nobody was sure of the best option. Decision making was further complicated because the lead Hughes doctor, Wilbur Thain, was off-duty, traveling in the Bahamas and Florida and then headed for a trip to South America.

There were also tax consequences that might arise out of local laws wherever Hughes might die to be considered. This issue was referred to a tax attorney in Houston, who delegated the work to an associate. His task was to scan the lawbooks to see whether there were any tax liability problems attached to any of the locations where Hughes might receive his hospital care.

While these problems were being assessed, there was some manifestation of impatience in Acapulco. Jack Real, one of the men around Hughes in the hotel, decided to bite the bullet and, acting on his own, made hospital arrangements for the billionaire in Bermuda. But Real had no status in the Hughes care regime, being neither aide nor functionary. Indeed, his presence in the entourage was generally resented. He was an old aviation buddy and former Lockheed executive whom Hughes liked to have on call from time to time to reminisce about the old days when Hughes had been a flying ace and the owner of Trans World Airlines. Real's initiative was not appreciated by the others. He was rebuked for exceeding his authority, and his hospital arrangement for Hughes was canceled.

In the meantime, with the crisis being handled by their superiors, Hughes's official keepers followed their familiar routines. On Friday, April 2, three days before his death, Hughes was dutifully handed the packet containing a week's supply of drugs. The next day, in one of his last conscious acts, he loaded his syringe with codeine and tried to shoot himself in the arm. He was too far gone to depress the plunger and appealed to two of his attendants to give him his fix. Appalled at his state, they refused his request and summoned one of the standby doctors, who went into the bedroom alone and closeted himself with the billionaire.

The next day, April 4, Hughes lapsed into his terminal coma. His breathing slowed and grew shallow, his face twitched uncontrollably, and his eyes turned up sightless in their sockets. His staff made a series of frantic calls, located Dr. Thain in Florida, and arranged for him to fly back to his dying patient on a chartered private jet. While they waited for Dr. Thain, Hughes grew worse, and at dawn one of the standby doctors, conscious of the fact that none of Hughes's physicians had a license to practice medicine in Mexico, put in an emergency call to a local doctor, Victor Manuel Montemayor.

He arrived at the Acapulco Princess Hotel at 5:45 A.M., examined the unconscious billionaire, and expressed shock and bewilderment at what he saw. Why were they keeping a critically ill old man in a hotel room instead of hospitalizing him? When his keepers explained that their patient disliked hospitals, Dr. Montemayor pointed out that the comatose Hughes was scarcely in any position to object. He would say later, "Even if you have a patient in a delirium who rejects medical help, you don't take any notice of the patient's objections. You administer the medical help." At the time he strongly advised the Americans to move Hughes to a hospital in the United States because none in Acapulco had adequate facilities for such a desperately ailing man. In another flurry of phone calls to California, the decision was finally reached to check Hughes into Houston's Methodist Hospital.

Dr. Thain arrived at the hotel at 8 A.M. after flying through the night. The jet that brought him from Florida was held at the airport, and an Acapulco ambulance was summoned to the hotel. Even after Thain's arrival, it was another three and a half hours before Hughes was moved to the airport. During this time and subsequent to Hughes's departure, two witnesses would later testify, there was extensive shredding of unspecified files.

The first call to Methodist Hospital was logged in at 8:15 A.M. and went to Dr. Henry McIntosh, the medical director. The call did not come from the Hughes staff in Acapulco, as might be expected given the eleventh-hour urgency of the hospitalization. Instead, someone first made a call to the Howard Hughes Medical Institute in Miami, where an executive named Kenneth Wright was instructed to call the Houston hospital to ensure that the hospitalization of the billionaire would be cloaked in the tightest security. Methodist Hospital is the teaching arm for the Baylor University College of Medicine, which for years had received research grants from Hughes's Medical Institute. Finally, Wright was assured and passed on in good faith the information that Hughes had lapsed into "a diabetic coma." Hughes had never had diabetes. If he were to die without an autopsy, however, this would provide an exculpatory explanation for his multiple needle tracks, which could be dismissed as the marks left by a diabetic's needle shots.

Dr. McIntosh was asked to assemble a special intensive care unit to guarantee that Hughes would be admitted under a fictitious name and to make certain that no word of his hospitalization leaked to the press or to any of the hospital staff not directly involved in his care.

Dr. McIntosh informed the hospital's president, Ted Bowen, of the call and swiftly selected a team of six doctors, including a diabetes specialist, and a group of nurses. The doctors were instructed to respect Hughes's well-known obsession with privacy. Arrangements were made for Hughes to be admitted as "John T. Conover of Atlanta, Ga.," but after another call in midmorning, this time from a Summa official in California, the home of the fictitious Conover was changed from Atlanta to Houston for unexplained "tax purposes."

The hospital team was waiting with an ambulance on the tarmac when the blue-and-white Lear jet whined in from the south and put down at a secluded spot at Houston International Airport at 1:50 P.M. Dr. Thain, still wearing the embroidered leisure shirt he had been wearing in Florida, disembarked with the dismaying announcement that Hughes had died in midair at 1:27 P.M., shortly after the jet had crossed from Mexico into Texas.

The body was taken to Methodist Hospital, some thirty miles from the airport, and a brief preliminary examination was conducted by Dr. Jack L. Titus, the hospital's chief pathologist, who noted that it was "remarkably emaciated and dehydrated" and estimated from the absence of rigor or liver mortis that the death had occurred within the previous three hours. The body was placed in a morgue cooler, under guard. Then Dr. Titus gathered with hospital officials to confer with the three men who had delivered the dead billionaire to Houston. Between them this trio had a formidable firsthand knowledge of Hughes's medical history going back some thirty years.

In addition to Dr. Thain, there was an elderly physician, Dr. Lawrence Chaffin, and a senior Hughes aide, John Holmes. Dr. Chaffin had been one of the doctors who treated Hughes after a serious plane crash in 1946. Chaffin subsequently moved out of Hughes's orbit, but he had come out of retirement some years earlier to join the entourage as a part-time standby doctor. John Holmes was the aide who had been closest to and most trusted by Hughes, and with reason. Holmes had supervised a system of fake prescription orders to keep his employer illegally supplied with narcotic drugs for his fixes. This system endured for almost twenty years until Dr. Thain took over the task of supplying the drugs by a more direct route.

Dr. Chaffin took no part in the drugs operation; indeed, he was opposed to it, but he had no wish to see Hughes branded an addict, even posthumously. At the same time, he knew that the multiple puncture marks on Hughes's body would probably call for some explanation. Some years later, Dr. Titus was required to testify under oath on the content of his initial discussion with Dr. Chaffin and Dr. Thain. Titus said he remembered asking the two Hughes physicians what they thought was wrong with their patient. They told Titus they didn't know but suggested the possibility of diabetes.

MANY HOUSTONIANS PERCEIVE their city as being in competition with Dallas, and the rivalry between the two cities goes both deep and high. When Houston built the largest skyscraper in Texas, Dallas promptly commissioned a taller one. But there was one aspect of Dallas's record that Houston's Methodist Hospital had no wish to emulate.

Fourteen years earlier, the assassination of President John Kennedy in Dallas had erupted into a lasting international controversy centering on the city's Parkland Hospital, where the president was rushed after the Dealey Plaza shooting. Several Parkland doctors, working for a frantic and futile few minutes, had observed a bullet wound in the front of Kennedy's neck and misread it as an entry rather than an exit wound. This mishap was complicated by the fact that the wound had immediately been obscured when enlarged for a tracheotomy tube. References to the neck wound as a possible "entry" when the shots from the book depository came from behind the president's car, suggested two gunmen and hence a conspiracy rather than the lone Lee Harvey Oswald named by the Warren Commission. This hurried observation spawned scores of books in the sixties and seventies that tumbled the Warren Report in public esteem amid acrimonious charges of plots, cover-ups, and unknown gunmen firing from the "grassy knoll."

With this monumental Dallas malfunctioning in mind, the Houston hospital staff was intent on handling the death of Howard Hughes with the strictest care, rectitude, and precision. "We wanted to make sure that everything was done right," said Dr. Titus. The hospital assigned a stenographer to record the conversations pre-

ceding the autopsy, and the key doctors dictated detailed memos
after it was concluded. All involved were instructed not to talk to
outsiders, especially the press, to avoid any mistakes or misinterpre-
tations. This abundant and unusual record, with the autopsy itself
and its X rays and exhibits, was then sealed away in a bank vault.
But even with all this care, Houston did no better than Dallas in its
testing hour, for the final autopsy report of Hughes's death mis-
takenly failed to disclose what was a highly significant aspect of
Hughes's dying condition.

Methodist Hospital was operating under fierce pressure, partly
from newsmen crowding the scene but, more important, from the
three disparate groups of people suddenly brought together by
the billionaire's abrupt demise—his family, the Hughesmen, and
the Houston medical establishment. Each group, it transpired, had
different ideas about how Hughes's postmortem arrangements
should be handled, both in medical and public relations terms. In
the end, a web of compromises was made that seemed to satisfy
most parties. But the real truth about Hughes's terminal condition
somehow slipped unnoticed through the floorboards.

HUGHES'S NEAREST OF kin was his eighty-five-year-old aunt,
Annette Gano Lummis, who resided in Houston, where her son,
William Rice Lummis, worked as a partner in the law firm of Andrews, Kurth, Campbell & Jones. When informed of the death of
her noted nephew, Mrs. Lummis asked her son to handle the funeral arrangements. He went to Methodist Hospital that afternoon and conferred with its officials and the three Hughesmen on
the scene, Dr. Thain, Dr. Chaffin, and John Holmes.

Lummis was shown Hughes's body, looked at it briefly, and
turned away. Later he recalled that he "saw only that he was dead
and extremely emaciated." He acknowledged that he was only
"mildly shocked" at the billionaire's condition, although he likened
it to that of General Jonathan Wainwright when he was released
after a long ordeal in World War II Japanese prison camps.

"I would not say I was emotionally involved," he explained later,
"because I had no emotional involvement with Mr. Hughes." His

reaction reflected the estrangement that had developed between his mother and Hughes, though there had once been some warmth. Hughes had originally lived with his Aunt Annette after he had been orphaned, and later, when he had moved to Hollywood, he gave her his Houston family home on Yoakum Boulevard as a present. Mrs. Lummis had written to him frequently thereafter, but she had stopped communicating with him when Hughes suggested that her letters should be routed through his secretary, Nadine Henley. After his plane crash in 1946, Mrs. Lummis hurried to Los Angeles, only to be turned away at the hospital without seeing him, apparently on Hughes's instructions. At the time of his death, Annette Lummis had not seen Hughes for thirty-nine years. Neither had her son.

Will Lummis, who would emerge as one of the major figures in the battle for The Money, bore a remarkable resemblance to the billionaire and shared some of his traits and attitudes. After Hughes's death *Texas Monthly* magazine ran an article entitled "Howard Hughes Lives—and His Name Is Will Lummis." Lummis had an attachment to privacy akin to that of Hughes, though without the pathological excesses, and he would avoid the press even after events propelled him into the public arena. Although his law firm, Andrews, Kurth, had represented Hughes on tax matters for many years, Lummis had not been engaged in this work. Other than one minor compensation case, he had had little to do with any of his famous cousin's interests. "He rarely talked about Hughes," said an associate, "and there were members of the firm who were not aware that Will was related to him."

The problem at the hospital, as Lummis saw it, was to comply with the law while getting Hughes decently buried with the minimum of public fuss. Unfortunately, these objectives were not reconcilable. "I simply did not want to have more notoriety about Hughes than was necessary," Lummis testified later. "It was just a sense of privacy." The Hughes doctors had explained the billionaire's deplorable condition to Lummis by reporting that he had been an extraordinarily difficult patient who resisted medical treatment and had "some propensity to self-medicate with a variety of proprietary medication, including aspirin."

The first task was to make sure that the emaciated figure in the hospital cooler was indeed that of Howard Hughes. Since Lummis had only been nine years old when he last saw Hughes, he knew that his initial viewing of the body could not serve as any kind of formal identification by a relative. And the identification required in this instance needed to be rock-solid.

The need for an unassailable identification of the long-invisible billionaire grew out of the many sensational stories that his invisibility had spawned and the magnitude of the money at stake. There was the persistent rumor that he had died years earlier and his death had been concealed by conspirators in order to continue control of his empire. One Texas group claimed to have a 1959 death certificate for Hughes, signed by a doctor. Others propounded that he had financed successful research for artificial prolongation of life and had himself preserved in a science-fiction deep freeze for revival in the future. There were tales of doppelgängers that had replaced him, a febrile notion given credence by Hughes's actual employment of doubles—one a Hollywood actor called Brucks Randell—back in the 1960s when the billionaire was eluding process servers in his court battles for control of TWA.

Some of these stories had the appearance of substance. When Hughes had been moved to Acapulco, nationally syndicated columnist Jack Anderson checked a "Hughes-is-dead" tip with Mexican officials. Aware that all incoming visitors were required to sign a tourist card, the officials asked Anderson for a known example of Hughes's signature and as a direct result discovered that Hughes's tourist card did not bear his own signature. But before this discovery was made, the Mexican authorities decided to check out the situation firsthand. A team of officials was sent to the Acapulco Princess Hotel, where they demanded to see Hughes to verify if he was alive—this was only four days before his actual death.

On that occasion the panicked Hughes aides managed to persuade them to go away. But the squad returned again soon, shortly after the dying billionaire was removed for the flight to Houston. The Mexicans second coming occurred just as the staff's shredding machine jammed. Foiled at inspecting Hughes, the Mexican officials seized thousands of surviving documents, a serendipity that played a major role in the subsequent unraveling of Hughes's darkest secrets.

At Methodist Hospital, the legal requirement for the identification of Hughes by a relative was temporarily resolved by a makeshift arrangement. Lummis returned to the body accompanied by John Holmes. The sheet was lowered to expose the face, and Holmes nodded his head to signify that this was indeed Howard Robard Hughes, which Lummis then attested. This secondhand identification was backstopped the next day by a more determinative procedure. On the instructions of U.S. Treasurer William Simon, who was aware of the potentially enormous tax sums at stake, fingerprints were taken from the body and forwarded to the FBI in Washington, which matched the prints on the file from a 1942 pilot's license application by Hughes. The corpse was indeed the remains of the once dashing, record-breaking flier.

There remained the question of what had caused his death. The two Hughes doctors had brought no medical records with them. Both Dr. Thain and Holmes informed Lummis and the hospital officials that Hughes had wanted to be cremated. Dr. Thain also said that Hughes did not want an autopsy. Had an autopsy been dispensed with, Hughes's long addiction to drugs would obviously not have been discovered.

Late in the day, the group at the hospital was joined by the Harris County medical examiner, Dr. Joseph Jachimczyk, who had been out of his office when the hospital first called to report the death of Howard Hughes. Dr. Jachimczyk would argue that even if Hughes's wishes were being accurately reported by his attendants, they could not lawfully be respected. He pointed out that since no Texas-licensed doctor had been attending Hughes, the death was legally a public coroner's case. Given the circumstances, he asserted that an autopsy was not only advisable but mandatory. In any event, a cause-of-death statement from two out-of-state Hughes doctors was not acceptable.

The medical examiner's insistence that the law be observed was a novel experience for Hughes's attendants. They were used to steering Hughes about the planet without even a valid passport—which required a contemporary photograph, something Hughes could not conceivably provide—and he had passed in and out of countries without the normal customs inspection. He had been licensed to run his Nevada casinos without the personal-interrogation grilling that others had to undergo, and no court, despite many efforts, had been able to put him on a witness stand.

While the debate about an autopsy went on, Dr. Thain and Holmes excused themselves to obtain further guidance from their California superiors by telephone. They came back and reported that the Summa high command absolutely insisted that Hughes be cremated. Otherwise, they argued, people would be demanding that the body be exhumed, and "you might as well put the body on an elevator."

Eventually, the medical examiner lost patience. He asked the Hughes attendants why they had brought the body to Methodist Hospital, an institution to some degree beholden to the Hughes organization for financial support. "Why did you come over here?" he asked. "What are you hiding?" He pointed out that he had a legal right to take the case and that some of the procedures they opposed were "unavoidable."

Dr. Jachimczyk said that he foresaw the gravest consequences if Hughes was cremated without a proper autopsy. "Someone will say that you killed him," he told them, "not that I'll say that or that I believe that, but somebody will say that. We need a complete autopsy. We need to keep everything straight." He then asked Will Lummis if he had objections.

"Only one," Lummis replied. "I want to avoid an elaborate autopsy . . . I want to avoid fanfare. I want to avoid photographs."

Lummis's concern was that if Dr. Jachimczyk took the case, the autopsy would become a public document, available to anyone for a nominal fee. This could only lead to what he dreaded most, public fuss. He had heard stories that the *National Enquirer* was offering anything from $100,000 to $500,000 for pictures of the wasted billionaire's body, and he did not want an autopsy that could feed an appetite for that kind of disclosure.

Dr. Jachimczyk offered a compromise. In hindsight this was a mistake, though at the time it seemed a very fair way of accommodating all the conflicting interests, at least all the private interests. He agreed that the Methodist Hospital staff could perform the autopsy at the hospital as long as he could observe the procedure. This would avoid the necessity of having to move the body and thus minimize the chances of any untoward publicity; the corridors of the hospital were already jammed with newsmen and photographers. He also agreed that the autopsy need not become part of the public record and that any disclosures should be subject to the discretion of the next of kin.

During these discussions, Dr. Thain volunteered his opinion that Hughes had died of a stroke. This unverified conclusion, unlike the decision to conduct what was effectively a secret autopsy, very rapidly became public. That evening, the official Hughes spokesmen in Los Angeles, besieged by hundreds of media calls, issued a terse formal statement that the billionaire had died of "a cerebral vascular accident," medical terminology for a stroke. At the time Hughes's body was still in the hospital cooler, still awaiting an autopsy decision. This suggested cause of death was never withdrawn or revised by the Summa Corporation though, as was the case with earlier intimations of "diabetic coma," no evidence for it was ever found.

The next morning, after consulting his mother, Will Lummis authorized an autopsy and ruled out cremation. Then the crank calls began to come in. A man who identified himself as "Judge Bell of Los Angeles" asserted that "Hughes's next of kin" had come into his court and demanded that the Houston proceedings be halted and the body be transferred to Los Angeles for an autopsy. He was in the process of issuing an injunction, he said, and would get back to them as soon as it was drafted. The matter was referred to the Andrews, Kurth firm, which learned after a series of telephone calls that there was no "Judge Bell" in Los Angeles and no next of kin closer than Annette Lummis. A woman called the hospital and warned that if "anyone cut into the body" it would be murder. Neither the woman nor "Judge Bell" was heard from again.

The autopsy was conducted in the afternoon, with Dr. Titus presiding over several assistants and Dr. Jachimczyk and an associate observing. The two Hughes doctors were also present. The procedure took almost two hours, and shortly thereafter Ted Bowen and Dr. McIntosh met with the press in the only media briefing the hospital conducted. Bowen announced that "the preliminary autopsy findings demonstrated that Mr. Hughes died of a chronic renal disease." Dr. McIntosh gave a terse explanation:

"Renal disease means kidney, two of them. Chronic means a long time. And failure means that they didn't work well. The kidneys have the responsibility of getting rid of waste products the body makes, and they come out in urine. The kidneys are marvelous organs, and when they don't function very well, the waste products accumulate. And unless something is done about it, the patient will die. And this is what I think happened."

In keeping with Lummis's wish to avoid sensationalism or "fanfare," the doctors avoided any comments on Hughes's lifestyle, though Dr. McIntosh termed Hughes's body "that of a man who lived a full life." An evidently satisfied Dr. Jachimczyk said, "As far as I am concerned, it's an ordinary death. It's an extraordinary individual involved, perhaps, but the death is like any other death." Dr. Chaffin would tell *Newsweek* that the autopsy showed that Hughes's brain was not only normal but "the brain of a very smart man." Stories of Hughes's long fingernails were dismissed; he had the "lovely fingers of an artist." It was evident that functionaries who had soaked the billionaire's hands and feet in warm water and trimmed his long-neglected nails in the scant hours before he was flown out of Acapulco had done an excellent job.

At the time of this public homage to normalcy, the final autopsy finding was still several days in the offing. There were still laboratory tests that had to be run, X rays that required examination, and a toxicological report was pending. While the news horde was gathered in the briefing room, a funeral director quietly transferred the body to a casket and moved it unseen and unphotographed to the mortuary. The next morning the billionaire was buried alongside his mother and father in Glenwood Cemetery in a private ceremony. The Very Reverend Robert T. Gibson, dean of Christ Church Cathedral, intoned over him: "We brought nothing into this world and it is certain we will take nothing out."

The press accounts of his death focused largely on the bizarre way he had lived. There seemed to be no big mystery about the actual death. To the outside world he was a seventy-year-old skinny hermit who fended off his doctors and whose kidneys had failed him, a common-enough complaint.

When Hughes's X rays were assessed, it was not thought necessary to tell the public, or indeed Will Lummis, that they showed broken fragments of hypodermic syringe needles in both arms. The family had no idea that Hughes was an addict. Similarly, when the toxicological report was completed on April 10, four days after the announcement to the press of kidney failure, no public comment was deemed necessary. The final autopsy report simply noted that "the toxicological studies show only a minor amount of codeine."

Events had somehow converged to totally relieve Hughes's keepers of their anticipated nightmare. They had brought in his wasted body with needle fragments embedded in his arms and had been spared the necessity of any public explanation. With their last services to their employer concluded, Dr. Thain and John Holmes flew off to California to discuss their future with their superiors. Whatever might be said about the quality of their care for Hughes, the two drug suppliers had been diligent in arranging that he would take care of them.

Seven months before Hughes died, they had been among a select group of twelve Hughes employees who had obtained "consulting agreements" from the Summa Corporation with Hughes's less than enthusiastic consent. Set at their highest salary rates, these agreements were designed to run for a minimum of five years. Thereafter, the beneficiaries could expect to be paid for further "consulting services" at one third of their salary for the rest of their lives. In return, they agreed to a secrecy clause prohibiting them from writing anything "embarrassing or harmful" to Summa or its personnel or providing such information to any writer or publisher.

As far as the Hughesmen were concerned, nothing of a remotely embarrassing or harmful nature to Summa had occurred at Houston's Methodist Hospital. The only serious casualty there had been the truth. But it would be another two years before the hospital, under pressure from court actions, was able to reveal that the official final autopsy report was seriously flawed.

The amount of codeine found in Hughes's body was not "minor" as stated. In point of fact, the toxicologist's original analysis, which had somehow been misconstrued, indicated the presence of enough codeine in Hughes's system to kill a man half his age. And this massive dose had somehow managed to find its way into the body of a man who had been in a coma for at least twenty-four hours before he died.

There was ample evidence in Hughes's wasted body to warrant an immediate criminal investigation within a few days of its arrival in Houston. But no law enforcement agencies were apprised of this at the time. They, like most of the public, like Will Lummis and like the rest of Hughes's family, believed what they had been led to believe—that Howard Hughes died an ordinary sort of death.

Eventually, after the walls of secrecy started to crumble, John Holmes and Dr. Thain and another doctor who had been with Hughes in Acapulco, Dr. Norman Crane, were all indicted for drug-supplying offenses. Dr. Thain would be acquitted but he would have to undergo the embarrassment of having two of his colleagues on Hughes's medical team—Dr. Chaffin and Dr. Crane —giving evidence against him at his trial.

2

—

A MAN AND HIS MONEY

THE DEATH OF Howard Hughes unleashed an enormous appetite for the facts of his life. This appetite had been building for many years as the rumors and manufactured stories about the invisible billionaire became ever more weird and fanciful. By the end, the character of the man had become so myth-encrusted that, in the words of Walter Kane, one of Hughes's oldest associates, "He had to die to prove he existed."

Newspapers coast-to-coast would eagerly take on the task of de-mystifying the man once described by *Fortune* magazine as "the spook of American capitalism." At last, it could be definitively asserted that Hughes had not spent the last twenty years in an icebox and that his empire had not been secretly manipulated and controlled by the Mafia or the CIA, although it had been well connected in both areas. The known facts, as opposed to the imaginative theories, about Hughes's bizarre life and times became the staple diet in America's leading publications for weeks on end. Most rich men are featured in obituaries when they die, but Hughes got something else—massive cradle-to-the-grave coverage. As a result, the extraordinary recluse suddenly became in retrospect the most accessible of all Americans.

One unwitting by-product of this outpouring of Hughes material was the provision of a solid bedrock of hard information for those inclined to launch a spurious claim to his money, or even forge his will. At the time, however, there was no hint of such untoward developments. Although there was speculation about what the billionaire's will might contain, there was no public suggestion initially that such a document might not even exist.

The main reason for believing that Hughes had left a valid will was based not on anything he had said on the subject, which could only occasionally be taken at face value, but on the one consistent trait he exhibited throughout an unpredictable life. This was his complete obsession with exerting personal control over every aspect of his existence. "I have never done anything," he once asserted, "because someone told me I had to." For such a man to die intestate and turn his empire and life's work over to the whims of countless others for dismemberment seemed, on the face of it, inconceivable.

Hughes first exhibited this insistence on absolute self-determination when, as an awkward, gangling boy of eighteen, he inherited the major interest in Hughes Tool Company in Houston, Texas, upon the death of his father. Legally, he was not qualified to exert his authority until he was twenty-one, and his relatives were opposed to "Sonny," as they called him, taking over the firm. "Sonny" went to court before a sympathetic judge, had himself declared a legal adult, and bought out his miffed relatives. This proved a remarkably shrewd move.

Hughes Tool was based on his father's invention of the "rock eater," an oil-drilling bit with 166 cutting edges fashioned on the principles of an egg whisk and far in advance of the competition not only in America but throughout the world. After the initial act of acquisition, Hughes evinced little direct interest in the company's affairs but was keenly appreciative of its profits, which amounted to $745 million during his lifetime. It was the golden cornucopia that financed his own more flamboyant business initiatives.

From his youth on, Hughes followed the practice of undiluted ownership, buying movie studios, companies, land, gambling halls, and hotels outright, with no partners to account to or consult. He would deviate from this at times, but only for short-term tactical reasons. His great wealth afforded him an almost limitless array of options bounded only by his ambitions, his desires, and—eventually—his internal flaws.

Hughes's initial relationship with The Money was genuinely creative, if a shade exhibitionist. He used it to try to overcome his innate shyness and find a popular place for himself in the world. The two most glamorous areas of American enterprise as he was growing up were the burgeoning aviation business and Hollywood, and Hughes set out to make his mark in both of them.

In Hollywood he would be denigrated by screenwriter Ben Hecht as "a sucker with money," but he would also establish himself as a producer, and sometimes director, who could struggle through to completing pictures that people really wanted to see. An early case in point is *Hell's Angels,* a 1930 movie about World War I pilots that was a long time taking off but eventually played to packed houses. Hughes spent $4 million on the project and fired two directors before taking control of the movie, which required the coordination of the aerial antics of eighty-seven planes. Three pilots lost their lives during the moviemaking process, and Hughes himself was involved in a crash on landing, suffering a concussion and crushing a cheekbone. The original leading lady, Greta Nissen, was another serious casualty, winding up on the cutting-room floor at a late stage because the talkies inconveniently arrived and Hughes wanted his picture to be up-to-date. He would reshoot all the love interest with Jean Harlow as his new leading lady. At the end of the shooting, Hughes set his editors the task of constructing a movie out of 25 miles of film, sufficient for 560 hours of screening. This was hardly cost-effective moviemaking, but it did establish his reputation as a young man who thought exceptionally big.

The other reputation he acquired was for driving the film censors up the wall, mainly by exposing larger acreages of female flesh to the camera than was deemed proper in those days. Hughes took a painstaking, almost clinical interest in how the breasts and hinted nipples of his female stars were presented. Indeed, he is probably best remembered in Hollywood for his diligent construction of a seamless cantilevered bra for Jane Russell in his 1943 movie *The Outlaw,* though Ms. Russell would later reveal that it was too painful to wear and that she secretly substituted her own undergarment without Hughes's knowledge.

Hughes never made anything resembling a cinematic masterpiece, but some of those films he produced, like *Scarface, Hell's Angels, The Front Page,* and *Two Arabian Knights,* which won one of the first Oscars (for Lewis Milestone's direction), still retain an impressive energy. His contribution was more idiosyncratic than qualitative, but it's certainly true that Hollywood would have been the poorer without him.

It was the making of *Hell's Angels* that led Hughes into a serious exploration of what he could do as a pilot. Aviators were the new heroes of the age, and Hughes determinedly set out to become one of them. In this area his success would be unequivocal. Public fascination with flying records had been at a high, almost feverish, pitch ever since Charles Lindbergh's flight across the Atlantic in 1927, and there were aviation races to be won and records to be broken at all levels. Hughes established a tiny subsidiary of Hughes Tool, called Hughes Aircraft, in California and began trying out, and refining, the different machines available and developing his own experimental designs. In this environment his obsessive preoccupation with detail that exasperated colleagues in the movie industry found its most practical outlet. From these efforts came the experimental H-1 (Hughes One), popularly known as the *Winged Bullet* and the fastest plane around. After establishing a series of speed records across the American continent, Hughes was ready for the big one. In July 1938, flying a Lockheed 14 modified to his own specifications, Hughes made it around the planet in three days, nineteen hours, and seventeen minutes—a new world record.

After his ecstatic ticker-tape welcome back in New York, the city's sanitation department was able to announce that another record had been established. Sixteen hundred tons of paper scraps had been thrown at Lindbergh on his return, but eighteen hundred tons fluttered down on Hughes's parade. Still only thirty-two, Hughes was truly, as one New York tabloid reported, "Public Hero Number One."

Hughes's popularity was not diminished, indeed, it was in many ways enhanced, by his reputation as a world-class woman chaser. He had arrived in Hollywood as a young married man, but his wife, Ella Rice, from a socially distinguished Houston family, soon backtracked to Texas and filed for divorce. As a single—or soon-to-be single—man, a multimillionaire, a budding aviation hero, and a filmmaker substantially taller and more comely than the average cigar-chomping movie mogul, Hughes was for years the prime Hollywood catch. Hughes's father had been a big-spending ladies' man, frequently seen squiring Mae Murray, an actress celebrated as "the girl with the bee-stung lips," but Howard would put his father's reputation in the shade. Indeed, no one could match his diligence in pursuit of the most desired love goddesses of the day. Among those who were romantically linked with Hughes were: Billie Dove, Jean Harlow, Katharine Hepburn, Ginger Rogers, Bette Davis, Rita Hayworth, Marilyn Monroe, Lana Turner, Susan Hayward, Ava Gardner, Yvonne De Carlo, Faith Domergue, Olivia De Havilland, Kathryn Grayson, Linda Darnell, and Jane Greer. Hughes would also find time to court many other young women whose names never appeared in a film credit. "Howard Hughes," Joan Crawford once commented, "would fuck a tree."

During the Depression years, Hughes's problem was how to spend money rather than how to acquire it. Hughes Tool, effectively run by Noah Dietrich, a young boxer-turned-accountant in whom Hughes reposed complete trust, took ample care of the money supply in a way that opened up new worlds for conquest. With the Hughes Tool profits, Hughes was able to acquire Trans World Airlines (TWA) and, after the outbreak of World War II, finance his cherished ambition to be a great plane maker. But the young man who had known only phenomenal success was now heading for his first conspicuous public failure.

As a result of some vigorous lobbying and lavish entertaining aimed at, among others, the president's son Elliott Roosevelt, Hughes was awarded two major federal contracts, one for the construction of a hundred photoreconnaissance planes and the other for three gigantic flying boats to be used as troop carriers. Unfortunately, Hughes's concept of the time he had to work on these orders bore no relation to the urgent pace of events. By the time hostilities ceased, the Hughes Aircraft plant in Culver City had managed to build only two XF–II photoreconnaissance planes, each still in the prototype phase, and just one giant wooden flying boat. Nicknamed the *Spruce Goose,* the flying boat had not ventured into the water, let alone the air. No Hughes aircraft ever made it into a battle zone.

Hughes would almost kill himself when he crashed an XF–II in a test flight in 1946, and, to add insult to his multiple injuries, he would be obliged to undergo a humiliating ordeal before a Senate investigating committee a year later. The senators in Washington wanted to know if the lavish entertaining that had helped secure Hughes's contracts amounted to bribery. They also wanted to know why the $40-odd million in taxpayers' money that had been channeled into Hughes Aircraft had produced so little for the war effort. In a personal appearance before the committee, Hughes managed to use his charisma to brilliant effect, presenting himself as an outraged and deeply misunderstood patriot. He would say of his flying boat, by far the largest plane ever built, "If it's a failure, I'll probably leave this country and never come back." He would then, to the chagrin of his congressional critics, go back to California and proceed to prove that the *Spruce Goose* could actually fly, albeit for only one mile.

In the wake of this public relations coup, there were even "Hughes for President" campaigns, but Hughes himself had found the public criticism deeply wounding and began to shrink more and more from contact with the real world. His career had always been pitted by strange absences, but after the unwelcome spotlight of the Senate hearing, his whereabouts became even less predictable. Hughes maintained an elaborate twenty-four-hour-a-day operations center on Hollywood's Romaine Street, a brilliant mechanism for transmitting his orders but not much help when it came to monitoring his own will-o'-the-wisp behavior. It was said that Hughes had become a resident of San Limbo, a small principality with one telephone in it, off the hook.

He never did become a great plane maker, but when he turned Hughes Aircraft over to the production of missiles and sophisticated electronic weaponry in the late 1940s, it acquired an extraordinary new lease on life. Over the years it would rival, and eventually eclipse, Hughes Tool as a wealth producer. Hughes, however, had very little to do with its great days. In 1953 he was quietly obliged to promise the firm's main customer—the U.S. Defense Department—that he would stay out of the running of Hughes Aircraft altogether. His decision making was thought to be too erratic for what had come to be regarded as a valuable national asset.

His fitful, remote control also helped make a shambles of his RKO movie studio, though the starlet recruitment system continued to function efficiently. Of all his enterprises Hughes was closest to TWA, but even here his waywardness created problems. It was his chronic indecision that caused TWA to be a late entrant into the jet age. And when Hughes tried to catch up, he was forced into a humiliating, and ultimately rancorous, association with a group of eastern bankers to raise the finance.

There were, in fact, two Hughes empires run on totally dissimilar lines. One consisted of Hughes Tool and Hughes Aircraft as an electronics concern, and they somehow managed to insulate themselves from the whims of their owner and run themselves on modern business lines. They produced The Money. The other consisted of the businesses in which Hughes took a personal interest—the movies, the airlines, the aircraft construction firms, and, ultimately, the gambling casinos of Las Vegas. These occasionally produced money, as was the case when Hughes scooped up $546 million from the sale of his TWA stock, but they were more generally characterized by losses, furious litigation and allegations of bad management, and inefficiency. David B. Tinnin would entitle his fascinating study of Hughes's storm-tossed years at TWA as *Just About Everybody vs. Howard Hughes.*

As it happens, Hughes was coming to precisely this view of the world himself. Uncomfortable with and suspicious of people who might be considered his peers, he took refuge behind minions who were unlikely to question his oddities. By 1957, when Hughes finally split with Noah Dietrich, his longtime financial guide, the billionaire was already seriously dependent on drugs and beginning to exhibit chronic phobias about germs. Newspapers had to be brought to him in stacks of three copies so that he could slide out the middle one—theoretically the least contaminated—by grasping it with a Kleenex. Hughes was already concerned that some executives in his empire might take steps to have him committed.

Out of these dilemmas, Hughes came up with a mechanically brilliant, but humanly destructive, solution. He effected a complete divorce between his public persona, which became pure image, and his private world, which ultimately became surreal. With The Money he invented his own personal Secrecy Machine to keep the world at bay. Part of this apparatus was a contraption, called Rosemont Enterprises, that harassed writers and publishers with lawsuits contending that Hughes alone owned and controlled the facts of his life and could forestall any unauthorized recital of his life story. More serious funding was required for the platoons of lawyers whose main task in life was to block or divert any action that might require Hughes's personal attendance in court. The scale of this activity can be judged by the fact that Hughes had sixty-five lawsuits pending against him and his business interests at the time of his death. But the main expenditure went to the creation of his own self-contained, face-to-face society of dependent aides, mostly Mormons, who would shield him from the world. The great wealth that had provided Hughes with an overdrive facility in pursuit of his youthful ambitions had, by his middle years, become the lubricant on his slide into an almost unique form of lunacy.

For a while, Hughes's retreat from the world would be mitigated by his marriage to Jean Peters, but her access to him—always limited—would cease altogether in 1966 when Hughes effectively shut her out by holing up on the top floor of the Desert Inn in Las Vegas. Naked for the most part and alone with his keepers, he exhibited what might be described as an untrammeled personality. Nobody opposed his will in the private world, and he became increasingly irate at manifestations of indiscipline outside it.

The Money was now working synergistically with his fears and flaws, inflating his hostilities and heightening his sense of vulnerability. In addition to his pathological fear of germs, he was now plagued with an abiding perception that "unauthorized individuals" were probing his thought processes. His need to do things in his own way deepened into an obsession to control everyone he dealt with and everything he touched. Afflicted for years with urinary difficulties, Hughes began to relieve himself in bed into Mason jars. On Hughes's instructions the jars were capped and stored in a closet, which eventually housed the greatest concentration of the billionaire's urine ever assembled. Nobody dared flush it away until Hughes moved on. Meanwhile, Hughes waged his relentless war on germs. He would write long, maniacal memos detailing exactly how his underlings should open and decant a can of fruit salad for him or how to retrieve his hearing aid from the bathroom cabinet ("It is to be removed using a minimum of 15 Kleenexes. . . . If necessary to use both hands, then 15 Kleenexes for each hand.") It was essential, at all times, to prevent what he designated "the backflow of germs."

When not presiding over such minutiae, Hughes compulsively watched movies—as many as six a day—which provided him with little two-dimensional worlds he could turn on or off at will or rerun as many as one hundred times if they pleased him. The real world, of course, was not so easily adjusted.

Hughes rapidly came to feel that his position as the number one casino owner in Nevada entitled him to virtual ownership of the state, with veto power over any legislation he found uncongenial. He would later extend this feeling to encompass the rest of America. Bribery had always played a pivotal role in Hughes's dealings, partly because he regarded it as an efficacious substitute for the chore of persuading people by talking to them, but it reached its apogee during his years in the Desert Inn. One of his casinos, the Silver Slipper, would provide the conduit for cash "campaign contributions" to county commissioners, legislative candidates, would-be governors, and other state dignitaries to tilt them into conformity. Bribes to national figures would be handled at a higher level of the organization, but always on Hughes's say-so.

In 1968 he made massive cash gifts to both the Democratic presidential candidate Hubert Humphrey and Republican Richard Nixon. He was even about to contribute to Robert Kennedy's candidacy before it was abruptly cut short by assassination, though Hughes had acknowledged that he wanted another Kennedy presidency "like I want the mumps." Other than a lifelong hatred of communism, Hughes had no discernible political philosophy, and he supported both liberals and conservatives—even when they ran against each other—in order to impose an obligation on whichever one won.

When, as occasionally happened, his money failed to shape the outside world in accordance with his wishes, Hughes felt that his "freedom" was being violated. He was enraged when a U.S. Supreme Court justice was nominated without his prior approval, affronted when the Nevada legislature contemplated a mild fair-housing law on behalf of the blacks he detested, and mortified when neither President Lyndon Johnson, nor his successor, Richard Nixon, could be persuaded to see sense and accept a million-dollar bribe in return for halting nuclear testing in Nevada.

It was Hughes's acute sense of being persecuted—by the tax authorities, by process servers eager to get him into court, and by presumed enemies within his own empire—that finally drove him into the long exile that would take him to the Bahamas, London, Vancouver, Managua, and, finally, Acapulco. Before taking off on his travels, Hughes characteristically told his chief executive to be sure to sort out the government of the Bahamas "to the point where it would be . . . well . . . a captive entity in every way."

Hughes never did manage to make a "captive entity" out of the Bahamas, but he did become one himself. Physically as well as mentally sick, he came to rely totally on his Mormon-dominated entourage for the business of carting him around the world and ultimately for getting him in and out of bed. He would go on rasping out his orders, but they would be less and less frequently adhered to. He still had The Money, but he was no longer in control.

3

—

AN EMPIRE WITH
FOUR HEADS

SEVEN DAYS AFTER the burial of Howard Hughes, there occurred a demonstration of the legal equivalent of formation dancing, Texas-style. Under the direction of Andrews, Kurth, the Houston firm that had represented Hughes for almost half a century, three teams of lawyers appeared simultaneously before courts in Los Angeles, Las Vegas, and Houston armed with almost identical petitions.

In each case the attorneys obtained what they wanted—appointment of special administrators in the three states where the bulk of the Hughes empire was situated, California, Nevada, and Texas. They advised the courts that Hughes was believed to have executed a last will but that it had not yet been located. Temporary administrators, they said, would facilitate the locating of the will and avoid "loss and waste of the estate." They would also, it was pledged, help maintain an "orderly operation" of the Hughes enterprises.

In Texas, Will Lummis and his mother were named temporary administrators. In Nevada, Lummis was named coadministrator with a local bank. In California, where an administrator must be a state resident, the court named Richard Gano, a cousin of Will Lummis. Subsequently, a court in Delaware, the state where Summa had been incorporated, granted Lummis control of the company's stock, which gave him the authority Hughes had exercised as sole stockholder.

The immediate effect of these actions was to preclude any public administrator from taking over the secrecy-shrouded Hughes empire. The precision and swift execution of these moves to control The Money gave rise to speculation that they were a predrafted contingency plan that awaited the death of Hughes to be put into effect. But William Miller, who became lead attorney for Andrews, Kurth in the marathon of litigation over the Hughes estate, says there was no preplanning, only rapid execution: "I drafted those court actions myself and knocked myself out working sixteen and eighteen hours a day, including the weekend."

A few months after Hughes died, Lummis moved with his wife from their quiet, orderly life in Houston's affluent River Oaks residential area to garish, neon-bathed Las Vegas, where Summa's main holdings were concentrated. Initially, the new administrator was regarded there as an oddity. According to a close friend, "Lummis is so conventional that he not only likes to stick with one wife, he also prefers to work with people who have only married one wife." This felicity clearly was not so readily available in what many Americans regard as Sin City. But what really rendered him most suspect was his manner. Las Vegas is a town where clout is greatly admired, and those who have it tend to flaunt it. But the new power in the Hughes empire showed no signs of conformity to this flamboyant standard. He was quiet and showed no disposition for pulling rank, even going so far as to park his own car when pulling up at a Summa hotel rather than delegate it to the car valets, an unheard-of modesty for a Las Vegas executive. The general impression of Lummis among Las Vegans was that of a decent, inoffensive man—the type that gets eaten alive in their city.

It's possible that Lummis shared this assessment. He was embarking on an unfamiliar and legally precarious series of tasks. He was undertaking the administration of an estate in which the true ownership was unknown. It was not even clear where the estate should be properly probated or how much it was worth. Nor was it at all clear how much it owed. "Every time the phone rang," said Lummis, recalling his early days as Summa's administrator in Las Vegas, "it was someone who said we owed them money."

Lummis also rapidly discovered that his pledge to ensure the "orderly operation" of the Hughes empire involved breaking new ground since orderliness had never been a feature of Summa's operation. Coupled with these uncertainties were some that Lummis himself had about his own abilities. He had a strong grounding in commercial law but no managerial experience to speak of and certainly none that seemed relevant to the Hughes empire. Summa had no less than sixteen operating divisions—ranging from airlines to ocean mining—but its real concentration was in the gaming industry, of which Lummis had no firsthand knowledge whatsoever. For the task of bringing order to these disparate concerns, Lummis was equipped with an uncertain lance: if a will turned up with a designated executor, Lummis would automatically be stripped of the authority to do anything.

The one apparent advantage of his position, for a while at least, was that he was a most welcome arrival as far as the existing Hughes management team was concerned. They, like the family, did not relish the prospect of the Summa empire going into public administration. Far better, they thought, dealing with one mild-mannered lawyer from Texas who would sort out any legal hassles over probate while they got on with running the show. Although Lummis's arrival created more congestion on the Summa bridge, it was thought that they could all steer a mutually beneficial course.

When Lummis moved into Summa, it was an empire that already had three heads. For the six years of Hughes's exile, Summa had been run by an executive triumvirate consisting of Frank William "Bill" Gay, Nadine Henley, and Chester Davis, each with long experience of survival in Hughes's weird and wondrous world. Unlike the aides and the functionaries, they did not attend to Hughes "on location," Summaspeak for wherever Hughes happened to be holed up. But throughout this period all the major deeds done in Hughes's name were executed by them. And, as Lummis would discover, they were firmly united in perceiving themselves as the natural custodians, and possibly the inheritors, of The Money.

The most complex member of this ruling group was Bill Gay, who had risen from the bottom of the empire to the top. Gay was a tall, thin-faced Mormon who had made and nurtured contacts at every level of the organization. He had begun working for it as supervisor of car drivers at the fabled old Hughes command post on Romaine Street in Hollywood, from which the billionaire had once run his affairs by remote control through a twenty-four-hour switchboard and brigades of messengers. After this modest start, Gay was singled out as a capable and discreet administrator, and would eventually find himself administering the Hughes Secrecy Machine. An early enthusiast of electronic eavesdropping techniques, Hughes maintained a squad of private detectives and other operatives charged with snooping in his areas of interest. Some of this activity involved business, but most of it was concentrated on his current amours and on the starlets he maintained "on the hook" to assure him that no misbehavior was occurring during his long absences. This work involved the preparation of many surveillance reports, which would be channeled to Hughes through Bill Gay. From this sensitive position, Gay moved up to management of the whole Romaine Street operation. Later he became vice president and, ultimately, chief executive.

But it had not been an effortless rise. En route to the top, he had sustained setbacks, rebuffs, banishments, and insults that would have sent a less resilient man to a psychiatrist's couch. Hughes was said to have a love-hate relationship with Gay, though to judge by the Hughes memos that surfaced after his death, there was not an excessive amount of the former.

Hughes even attributed to Gay the failure of his marriage to Jean Peters, citing "his total indifference and laxity to my pleas for help in my domestic area, voiced urgently to him week by week throughout the past seven to eight years . . . I feel he let me down, utterly, totally, completely." In this instance Gay was serving the vital role of scapegoat. It was Hughes who neglected his wife and sought somebody else to blame. Gay was also excoriated when his staff failed dismally in a hunt for Mrs. Hughes's lost cat. The cat returned of its own volition one day after Gay's reprimand. On another occasion, Hughes ranted on at Gay when his messengers failed to promptly procure copies of some aviation magazines Hughes had requested: "This is typical of our whole slovenly indifferent way this entire operation of mine is handled and I can name so many more parallels I would be here the whole stinking day doing it . . . It just saps my guts and my ailing constitution. The damage it does to my system psychologically is beyond imagination."

Gay seemingly accepted his role as a front-line whipping boy. He had no great gift for business, but he was particularly adept at making career-wise staff appointments. Five of the six aides assigned to Hughes's personal care were Mormons, and they all looked to Bill Gay for leadership. Gay was also instrumental in the appointment of Dr. Thain, Hughes's lead doctor and drug supplier in the last years of his life. Dr. Thain was Gay's brother-in-law.

Gay was hired for his first job with the Hughes organization back in 1947 by Nadine Henley, who would take a keen interest in Gay's progress and go far herself. As the chief secretary at Romaine, she would act as Hughes's personal secretary on his infrequent visits to the command headquarters. She described herself as "Madame Nitpick" because of her attention to detail, and Hughes liked that. From time to time she worked on drafts of his will, though none was ever signed. Hughes would also encourage her to become his "eyes and ears" at his Medical Institute when he went into seclusion, and her status grew with this role. She would move up to a vice presidency of her own and bring a feminine touch to what was an overwhelmingly male high command. A plump woman who affected blond bouffant hairdos, she rarely, unlike Gay, caught the rough edge of Hughes's tongue. But, like Gay, she was indispensable, as one of the repositories of Hughes's most cherished secrets.

The third member of the executive trio was Summa's general counsel, Chester Davis, a strongly built, skilled trial lawyer whose aggressive, abrasive character contrasted with Bill Gay's low-key qualities. In Hughes's circles, they were covertly referred to as "Godzilla and Bambi." In the bitter lawsuits between Hughes and eastern financiers over TWA, Davis had achieved a stunning reversal of a $145 million judgment against Hughes in the final appeal to the U.S. Supreme Court, relieving Hughes of an enormous default penalty and enhancing his own standing in the empire. Like Hughes, Chester Davis had some closely guarded secrets. A graduate of Harvard Law School, he had married an heiress of the Ferry seed fortune and was presumed by everyone who knew him to have come from an old-line WASP New Jersey family. In fact, he had been born in Rome as Cesar Simon, the son of an Italian mother and an Algerian Jewish father. When his father died, his mother brought little Cesar to the United States at the age of ten and married Chester Davis, Sr., a moneyed New Jerseyan, who adopted him.

Together, the Summa triumvirate had more than seventy-five years' experience in the disorienting world of Howard Hughes. Two of them—Gay and Henley—had memories going back to the era when Noah Dietrich had been Hughes's financial czar. And both had moved up a few notches when, in 1957, Dietrich had ended his thirty-two-year reign by asking for something Hughes felt compelled to refuse—stock options in his companies. But the thing that tied the triumvirate together was its success in derailing Hughes's next favorite, big Bob Maheu, the tough guy drafted by the billionaire to oversee his manic buying spree in Las Vegas. Hughes's partiality for Maheu, whom he would describe as his alter ego, was a direct threat to his own ancien régime. And Maheu was the kind of man who could not be easily pushed off the hill. He had a long record as a successful investigator for the FBI and private clients, though he was most celebrated for one of his failures, as the man who recruited three Mafia leaders for the covert CIA plot to assassinate Fidel Castro as a complement to the Bay of Pigs operation.

With Hughes's deep attachment to him and his independent status in the empire—he was accountable only to Hughes—Maheu fell afoul of the Gay-Davis-Henley axis. Using the personal aides Gay had put in place at the billionaire's side, Gay and Davis systematically undermined Hughes's trust in Maheu with reports that he was wasting funds and structuring an organization of his own inside the empire. Disillusioned and bitter, Hughes left a proxy authorizing Davis and Gay to oust Maheu, which became effective after he himself had decamped to the Bahamas. Armed with this corporate guillotine, Davis took up his battle station in the Sands Hotel, which he had been told erroneously Maheu had had wired for sound. Davis let out a Godzilla-like roar directed at the fancied microphones in the ceiling: "If you're up there, you son of a bitch, you're going to jail."

Instead, Maheu went to court, adding to the growing legion of litigants against Howard Hughes. With Maheu gone, Hughes lost his last window to the outside world. Shortly after Maheu's departure, a reluctant and ailing Hughes was persuaded to sell off Hughes Tool, ostensibly to ease cash-flow problems. This proved a remarkably maladroit business decision—within a year the value of Hughes Tool had swollen to three times the $150 million sale price—but it did help tighten the triumvirate's control on Hughes's empire. Hughes Tool had always tended to operate as an independent barony within the overall scheme of things. Once it was gone, the board decided to rechristen the Hughes empire as Summa. Hughes liked to label all his enterprises with his own name—Hughes Aircraft, Hughes Helicopters, Hughes Air West, Howard Hughes Medical Institute—and did not like the new name. He preferred the appellation Hughes Resort Hotels, which had the attraction of having the same abbreviation as his initials, H.R.H. But the name Summa was retained. At this stage, what Hughes did or did not like was a matter of decreasing relevance.

In addition to their grip on Summa, Gay and Davis had gained control of the much larger pile of wealth represented by the Hughes Aircraft stock held by the Howard Hughes Medical Institute. On Hughes's death they had assumed full power at the institute as the result of a murky revision of its bylaws when Hughes was in his drug-accelerated decline. This revision, drafted by Chester Davis, provided that Davis and Gay would exercise Hughes's authority "in the absence of the trustee." And Hughes, on the arrival of Lummis in Las Vegas, was incontrovertibly and irretrievably absent.

Lummis knew next to nothing of this background when he moved in, but he was struck almost immediately by a peculiar feature of Summa's boardroom setup. To his knowledge, it had no known parallel in the history of mature American business corporations. None of the directors of Summa had any business managerial experience outside the empire of which they had gained control. This applied to the ruling triumvirate and to the two other members of the five-man board. The two were personal aides who had carted the ailing Hughes around from "location" to "location" during his exile. One was John Holmes, a former cigarette and floor-polish salesman and the only non-Mormon in the circle of aides. The other was Levar Myler, a dour, bespectacled onetime airplane mechanic. Both, like Gay and Mrs. Henley, had made their start with low-level jobs on Romaine Street, moving from $70-a-week paychecks to executive salaries in the $110,000-a-year league.

Lummis did not immediately deduce from this that the company was poorly managed, but it did alert him to the fact that he was now in a business that played with its cards pressed close to its chest. It also seemed to him that this passion for promotion from within had the disadvantageous effect of narrowing the range of expertise at the top. His first serious move as administrator therefore was to advocate some adjustments in this area, and a formula was found that seemed satisfactory to all concerned.

Lummis was named chairman of the board, and Gay continued as chief executive officer and also assumed the title of president. The five existing board members were all confirmed in their posts, but the board was expanded to eight. Lummis introduced Mickey West, the Andrews, Kurth partner who advised Hughes on tax issues and who was said to have only two passions in life—shooting quail and dodging taxes (legally of course). Lummis also appointed William Rankin, a veteran Summa financial officer, adding a novel element of conventional business experience to the board. With this new structure, the three old heads of the empire still held a five-to-three majority over the new, titular head of the board in any show-down. But nobody, at this stage, was thinking in such unseemly terms.

What everyone was thinking was that a valid will would show up that would dictate what had to be done. The framework for a com-prehensive will search had been established shortly after Hughes's death by the probate court in California, where Will Lummis's cousin, Richard Gano, had been appointed administrator. Gano had been mandated by the court to conduct the search, and he asked the New York law firm of Davis & Cox to assist in this enterprise. Davis & Cox was Chester Davis's law firm and, as such, powerfully motivated in the quest for a Hughes will. Repeatedly, and as late as 1973, Hughes had expressed his intention of leaving his entire per-sonal estate to the Howard Hughes Medical Institute. Such a will would have effectively placed all Hughes's assets under the control of Davis and Gay, leaving Lummis with nothing to administer.

The will search logically began at the Romaine Street communi-cations headquarters, a two-story stucco building occupying a full block in a seedy section of Hollywood. Though largely unused in the last decade of Hughes's life, it was still a treasure-house of his effects. Its contents had been slightly thinned in 1974 as a result of a celebrated burglary that resulted in the loss of many documents and Nadine Henley's butterfly collection, but there was no report of a will being stolen at that time. It was generally, though not uni-versally, thought that the burglary was an inside job designed to weed out documents that might be embarrassing to Hughes if they were demanded by the courts. The chances were that if Hughes had entrusted his will to be kept at Romaine, it was still there somewhere. The building still housed vast undisturbed files of Hughes's documents, and all his movies, in special air-conditioned vaults, and odds and ends of his possessions.

This cluttered out-of-the-past attic was combed over and vaults were broken into. Nothing promising was found except two safe-deposit-box keys bearing the number 47 and no other identification. This discovery set off a long search of every bank Hughes had been known to have patronized. It yielded nothing. Every lawyer Hughes had ever consulted was questioned about a will, and, when a known attorney had died, his relatives or surviving partners were questioned. Hundreds of Hughes's colleagues, associates, and employees from his prehermit days were interviewed, and scores of hotels where he stayed—from the Beverly Hills Hotel to the Waldorf-Astoria in New York and the Mizpah Hotel in Tonopah, Nevada—were checked. Classified ads were inserted in forty newspapers from coast to coast: "Howard Robard Hughes Jr., son of Howard Robard Hughes Sr. and Allene Gano, born Dec. 24, 1905, died April 5, 1976. Anyone having information regarding this death, please phone 213 986-7047."

Summa even enlisted the extrasensory perceptions of a Hollywood psychic named Peter Hurkos, a man of considerable prestige in the movie colony, where stars often consult astrologers, numerologists, and suchlike on major career decisions. Hurkos had come to Hollywood after a well-publicized career in Europe, where he claimed to have solved a number of baffling murders, jewel thefts, and missing-persons cases through his gift of second sight.

By his own account in *Psychic: The Story of Peter Hurkos,* he had acquired the ability to see the unseen when he fell from a ladder while painting a house in his native Netherlands. In the hospital he discovered that he now had, in addition to a skull concussion, what he asserted scientists hailed as "the most highly developed psychic gift in the world." He could even solve mysteries by holding an object associated with a person, such as a ring, watch, or article of clothing. Holmes procured a pair of Hughes's shoes, but when Hurkos held them and peered into the unknown he saw nothing, possibly because Hughes had shuffled around in old slippers and had never worn the shoes.

With so much at stake, Hurkos proceeded down another psychic avenue. There were rumors that Hughes had stashed his will in a Houston bank years earlier without telling anybody which one. Hurkos had often, according to his autobiography, discovered the whereabouts of missing persons by holding a photo of them to his head and reading the scenes the pictures triggered. If the missing will was hidden in some lockbox in Houston, then Hurkos, it was reasoned, might be able to locate it from a photograph of the bank.

Andrews, Kurth was instructed to sally forth and photograph Houston banks, an assignment that still evokes wry head shaking among the partners of the conservative firm. The attorney and photographer they dispatched soon ran afoul of the law. Police surmised that they were casing the banks for a heist, and they had difficulty explaining that they were innocently trying to help a Hollywood psychic locate Howard Hughes's will. When they completed the assignment, the photos were forwarded to Hurkos. Again they yielded nothing. To his true believers, this established that the will was not in a Houston bank. Hurkos was not so categorical. He modestly acknowledged that his second sight was not flawless but worked only 85 percent of the time.

While the psychic will-hunt was going on, the first of a series of purported wills turned up in a place where no one would have thought to look. It appeared in the world headquarters of the Mormon faith in Salt Lake City, Utah, where it was found lying on a junior employee's desk. The will named old Noah Dietrich, Hughes's original right-hand man, as executor of the Hughes estate. If the will were found to be valid, all four heads of the empire could find themselves deposed or operating under the thumb of a man Hughes had discarded almost twenty years earlier. At first, both Lummis and the triumvirate viewed this threat lightly, but it would grow and grow in menace over the next year.

4

—

BIRDS IN THE HAND

THE ONE THING that could be confidently predicted of a Hughes will, when and if it was found, was that it would not contain a cheering message for any of his relations. Hughes was manifestly not a family man and showed no signs of family sentiment even in his dying days. When Dr. Thain, his last physician, was asked to testify on Hughes's intentions with regard to his relatives, he said, " 'Nothing.' He didn't want them to have 'one goddamn fucking dime'—if I may quote him explicitly."

There is no reason to believe the doctor misquoted Hughes on this point. It was only a degree more savage than what Hughes had said on this subject many times previously. His aversion to his relatives in the Houston area seems to have taken hold after his divorce from his first wife, Ella Rice, and remained constant down through the years. In one of the many draft wills composed by Nadine Henley on Hughes's behalf but never signed, Hughes went so far as to bequeath his old Houston family home on Yoakum Boulevard to his aunt Annette Lummis. But since he had already given the same house to Mrs. Lummis twenty years earlier, the thought was less generous than it appeared. On the subject of his other relatives, the draft will said: "I have intentionally omitted making provision for all of my heirs who are not specifically mentioned herein and I hereby generally and specifically disinherit each, any, and all persons whomsoever claiming to be or who may lawfully be determined to be my heirs at law, except such as are mentioned in this will."

Aside from Aunt Annette, Hughes did not really know any of his relatives. He had a fair number of first cousins in the Houston area and dotted around the country, but they played scarcely any part in his life. The one he probably knew best was Will Lummis, with whom he had two encounters before Lummis was ten years old. After their first meeting at the Yoakum house, when Lummis was four, Hughes wrote uncharacteristically to his aunt to say what an "adorable" boy her son William was. As Hughes's views on children closely paralleled those of W. C. Fields, this was indeed an accolade. Their second meeting, also at Yoakum, occurred when Lummis was nine. By this time, Hughes was being lauded as the heroic around-the-world aviator and Lummis was perhaps a shade less adorable. Lummis's only distinct recollection of this occasion was of the great aviator telling him, "Goddamnit, boy, get off my porch."

Hughes's antipathy for his family, however, had no relevance as far as the laws of inheritance were concerned. And with every day that passed without the discovery of an unchallengeable will, his family came more and more into the reckoning as claimants for The Money. So did the Internal Revenue Service. Without a will, the IRS could claim over 70 percent of the estate's value. Indeed, this aspect of intestacy was the main reason for believing that there was a Hughes will leaving everything to his tax-exempt Medical Institute, a move that would have left the IRS virtually empty-handed.

But even after tax there would be many millions to distribute. Without a will, the Hughes estate would go to his relatives, regardless of Hughes's intentions. There was, however, a wide measure of uncertainty over which relatives might benefit and which

ones would wind up with nothing. And uncertainty in this area
was something that Will Lummis was anxious to avoid. There was
no point in members of the family positioning themselves to benefit from The Money if they subsequently threw large chunks of it
away by litigating against each other.

A few weeks after Hughes's death, Lummis summoned all the
potential heirs he could think of to a conference. There were fifteen that he knew of apart from himself and his mother. They were
all on the maternal side of the family and all first cousins of
Hughes, like Lummis, or first cousins once removed. At the meeting he warned those assembled that the occasion might well prove
to be academic, in that, if a valid will surfaced, their interest would
probably cease altogether. He also warned of the possible perils if
it turned out that they were entitled to a share of Hughes's fortune.
"This is found money," he insisted, "the kind of money you might
find in the street, and we shouldn't fight about."

The problem, he told them, was that, in the event of Hughes's
intestacy, the disposition of his estate could go one of several different ways. Before any distribution could take place, there would
have to be a legal determination of Hughes's domicile or chief residence, and this could be years away given Hughes's peripatetic
life. California, Texas, and Nevada were all in contention on the
domicile issue, and there could well be other states wanting to get
into the act. All of these states had their own inheritance laws, dif-
fering from each other.

In California and Nevada, the entire estate would go to the
nearest of kin. This would be Will Lummis's mother—provided no
undivorced wives, children, brothers, or sisters unexpectedly appeared out of Hughes's distant past.

But if Texas was declared his residence, a radically different
order of inheritance would prevail. The estate would be split
equally between his maternal and paternal relatives, through his
first cousins once removed on either side. In short, if there was one
paternal heir and a score of maternal heirs, the heir on the father's
side of the family would get 50 percent of the estate and the twenty
maternal heirs would divide the remaining 50 percent.

What Lummis wanted from the meeting was agreement that they should act in concert, no matter what domicile was eventually decided for Hughes. In furtherance of this common cause, Lummis was able to announce that his own mother, Annette, had generously agreed to waive her rights to be the sole heir—under the laws of California and Nevada. This should ensure shares for everybody. Lummis persuaded his cousins of the merits of this approach, and they agreed that, in the future, there should be "one family spokesman" on these issues and "a designating authority" to deal with legal matters. Will Lummis was formally appointed spokesman and designating authority and would soon find himself exercised in both capacities.

Shortly after the accord between the maternal relatives, there appeared three claimants from the paternal side of the family. While Lummis had an accurate list of potential maternal heirs, he knew nothing about those on Hughes's father's side of the family. He had never even heard of the three newcomers.

They were the three granddaughters of the well-known screenwriter and novelist Rupert Hughes, the brother of Howard Hughes's father—Agnes Lapp Roberts, Elspeth Lapp DePould, and Barbara Lapp Cameron. As first cousins once removed from Howard Hughes, they were proper claimants to half the fortune if Hughes was ruled a Texan. If he proved to be a Californian or a Nevadan, they would have no claim whatever. Lummis examined their credentials and became convinced they were authentic. The problem was deciding exactly how they should fit into the fail-safe system that the maternal heirs were in the process of constructing for themselves.

Negotiations with the paternal trio came down to examining odds and probabilities. They had only one chance in three—Texas versus California and Nevada—of inheriting anything. The odds were thus two to one that they would wind up in the cold altogether. Instead, Lummis and the maternal relatives offered them what lawyers call a "bird-in-the-hand arrangement," which the paternal heirs found acceptable. They agreed to a guaranteed one fourth of the estate, regardless of where the legal wheel of fortune stopped on the domicile issue. While this was less than the possible half if Hughes was declared a Texan, it was preferable to the zero forthcoming if the domicile spin stopped on California or Nevada.

This exercise in sanity was then reduced to writing in a sixteen-page "Settlement Agreement" filed in the Houston probate court in July 1976. It provided that Lummis's mother, as the heir most apparent—and sole heir in California and Nevada—would receive only 25 percent of the estate. Fifty percent would go to the remaining maternal heirs—or approximately 3 percent each to sixteen cousins. The remaining one-fourth would be split three ways among the three Rupert Hughes granddaughters—8⅓ percent of the estate for each.

The agreement spelled out its reason for being:

"The parties understand that the question of domicile may take years to resolve by litigation and believe that protracted litigation necessarily would involve serious adverse consequences to each of them and it is in their best interests to resolve as between themselves their conflicting claims based on domicile. There would be substantial financial and emotional strain on the parties and their families, uncertainties and difficulties with the management of Summa Corporation (which is the principal asset of the Estate) and the possibility of substantial diminution of the value of the Estate . . . In view of the problems outlined above, the parties have conducted extensive negotiations in an effort to settle their respective claims regarding the Estate, which are conflicting, to the end that they may receive agreed portions of the Estate regardless of the ultimate resolution of the question of the Decedent's domicile."

The agreement had some teeth to it as well. If any of the signers took any court action to contest or attempt to defeat any provision "without the consent of the designating authority," i.e., Will Lummis, they would be deemed to have breached the agreement and forfeit their share, which would be assigned to those who stayed in line.

As a result of the unexpected appearance of the three paternal heirs, a provision was devised for handling any future surprise claimants. If any additional maternal heirs turned up, the maternal side would incorporate them into their share and the paternal heirs would do the same for any additional heirs from their side of the family.

Before the year was out, two more claimants on the paternal side did indeed show up, this time out of the farthest reaches of the genealogical ballpark. They were a brother and sister, Rush Hughes, seventy-four, and Avis Hughes McIntyre, seventy-six, and by their own admission they had no blood relationship whatever to Howard Hughes. Instead, they were the stepchildren of novelist Rupert Hughes, the grandfather of the three earlier paternal-side prospective heirs. Rupert Hughes had been married three times. Rush and Avis were children of his second wife by an earlier marriage. Rupert Hughes, however, had never adopted them and had not even mentioned them in his own will.

What Rush and Avis had was an innovative lawyer by the name of George Dean, who had been a friend of Avis McIntyre's for years. Mrs. McIntyre, who lived in Montgomery, Alabama, had an exceptionally lively mind, which she kept well informed on current events, including the affairs of Howard Hughes. When it seemed possible that Hughes had left no will, she called her friend Dean and asked if he would care to enter her brother and herself in "the rat race" for Hughes's fortune.

George Dean was an unlawyerlike lawyer, rarely seen toting a briefcase. He was primarily a strategist, rather than a "whereas" drafter. He had a sharp mind and an equally sharp wit, which he frequently turned against his own foibles. Like Scaramouche, he was "born with the gift of laughter and a sense that the world is mad." Long a resident of the Deep South, he was active in a number of civil rights cases and also put together several landmark cases on behalf of derelict and retarded patients committed involuntarily to state mental hospitals. In taking the case against the Hughes estate, Dean said, "I went from working for the poor nuts to a case involving the richest nut."

He assembled a team of young lawyers, including T. Norton Bond of Pensacola, Florida, who established close contact with

Avis's brother, Rush, and Robert Roch and Wayne Fisher, partners in the new hard-driving Houston firm of Fisher, Roch & Gallagher.

The case they constructed for Avis and Rush centered on a little-known and rarely invoked legal doctrine called "equitable adoption" which only prevails in certain states. It is comparable to the doctrine that established the rights of an unmarried common-law wife—if she is treated as if she were a wife, under certain circumstances she acquires the rights of a wife. The equitable adoption theory extends similar rights to children who are taken into a family but not adopted.

When the Dean team filed the claims of Rush and Avis in the Houston probate court, they understandably pushed for Texas to be declared Hughes's domicile. Otherwise, they faced the same plight originally faced by the three Rupert Hughes granddaughters—unless Texas was ruled to be the billionaire's home, they would have no claim at all. By this time, Will Lummis and his line of maternal relatives were contending that Hughes's four years in Nevada had made him a legal Nevadan. In Nevada, unlike California and Texas, there was no state inheritance tax.

There ensued a series of court skirmishes, with Lummis and Rupert Hughes's granddaughters questioning the claim of the two nonrelatives. There were things to be said on both sides of the equitably adopted pair. Rupert Hughes had educated them and, by Avis's account, had wanted to adopt them but had been blocked by their natural father, an engineer named George Bissell.

Avis testified that Rupert Hughes and his lawyers "had contacted my father and he said absolutely not. He would not under any circumstances permit us to be adopted. . . . But from then on, Rupert asked if we would like to change our name to Hughes because that's what he would like and that we were his children and that was that."

Rupert Hughes, the person who could authoritatively resolve the matter, had died in 1956 at the age of eighty-four, and Avis conceded that she had no documents to support her claim. But the Dean team dug back into the early days of Hollywood and produced two aging movie queens, Colleen Moore and Eleanor Boardman, who supported Rush's story of the adoption-by-declaration. Each testified that Rupert Hughes, who wrote many movie scripts, had introduced Rush to them on Hollywood sets in 1921 as "my son."

On the other hand, neither Avis nor Rush had filed any claim against the estate of Rupert Hughes when he died and left them out of his will. Their claim of equitable adoption had first surfaced as it pertained to the estate of Rupert's nephew Howard, where the stakes were incomparably higher.

Once again, Will Lummis decided that the threat of disruption between potential heirs needed to be headed off at the pass. A year after the first settlement agreement had lined up the maternal relatives and the first three paternal relatives, a supplemental agreement was signed taking care of Avis and Rush. Although the original contract specified that the paternal relatives would accommodate any newcomers from their side of the family, once again the maternal side, persuaded by Lummis, dipped into its prospective share to avoid any friction.

Avis and Rush were each cut in for 4¾ percent of the estate, which naturally required a new arithmetic of expectation for the other parties. To help accommodate the 9½ percent for the paternal newcomers, the three paternal granddaughters reduced their share from 25 percent to 19 percent. The remaining 3½ percent was yielded by the seventeen maternal heirs. The overall breakdown was 71½ percent to the maternals and 28½ percent to the enlarged paternal group. And the full cast list now consisted of Hughes's Aunt Annette, twelve maternal first cousins—including Will Lummis—four maternal first cousins once removed, three paternal first cousins once removed, and two paternal first cousins-by-equitable-adoption.

Given the normal course of estate battles—and the number of relatives involved in the Hughes estate—these accommodations and arrangements constituted a remarkable, and even unique, display of restraint, grace, generosity, and good manners. Of course, with so much money involved, not everyone saw it that way. In the bitter and prolonged heirship battles to come, these agreements were assailed by outsiders-who-wanted-in as coldhearted and cynical moves, a callous "cutting up of the Hughes estate before his body was cold," as one attorney phrased it.

The Lummis agreements, however, were in no sense automatic qualifications for The Money. The apparent heirs would have to be declared legal heirs by the courts before they could receive a cent, and that could not happen until after the courts had determined Hughes's domicile. All the agreements ensured was that whatever grappling, kneeing, or jostling occurred in the courts, the relatives would not grapple, knee, or jostle each other.

Meanwhile, the Houston probate court had made it abundantly clear that it was not about to take anything that Lummis and his family might assert about their ancestry on trust. One of the first moves made by probate court judge Patrick Gregory in Houston was to appoint an "attorney *ad litem*" with the specific task of delving deeply into Hughes's family background to ensure that no heir—apparent or otherwise—was overlooked. The appointed attorney, O. Theodore Dinkins, Jr., an authority on the Texas probate code, immediately gave notice of his intention to conduct one of history's more exhaustive *ad litem* investigations. He recruited a bright young assistant, Suzanne Finstad, and a professional genealogist, Mrs. Mary Smith Fay, and together they trekked off into all the murkier corners of Hughes's past. Their task, as described by Ms. Finstad, who would later write a book about this odyssey, was "to locate any and all rightful heirs of Howard Hughes—people who, if they existed, were either not aware of their relationship to the dead magnate, or chose, for whatever reason, not to pursue it." In short, they had a license, a duty even, to find heirs who could totally upset Will Lummis's carefully arranged applecart of claimants.

They were also exceptionally well funded, because in the probate court's view, Dinkins was rendering a service to the estate, and it was deemed proper that the estate should be charged for the *ad litem* research. The research would take almost five years and consume more than $700,000 of Hughes's fortune, an investigative fee far exceeding the value of most probated estates. For Lummis, in the position of financing an operation that could result in his disinheritance, it was a worrying time, but there were enough other problems to occupy his mind.

Some of these came in the shape of John Hill, the ambitious Texas attorney general. Aware of the millions at stake in the domicile issue, Hill filed papers in Judge Gregory's court asserting that the billionaire was a Texan and that Texas was entitled to collect his state inheritance tax, which is 16 percent of the estate. Lummis, of course, was still hoping that inheritance-tax-free Nevada would prove to be the domicile, but Hill had a profoundly low opinion of that idea. He also had the organization to do something about it, putting together yet another team of lawyers headed by a bright and energetic thirty-two-year-old assistant named Rick Harrison. Harrison's task was to dig up everything he could on Hughes that might assist Hill in court.

Prior to Hughes's death, Harrison had shared the conventional public view of the billionaire as an eccentric business genius. But when he began digging into his affairs, he got a series of odd blips on his legal radar—contradictory stories from the Hughes keepers, evasions of known facts, the resistance of Summa's counsel, Chester Davis, to the production of witnesses and vital documents. He quickly concluded that there was something odd behind the long Hughes charade and, fascinated at what he was finding, went beyond the routine legal moves of asserting the Texas tax claim and focused on the hidden story of the way Hughes had lived and died. His curiosity and persistence turned up evidence that Hughes was something other than a reclusive businessman.

Aware that Mexican officials had seized thousands of Hughes documents immediately after the dying billionaire had been taken out of Acapulco, Harrison set about acquiring them. Doing so required a kind of legal double play. The documents had all been Xeroxed by U.S. officials at the request of Treasury Secretary William Simon for scrutiny by the Internal Revenue Service, but the IRS was notoriously grudging when it came to sharing information. Harrison importuned Simon to help him, and after a formal request from the governor of Texas, the IRS gave copies to Attorney General Hill's office. Initially, Harrison found himself working with bad-quality photocopies, but he was able to decipher a sad thought written in Hughes's hand—"Nobody gives a damn about me, all they want is my money." But the document that really riveted Harrison's attention bore a late 1973 date and noted that Hughes was inquiring of his aides, "What is Watergate?"

By this time Watergate had been the subject of front-page and prime-time coverage for months. Moreover, there was substantial public evidence that the Hughes empire was involved in Watergate up to its ears. The two telephones tapped by the Watergate burglars in the Democratic Party's committee office both belonged to people with strong Hughes connections—Spencer Oliver was the son of Robert Oliver, who had been a Washington lobbyist for Hughes Tool, while Larry O'Brien, the Democratic National Committee chairman, had been taken onto the Hughes payroll at $15,000 a month after the death of Robert Kennedy. O'Brien would go on to earn some $300,000 for his discreet assistance on various Hughes projects.

There were also other Hughes ramifications that came to light through Robert R. Mullen and Company, a P.R. agency in Washington, D.C., that employed E. Howard Hunt, one of the main characters deployed by the Nixon White House on a variety of "dirty tricks" activities against Democratic opponents. The Mullen agency's principal client was Howard Hughes. It was headed by Bob Bennett, a flexible and energetic Mormon who was on excellent terms with Bill Gay, the CIA, and influential sections of the Washington media. No identity had been disclosed for Deep Throat, who had fed *Washington Post* reporters Carl Bernstein and Bob Woodward a series of damaging Watergate revelations. Bob Bennett, Hughes's man in Washington, seemed like an excellent candidate as far as President Nixon was concerned, but he denied the role.

It was also clear that Nixon's own motivation, which set Watergate events in motion, was deeply colored by his dealings with Hughes, which had been both beneficial and hazardous in the

past. Nixon would attribute his defeat in the 1960 election against
John Kennedy to a late campaign revelation about a $205,000
"loan" channeled to his brother Donald by Howard Hughes. Further revelations about the loan adversely affected Nixon's chances
in the 1962 race against Edmund "Pat" Brown for governor of
California. Again Nixon lost the election. This much was history.
But Nixon also had reason to be apprehensive about what the
public might think of a more recent secret act of generosity—
$100,000 handed to his close friend Bebe Rebozo by a Hughes ex-
ecutive, which might be construed as an undeclared campaign
contribution. Larry O'Brien's presumed knowledge of this bag job
helped make him a White House target. The fear was that O'Brien
might use his knowledge to turn the 1972 presidential election
over to the Democrats with another Nixon-Hughes money scandal. Hence the tapping of his telephone as part of the first undetected Watergate burglary. The second burglary, dictated by
pressure to locate O'Brien's "shit file" on a Nixon-Hughes connection, was the one that went awry and ultimately led to the top-
pling of a president. Bob Haldeman, Nixon's White House chief of
staff, would say, "On matters pertaining to Hughes, Nixon sometimes seemed to lose touch with reality." Nixon apparently became convinced that Watergate was a plot against him engineered
by Hughes in conjunction with the CIA.

As Harrison studied the Hughes documents, he was at first incredulous that Hughes should apparently know so little about
what was going on in his name. But there seemed to be absolutely
no doubt about it—the demon prince of Watergate didn't even
know he was in the play. Harrison's next thought was that there
might be many other aspects of his existence that Hughes was not
altogether aware of—things like where he was and where he was
going, matters of some relevance to a domicile investigation.

Some light would soon be shone in this area. In December 1976,
an unexpected rift cracked the wall of secrecy that Gay and the
Mormon aides had erected around the billionaire. In its December
13 cover issue, *Time* magazine carried extensive excerpts from a
book featuring the revelations of two low-level functionaries from

the traveling Hughes asylum, Gordon Margulis, a waiter, and Mell Stewart, a barber and male nurse. The book, *Howard Hughes: The Hidden Years,* depicted the wretched conditions in which the billionaire had spent his last years, and set forth his longtime dependency on drugs and his physical decline, until he looked, in Margulis's graphic phrase, "like a witch's brother." Although neither Margulis nor Stewart was privy to the empire's financial affairs, they gave a gritty, day-to-day insider's account of Hughes's deterioration in exile and raised questions about his mental competence. Since they were the first insiders to talk, their revelations became an international best-seller, and they were widely booked on television talk shows.

One of their anecdotes underlined the awesome power of a Hughes whim before his decline. It involved Baskin-Robbins banana nut ice cream, Hughes's favorite flavor, which he ate every day in his years in his Desert Inn hideout. When his supply dwindled, his aides were dismayed to learn that the manufacturer had discontinued the flavor. In a panic, they appealed to the maker to turn out a special order and were told that the minimum would be 350 gallons. Ordered by their superiors to "Get it at once!" they had a truckload rushed out from the Los Angeles factory and unloaded into the Desert Inn just before Hughes finished his supply. The next day Hughes commented that it was time for a change and "From now on it's French vanilla." It took the resort months to get rid of its huge surplus supply of banana nut ice cream.

Why Margulis and Stewart disclosed Hughes's secrets was, once again, entwined with The Money. Although they performed the more unpleasant tasks of personally taking care of the declining billionaire, they were the lowest-paid of the fifteen-man entourage. "Mell and I did the scut work," said Margulis, "and Gay's aides got the big money." Neither had been hired by Gay, but they had been co-opted because they had each encountered Hughes face-to-face. When the Gay-dominated Summa board had passed out contracts and lifetime consulting agreements shortly before Hughes's death, Margulis and Stewart had been passed over. Unlike the aides and the doctors, they were not bound by the secrecy clause of these agreements and were free to talk, write, and publish.

In addition, they had resented the way Hughes was controlled and furnished with drugs. Three weeks after his death, they sought out the coauthor of this book, Jim Phelan, to disclose what they had seen.

When the *Time* story hit the newstands and the Margulis-Stewart disclosures moved into the bookstores, a Summa public relations executive asked Bill Gay, "What are you going to do to counter this new book about Hughes?"

"I'm not going to do anything," said Gay. "Who cares about what a waiter and a barber have to say."

Later, in a deposition, Will Lummis said that he confronted Gay about the *Time* article. "Mr. Gay assured me that everything in this article and the forthcoming book . . . was false." Asked by an attorney if Gay specified what was false, Lummis replied, "No, I did not cross-examine the man." Gay was supported in his dismissal of the Margulis-Stewart account by the two aides he had put on the Summa board, Holmes and Myler.

"They said the allegations were absurd and false," Lummis testified, "and that Mr. Hughes was firmly in control of himself and his affairs, fully aware of everything going on in his business, up to the moment of his death."

At that time, because of the bungled autopsy, Lummis knew nothing of the true level of codeine in Hughes's corpse or of the broken needles embedded in his arms. He accepted the assurances of Gay and the aides that all had been well in the billionaire's last days.

Lummis was on a learning curve as far as the Hughesmen were concerned, and still fairly low on it. He did, however, make an appointment that would accelerate his education. Impressed with the way George Dean and his colleagues had handled the less-than-rock-solid case of Avis and Rush, Lummis recruited Dean for his own legal team at Summa. Like Rick Harrison, George Dean had a lively curiosity about Hughes's terminal years and none of the sense of family privacy that restrained Lummis. He went aboard at

Summa eagerly, sprinkling the wit and wisdom of Lyndon Johnson about how nice it was to be in a large tent "and pissing out for a change."

The irony of being paid by a large corporation for doing what he liked best—stirring things up—appealed to Dean enormously. "I soon became a very thin tail wagging a ninety-pound dog," he would recall. Once, when asked what this tummler of an attorney did at Summa, Nadine Henley turned her eyes heavenward and replied, "Mr. Dean does *everything*."

5

—

MELTDOWN

THE NEW CHAIRMAN of Summa was hampered by an old problem. Employees long steeped in the doctrines of secrecy were reluctant to come forward and tell a newcomer what they knew. All the same, Will Lummis applied himself diligently to the task of finding out exactly what he was supposed to be administering. It was an exercise that would lead him from curiosity, through bewilderment tinged with fascination, and finally into a state of acute alarm.

Though no expert on business organization, Lummis found it strange that a commercial empire with its headquarters and most of its holdings located in Nevada should, in effect, be run from offices on either side of the continent. Bill Gay and Nadine Henley habitually worked out of offices near Gay's home in Encino, California, while Chester Davis could most often be found in the offices of his Manhattan law firm or on his farm in upstate New York. Apparently, Hughes's example of remote control by telephone had been thoroughly mimicked by his subordinates, though not, Lummis came to think, with such good reason.

Lummis was also disconcerted to find that the Gay-Davis-Henley ruling triumvirate was less cohesive than it appeared. Of the three, Lummis got on best with Nadine Henley, who also took to Lummis, partly because, she said, "some of his mannerisms remind me so much of Howard." But Mrs. Henley was a facilitator rather than an initiator; she would take her lead from Davis or Gay. But from Mrs. Henley and some of the company's less-inhibited financial officers, Lummis was able to establish at an early stage that Summa had problems, the most notable being that it wasn't making any money, indeed, quite the reverse. Lummis therefore set his new codirector, Mickey West, the task of gingering up the finance department to produce a financial report on the company's performance going back to 1970, the year Hughes went into exile. This internal inquiry took many months to complete. Meanwhile, Lummis asked around.

On a visit to Encino, Lummis asked Bill Gay privately what he thought Summa's problem was. Gay said he thought that Chester Davis was the problem. Gay complained about Davis's soaring "mystery fees" while cases were allowed to drag on unsettled. But that was only part of the problem. Even though Gay was now president of Summa, he felt he "couldn't control" Davis because of his arrogant view of his role as general counsel. Davis always insisted that legal affairs at Summa were his exclusive turf and no one else's business. And, as Lummis already knew full well, there were not many aspects of Summa without a legal problem.

Very shortly after this illuminating conversation, Lummis took Chester Davis quietly to one side and asked him what *he* thought Summa's problem was. Davis said that he thought that Bill Gay was the problem. He told Lummis, "The estate can be thankful that I have been keeping a close eye on Gay over the years." Gay had a lot of "grandiose projects" in mind, but fortunately Davis had been "sitting on the lid."

Lummis was obliged to deduce that whatever it was that provided the Gay/Davis axis with its corporate authority, warm fellow feeling was not it. As a result, Lummis became keener than ever to acquire objective information and, where possible, to see for himself what was going on. In this pursuit he was hampered by the compartmentalization of his empire that Hughes had fostered and the Gay-Davis-Henley trio had continued. Internal communications within Summa were not just flawed, they were deliberately crimped except in transmitting orders from the top. A worker in one cubbyhole had no idea what was going on in an adjoining cubbyhole and was not encouraged to find out. The few who had some inkling of a bigger picture were often not eager to discuss it. In many cases, Lummis unnervingly found, there was not much cheerful to discuss.

Summa boasted no fewer than sixteen operating divisions, but their operation was less than impressive. In the ranching division Lummis could find only one active rancher, who complained of a miserable, housebound existence as he wrote memo after memo to various Summa executives asking for a tractor. Lummis ordered his tractor. In the land-mining division, Lummis found a rich profusion of rights but no sign of any gold or silver actually being mined. He would later discover that almost all the expensively acquired rights were, in fact, useless. It was a similar story in the ocean-mining division, which had earlier achieved some notoriety as the cover for the Jennifer Project, a $500 million CIA initiative designed to retrieve a sunken Russian submarine from the floor of the Pacific Ocean near Honolulu. The lead vessel on this top secret mission was called the *Hughes Glomar Explorer,* and the discovery of its true purpose in 1974 had a dramatic media impact, but its commercial effect was minimal. Lummis was impressed with the weight of press cuttings but could detect little sign of any wealth being extracted from the seabed by Hughes's ocean-mining operation. The largest Summa division of all was the gaming operation in Nevada, the business Lummis knew least about. Repairing his ignorance on this subject became Lummis's major priority.

LAS VEGAS BLOOMS with gaudy splendor in the desert because it is irrigated by the money pumped in from tourists by the casinos; without it Vegas would revert to the lizards and the coyotes, its original inhabitants. Its casinos prime their pumps with the fantasy of instant riches for the credulous and hopeful. But they rely on something called the "vigorish" to ensure that the casinos, not their patrons, will prevail. Vigorish is the house edge, the mathematical odds in favor of the casinos. The odds are built in and as dependable as the proposition that one hundred is larger than ninety. Casino patrons may prosper temporarily, even spectacularly, but, in the long haul, the vigorish guarantees that the losers will outnumber the winners. The way to make money in Nevada is to own a casino.

But buying a casino is only the first step toward making money; a more imperative requirement is knowing how to run it. For the vigorish is constantly under threat. There are professional cheats, called "cross-roaders," who employ such deplorable tactics as counterfeiting chips or slipping their own crooked dice into a game. There are teams that cluster around a slot machine to conceal a technician who drills a hole in the machine and jiggers a jackpot. There are dishonest dealers called "chip eaters" who yawn and slip a hundred-dollar chip into their mouths before taking a break in duty. Other dealers may team with confederates across the table and systematically overpay their winning bets. There can be collusion in the counting rooms, with winnings skimmed off before they are tallied or reported. Running a successful casino requires that those running it be knowledgeable, suspicious, and eternally vigilant.

Hughes's predecessors at the Desert Inn, reputed the number one "class joint" on the Vegas Strip, were just such a body of men. They were headed by an old patriarch, Morris Barney "Moe" Dalitz, whose parents had wanted him to become a violinist but who had segued instead into rum-running and illegal gambling in Ohio and Kentucky. Lured west by the early blooming of legalized gambling, Dalitz had fetched with him three seasoned colleagues, all as vigilant at guarding the vigorish as a Spanish duenna protecting a sixteen-year-old maiden.

Hughes had rented the entire ninth-floor penthouse at the Desert Inn on his arrival in 1966. As the Christmas–New Year holidays approached, Dalitz and Company disapproved of their new tenant occupying all the valuable space. They wanted the penthouse suites for high-rolling customers, not a hermit with nonswinging Mormon aides who never patronized the gambling tables. When they prodded Hughes to find other quarters, he solved his housing problem with the élan of a Walter Mitty: He bought the Desert Inn. He then bought six more casinos, prompted by a kind of vigorish of his own. The IRS had a tax rule that imposed steep levies on passive profits, and this made the $546 million Hughes had just realized from the sale of his TWA stock highly vulnerable to the taxman's attentions. The taxes imposed on active investments, however, were very much lower. By investing huge cash sums into the Las Vegas economy, Hughes trimmed the IRS odds against him.

This all made sense, albeit of a bizarre kind, to Lummis, but the puzzling part was what happened to the casinos after Hughes acquired them. No doubt there were problems associated with the controversy over Bob Maheu's eviction, but from the end of 1970 Hughes's casinos should, logically, have become settled, moneymaking machines. But the provisional figures showed that Hughes's gaming empire, consisting of the Desert Inn, Landmark, Castaways, Silver Slipper, Sands, and Frontier in Las Vegas and Harold's Club in Reno, had collectively lost money in every year of Hughes's exile. Yet during the same period all their major competitors had scored large profits every year. Whatever happened, Lummis wondered, to the vigorish under Summa?

Such a long losing streak by the house was not only weird, it was against known odds. As he patiently turned over Summa's long-hidden fiscal hole cards, Lummis could see that there were not enough ins and far too many outs. One did not need to know the back-line odds on a dice table or the house advantage in dealing blackjack from a four-deck shoe to understand that if the house keeps losing, it will go broke.

Lummis asked Gay, who had taken charge of the Nevada operation after Maheu's ouster, what the problem seemed to be. Gay told Lummis that it all stemmed from the "constraints" placed on him by Hughes, who had blocked all his efforts to finance improvements in Las Vegas. One consequence of this was that the

Department of Health had shut down ninety rooms in the Desert Inn back in 1974, earning Summa an unenviable reputation as the first Las Vegas Strip slumlord. Gay assured his chairman that if he would only sanction the appropriate level of capital expenditure in the future, renaissance could not be long delayed. Lummis was not reassured. As far as he could tell, all the strategic decisions in Las Vegas had been made by Gay, and, in retrospect, they did not look supremely bright.

After getting rid of Maheu, Gay had summarily removed a number of seasoned gambling executives and replaced them with Mormon cronies as unschooled as he and Davis. At the Desert Inn, he had installed a onetime car dealer from Utah. At the Landmark, he put a lawyer in charge. He brought out his son, a recent Harvard graduate, and two of his son's fresh-faced classmates and gave them key positions in the hotel and casino organization. Even when he retained experienced hands, he intruded into their operations and frequently overruled their decisions. Some of them quit and took their know-how over to rival casinos, diminishing the Summa efficiency and enhancing that of its competition. Lummis eventually concluded, "Gay appeared to me to be a man who badly needed assistance and had surrounded himself with people who were really unable to give it to him."

While Lummis was piecing together the story of the casino disasters, one of his agents roamed the country conducting a census of Hughes's aircraft. They ranged from a flock of modern JetStars to an ancient Sikorsky amphibian that he had crashed in 1943 trying to land on Lake Mead. At various locales around the United States, he had new and old planes under guard, untouched and by his orders untouchable. The flagship for this grounded aerial circus was the *Spruce Goose,* the giant wooden flying boat constructed to ferry troops over the Atlantic in World War II but not completed until two years after the war ended. After Hughes had flown it once, for a mile, it had been tucked away in a windowless hangar in Long Beach, California, under armed guard. There a secretive crew of workmen had maintained it in its pristine and inexplicable splendor for thirty years at a cost to Hughes of $50 million. Stashed elsewhere were Hawker Siddeleys, Aerocommanders, Grumman Gulfstreams, Cessna Golden Eagles, and Convair 880s. Most of these planes had motors corroding from neglect, but there was also a well-maintained group of corporate jets for the top Summa executives, who ferried friends, relatives, casino entertainers, and themselves where fancy beckoned. "If you flew commercial," said a former Summa vice president, "you were a low-grade fellow indeed."

The catering on these aircraft was superb, as were the details. The handblown glassware and the table napkins were designed by leading designer Mario Zamparelli, who was esteemed very highly by Bill Gay. Lummis, something of a puritan in matters of executive display, became quite fascinated by the uses and misuses of Hughes's air power. Eventually, he managed to persuade Paul Winn, a former aide to Bill Gay, to describe in affidavit form the kind of flexibility the aircraft afforded. Winn chose Gay and Davis's 1972 trip to Europe. Its ostensible purpose was finding Hughes, then holed up in Vancouver, a new "location" to live.

"Gay's wife, Mary, their child, and another executive's wife and three children were already in Monte Carlo," Winn related. "We flew to Nice and rented luxurious suites at the Hôtel de Paris in Monte Carlo. Mrs. Gay told us that the kids were 'driving her crazy,' and Mr. Gay said he wanted to see about buying a watch. Consequently, the pilot was instructed to fly Mr. and Mrs. Gay, Davis, and me to Zurich, where we stayed overnight at a luxurious hotel. We also kept our suites in Monte Carlo. . . . During this European 'business trip,' we flew to the island of Majorca so Chester Davis and his daughter, Beatrice, who had joined us, could visit another of his daughters there.

"In 1973, while on a trip to Europe in the corporate jet with Gay, his wife, and others, Mrs. Gay suggested a flight from London to Tours, France. She had seen a clock in an antique store there the summer before and thought that Gay would like to obtain it. The group flew to Tours, hired two taxis for the day, and traveled to the antique store on the outskirts of town.

"On another occasion," Winn said, "I was asked to accompany Gay and two others on a trip to Salt Lake City because they needed a fourth to play gin rummy. It required that I incur hotel expenses for the night before returning."

The picture that Lummis was getting was of an exceptionally benign way of life as far as Summa's high command was concerned. And this would be reinforced by analysis of some of its property acquisitions. A year after taking over at Summa, Gay had arranged for the purchase of a plush residence in Miami Beach, again "to provide a home for Hughes." It was extensively redone and redecorated, and a tennis court and swimming pool were added, although Hughes didn't play tennis and after 1973 could not even walk, much less swim. The billionaire never took up residence there. Instead, Gay, Davis, and the Hughes aides used the house for recreation and occasional "business meetings" to which the participants would be whisked by corporate jets and then whisked back to their posts, the aides to monitor the deteriorating billionaire on "location" and Gay to Encino or Las Vegas or wherever.

Lummis was also a bit mystified to find Summa responsible for the Xanadu Princess Hotel out in the Atlantic on Grand Bahama Island, which didn't seem to fit even into Hughes's logic-defying scheme of things. It had once been a "location," but Hughes had not been in the habit of buying "locations" after moving into exile. Hughes had purchased the Princess for $7,980,000 in a transaction negotiated by Chester Davis. It was an attractive hotel but, according to an independent valuation drawn to Lummis's attention, worth little more than half what was paid for it.

Bill Gay's office at 17000 Ventura Boulevard in Encino was not exactly a new acquisition, but it had an interesting history. When Hughes got news that Gay had quartered himself so conveniently close to his own home, he went into another of his rages against his chief executive and ordered that the Encino office be shut down. Apparently, he thought that Gay should position himself closer to the action in Las Vegas. The aides had then mollified

Hughes by saying there was nothing of any consequence in Encino, "just a little office over a barbershop." Lummis knew
nothing of this history when he went to see Gay in Encino and saw
how elegantly the office block had been refurbished, with Mario
Zamparelli's touch on all its floors. The vestibule had an impressive parquet floor, inlaid with chips of oak, walnut, and teak. The
conference hall had silk draperies and mohair fabric on the walls.
The bathroom fixtures were in tasteful onyx. Although Bill Gay
clearly qualified for television's *Life Styles of the Rich and Famous,* he successfully avoided such scrutiny. ABC's 20/20 once
spent weeks trying to get him on camera but had to settle for a
shot of him being tailed by a car with TV reporter Geraldo Rivera
shouting questions at him and getting no answers.

Lummis's relations with Gay, however, were not discordant
from the outset. While Gay was less than forthcoming about
Summa's financial meltdown, he maintained a show of civility to
the new chairman. Chester Davis was another story.

Although Davis had endorsed the legal processes that made
Lummis the administrator and Summa's sole stockholder, it became rapidly apparent that he viewed Lummis as Summa's ser-
vant, not its master. To Davis, Lummis's titles were essentially
honorifics, designed to keep the legal situation on hold until a
Hughes will showed up. And Davis was confident (a) that it would
show up and (b) that its main provision would be the bequest of
the estate to the Howard Hughes Medical Institute, which he controlled with Bill Gay. At that point it would be bye-bye, Mr. Lummis. With this scenario in mind, Davis saw no reason why Lummis
should involve himself in the nitty-gritty of Summa's affairs, especially not in Davis's affairs as Summa's general counsel.

The first of many flash points between them was the backlog of
unfinished legal business. Lummis had a natural lawyer's curiosity
about the sixty-five pending actions involving Summa, but, more
important, he needed to know about their status in relation to the
estate, which would have to pay out on the ones that went sour.
He would ask Davis to give him some idea of what was going on
by designating which actions were frivolous, which required set-

tlement, and which needed to be fought in the courts. He never got a straight answer, though it was his firm impression that the only case receiving Davis's earnest attention was the stock-rigging case involving Hughes's purchase of Air West. In that case Davis himself had originally been indicted, along with Hughes.

Lummis told friends he had never encountered a lawyer quite like Davis. Davis was a nonstop, rapid-fire talker who dominated whatever conversation arose without necessarily communicating anything. "As his mind worked, his mouth worked," Lummis said of him. "The result was a monologue of some duration focused on matters of very little relevance or importance." When Lummis did manage to obtrude matters of importance, Davis would either become evasive or tell Lummis that he was seeking information "he wasn't entitled to." By the fall of 1976, Lummis decided that Davis really should know who the boss was. He therefore wrote Davis a "very detailed" letter outlining the general counsel's areas of responsibility and instructing him to adhere to the directions Lummis set forth. Davis didn't bother to acknowledge the letter or reply to it. Lummis observed dryly to a friend that his general counsel was an unusual kind of lawyer of the type "that was not used to receiving instructions from his client."

Lummis was bemused by Davis's manner, but clarification of his general counsel's motives soon emerged. In December 1976, the chairman of the board of Summa learned that Summa's own general counsel intended to attack him in court with a novel will suit. Lummis discovered this, not from Davis, but from an article in *The New York Times,* which reported that the Howard Hughes Medical Institute, controlled by Gay and Davis as the sole members of the executive committee, planned to probate a "lost will" lawsuit with the intent of awarding the Hughes personal estate to his Medical Institute.

The suit, filed in January 1977, contended that Hughes had executed a valid will leaving his entire estate to his Medical Institute and that it was still in existence and had not been produced by the "person or persons" in possession of it. If the will failed to appear, the suit declared, "then it has been lost or destroyed without the knowledge or consent" of the billionaire. The institute sought the opportunity to prove this and admit the "lost will" to probate.

The legal theory behind this was spelled out in a number of court decisions, one of which found that "wills are carelessly lost and misplaced and a reasonable opportunity should be given to establish such a will. Likewise, wills are suppressed or destroyed for an ulterior purpose. The defeat of that purpose ought not to be made too difficult or impossible." While the suit made no accusation against Will Lummis or any other identified parties, if it were sustained it would effectively end the quest of the Hughes relatives for any part of The Money.

On the day he read of the forthcoming "lost will" suit, Lummis had a previously scheduled meeting with Davis on other matters. It turned into what Lummis termed "the most appalling meeting I have ever attended." Lummis conceded at the outset that he knew of Hughes's frequently expressed wish to give his estate to the Medical Institute. He was also more than ready to honor a will containing this provision. But where was the evidence for the existence of such a will? Davis told Lummis it was really none of his business.

Stiff-armed by Davis, Lummis went off fuming to himself and wrote the general counsel an uncharacteristically "very hot letter" that he characteristically thought over and did not mail. Instead, he asked Davis to resign as director of Summa. Davis at first agreed to leave the board, taunting Lummis that "this would give me more time to work on the 'lost will' case." Shortly thereafter, Davis told Lummis he had changed his mind and would not quit the board. With a restraint that Chaucer's Patient Griselda might envy, Lummis held off and let Davis continue—for a time—both as Summa general counsel and Summa director.

Relations between the two men were strained even further by Lummis's subsequent discovery that many of the expenses of Davis's farm in Unadilla in the state of New York had been routinely charged to the Summa account. Indeed, the scale of these charges led some Summa employees to suggest that the company's profits had been eaten by Chester Davis's pigs. There was, however, no truth in this. Davis kept only horses at Unadilla.

By January 1977 Will Lummis knew that the situation at Summa called for a thorough housecleaning. He was restrained, according to an Andrews, Kurth colleague, by three factors. First, with John Hill and Rick Harrison vigorously pushing for Texas to be declared the taxable Hughes domicile, Lummis needed the testimony of the Hughes people in support of a taxless Nevada. One of Lummis's earliest actions after Hughes's death had been to convene a meeting of the aides and doctors in the Century Plaza Hotel in Beverly Hills, where an Andrews, Kurth attorney led a discussion about Hughes's domicile and its relationship to tax issues. A number of them recalled that Hughes had expressed a fondness for Nevada and a dislike for the climate in his native state. Second, Lummis was inhibited by the fact that many of the people he had been keen to remove had what seemed, at the time, valid contracts with Summa. And, finally, Lummis was not certain that his authority at Summa would be legally sustained, and if he took any drastic actions there and got sued, he might incur substantial legal damages.

The economy moves that Lummis did make were for the most part uncontroversial, though less than respectful to the memory of Howard Hughes. Aside from the *Spruce Goose*—a special case—he sold off the stashed-away fleet of airplanes, saving about $2 million a year in hangar fees, maintenance, and lease-purchase fees. He also reduced the Summa corporate jet fleet to a single plane and set an example by flying commercial when traveling alone or with small groups of colleagues.

Some saving was also effected by curtailing the traditional role of the Silver Slipper in the Hughes organization. Summa representatives who went there to arrange a payoff for a local official or politician were redirected to one of the estate's lawyers, who told them, quietly but firmly: "We don't do that anymore."

Lummis also saw no reason for the perpetuation of Rosemont Enterprises, the book-aborting device Chester Davis had contrived back in the 1960s in an effort to halt publication of anything written about Hughes without his approval. Its resources financed lawsuits against publishers who presumed to issue any "unauthorized" accounts of Hughes's life on the grounds that the billionaire had conveyed biographical rights to Rosemont and any other publication would violate that company's "property." From its first lawsuit, against Random House for its publication of a Hughes biography by John Keats in 1966, Rosemont had a record of failing in court, although the prospect of expensive litigation had a chilling effect among publishers unwilling to take on this financial hazard. Chester Davis was all for continuing Rosemont's life beyond Hughes's death, but Lummis shut it down and retrieved the $300,000 still in its account.

These initiatives, while constructive, were about as effective as the thrusting of fingers into a burst dyke. And Lummis realized as much when the internal financial report, steered by Mickey West, came through in the spring of 1977. The situation was even worse than Lummis had feared. Summa was losing money at a rate that could make inheritance an academic question, as what was left of it could all be consumed by pending lawsuits and, more drastically, by tax. This was because inheritance taxes, both federal and state, would be levied on the estimated value of Hughes's estate at the time of his death. The estate's only significant asset was Summa, and if that plunged in value, the estate could find itself forced into a fire sale of Summa's component parts and still be unable to meet the bills.

In the five years and nine months since Hughes had gone into exile, Summa's net operating losses totaled $131 million, and not a single year was in the black. During the last two years, the company had dropped over $50 million, and the trend showed every sign of continuing. The report noted that in the 1971–1976 period, "None of the major competitors of Summa in Nevada suffered an operating loss for even one of the years involved."

While profits had declined, top executive salaries had held up very well, and bonuses were paid in most years. Bill Gay's annual earnings had risen from $110,000 in 1970 to $400,068 in 1975.

The latter figure included a bonus of $188,583. There did not appear to be any perceptible correlation between the company's performance and the level of bonuses approved by Summa's board. Chester Davis's legal fees, logged in at $860,732 in 1971, ascended to $1,712,773 in the billionaire's last year.

The truly alarming aspect of the report, as far as Lummis was concerned, related to Summa's liquidity. The report noted that in the ten years from 1966 to 1976 the Hughes organization had received cash of approximately $715 million, mainly from the TWA windfall and the sale of Hughes Tool. This money had all been directed to the benefit of Summa, but only a small proportion of it survived in liquid form. According to the report the liquid assets of Summa had nose-dived to $94 million and were still proceeding rapidly downward. By normal business standards this was still not an illiquid position, but the problem was that Summa was not a normal business corporation. The report stated that Summa was already vulnerable as a result of its reduced liquidity because the company had been able to survive only through the interest earned on its cash. In other words, Summa was an organism grown accustomed to living on its fat, and the fat was fast running out.

A year after Lummis's attorneys had raced into court and put him in Howard Hughes's shoes, Lummis found himself sinking into the chaos the billionaire had left behind. He had a financial projection "that by year-end in 1977 we would be out of money and unable to meet the Summa payroll." He had a chief executive officer, Gay, who was agitating for spending fresh millions with no apparent concern about where the money would come from. He had a general counsel who told him to mind his own business and was backing a lawsuit that would strip the estate Lummis was administering of all its assets. He was paying out large salaries for untrained aides who no longer had any function. To disturb him further, he discovered the Las Vegas climate did not agree with him and exacerbated his allergies.

Just when he thought that things could not get any worse, they got worse. The time bomb of the "Mormon will," which named old Noah Dietrich as Hughes's executor, began to tick ominously in the Las Vegas probate court. In addition to fighting against Chester Davis's "lost will," Lummis now had to contend against the "found will" that had materialized under such strange circumstances at the Mormon Church headquarters in Salt Lake City.

Next, Lummis and his kin were propelled into a new legal arena, where the leading character was filling-station operator Melvin Dummar, who claimed to have retreated up a lonely road in deserted northern Nevada merely to relieve his bladder and had found instead the prone figure of Howard Hughes, alone, abandoned, a billionaire without a penny in his pocket but a billionaire with a long memory and a heart of gold.

6

—

THE DESERT SAMARITAN

THE MOST WIDELY publicized will of recent times showed up out of nowhere on the afternoon of April 27, 1976, twenty-two days after the death of Howard Hughes. It landed, soft as a feather, on the corner of the desk of a minor employee of the Mormon world headquarters in Salt Lake City, and no one witnessed its arrival. The employee discovered it on his return to his small office on the twenty-fifth floor. It was a crisp, new, sealed envelope from the nearby Mormon Visitors Center addressed to the church president, Spencer Kimball. Puzzled as to why it had been delivered to him, the employee took it down the hall to Kimball's secretary, who sliced it open and found inside a handwritten note and another, much older-looking envelope.

The note said, "This was found by Joseph F. Smith's house in 1972 thought you would be interested." Joseph Smith had been president of the Mormon Church in 1972.

The handwriting on both the note and the outer envelope were in the same slanted style. But on the inner, older-looking envelope was written, in different handwriting, a message that sent the secretary scurrying to President Kimball:

Dear Mr McKay,
    please see that this will is delivered after my death to Clark
County Court House Las Vegas Nevada.
                                          Howard R. Hughes

David McKay had been president of the church for many years before Joseph Smith.

In the inner envelope was a three-page will, handwritten on yellow, legal-sized paper and dated March 19, 1968, when Hughes had been holed up in the Desert Inn penthouse. The will directed the division of the Hughes estate as follows, with misspellings and punctuation intact:

I Howard R. Hughes being of sound and disposing mind and memory, not acting under duress, fraud or undue influence of any person whomsoever, and being a resident of Las Vegas, Nevada, declare that this is to be my last Will and revolk all other Wills previously made by me—
    After my death my estate is to be devided as follows—
    first: one forth of all my assets to go to Hughes Medical Institute of Miami—
    second: one eight of assets to be devided among the University of Texas—Rice Institute of Technology of Houston—the University of Nevada—and the University of Calif.
    third, one sixteenth to Church of Jesus Christ of Latterday Saints—David O Makay—Pre
    Forth: one sixteenth to establish a home for Orphan Cildren
    Fifth: one sixteenth of assets to go to Boy Scouts of America—
    sixth: one sixteenth to be devided among Jean Peters of Los Angeles and Ella Rice of Houston—
    seventh: one sixteenth of assets to William R. Lommis of Houston, Texas—
    eighth: one sixteenth to go to Melvin Du Mar of Gabbs Nevada—

ninth: one sixteenth to be devided amoung my personal aids at the time of my death—

tenth: one sixteenth to be used as school scholarship fund for entire Country—

the spruce goose is to be given to the City of Long Beach, Calif.—

the remainder of My estate is to be devided among the key men of the company's I own at the time of my death.

I appoint Noah Dietrich as the executer of this Will—

> signed the 19 day of
> March 1968
> Howard R. Hughes

Because the will named the Mormon Church as a beneficiary and was found at its headquarters, it posed a delicate problem for church officials. If forged, it could damage the church's reputation. Employees were interrogated about how the will had got up to a desk on the twenty-fifth floor. The lone clue came from a clerk on the main-floor information desk, who had a dim recollection that a "well-dressed woman in her forties" had come in carrying an envelope and asked for the location of President Kimball's office.

A local handwriting expert was summoned, and after a quick look at the will and some published examples of Hughes's handwriting, she declared that the will seemed authentic. On April 29, after much agonizing, the church officials delivered the will to the Las Vegas probate court, along with a caveat that the church was not taking a position on its authenticity.

For days the media had been buzzing with speculation about the existence of a Hughes will and what might happen to his fortune if one were not found. Delivery of the document to the court authorities in Las Vegas created a media sensation, and front-page and prime-time stories appeared across the United States and abroad. The *Los Angeles Times* headlined the discovery: HOWARD HUGHES "WILL" LEFT BY MYSTERY WOMAN AT MORMON CHURCH.

To the public, the story of the Mormon will and its strange appearance made superficial, even attractive, sense. Hughes's attachment to Mormon aides was one of his most familiar quirks. It was common knowledge that his flying boat had long been hangared in Long Beach and that Noah Dietrich had been his trusted money-man for over thirty years. It was well known that Hughes wrote notes, memos, and such on yellow legal pads. Moreover, the text of the document showed some sentimental remembrance of Hughes's two former wives—Ella Rice and Jean Peters—and generally struck a popular chord by allocating well over half the estate to charitable and quasi-charitable enterprises. If some of the bequests were odd, so notoriously was the man whose name was on the will. And since Hughes had mysteriously vanished years ago into absentia, it seemed fitting that his last testament should mysteriously materialize out of nowhere.

To those with more than a cursory knowledge of the world of Howard Hughes, the will was shot through with incongruities. Whatever his other oddities, Hughes in 1968 had a meticulous writing style and an expert grasp of legal terminology. He could recite dense passages of the tax laws and was not likely to bequeath a portion of his estate to such imprecise beneficiaries as "the key men of the company's I own." While he occasionally misspelled words, he was a better-than-average speller. Yet there were fifteen flagrant spelling errors in the Mormon will, along with errors of capitalization and grammar. He was certainly aware that his aunt's family, with whom he had lived as a youth, was "Lummis" and not "Lommis." He detested the term *Spruce Goose* for his beloved flying boat, and people around him were careful never to use it. Furthermore, in 1968, the date on the Mormon will, Hughes was in no position to bequeath the plane to Long Beach or indeed any other city as it was still the property of the United States government. He would eventually acquire title to the plane from the General Services Administration for $700,000, but not until some six years later.

Finally, there was the designation of Noah Dietrich as "executer." After their bitter split in 1957, Hughes had never again communicated with Dietrich. Dietrich had successfully sued him for a million dollars after the split and had a second suit on file when Hughes died. For Hughes to choose Dietrich as executor after their angry bust-up was about as likely as Richard Nixon picking John Dean to administer his estate after Watergate.

When news of the will broke, Dietrich had it read to him over the telephone and branded it a fake, citing the reference to the *Spruce Goose* and the gross misspellings. But then a reporter flew to Los Angeles with a Xerox of the will, and Dietrich instantly executed a 180-degree turn and pronounced it authentic. He called his long-time attorney, Harold Rhoden, a quick-witted, formidable trial lawyer, told him that the handwriting was unquestionably that of Hughes, and summoned him to an imminent press conference.

Dietrich, a peppery little white-thatched man, was then eighty-seven but still possessed of a strong sense of destiny. For years, when not litigating against Hughes, he had nourished the fantasy that some day Hughes would relent and restore him as his money genius. In his thirty-two years of service, Dietrich had become as familiar with Hughes's handwriting as his own. "There's no question," Dietrich told a throng of reporters, "it's his handwriting and his signature. It's the real thing."

Asked why Hughes had named him, of all people, as his executor, Dietrich replied: "Because he knew that I knew more about his business than anyone else did—a hell of a lot more than he did. He trusted me. He never trusted anyone else. He always respected my expertise in financial matters. He respected my ability and my integrity."

"And your modesty," Rhoden impishly added.

The feisty old industrialist and his wisecracking attorney made an undeniably good team. Rhoden, Chicago-born and a B–24 tail gunner in World War II before he scaled the legal ladder, was rarely at a loss for words, many of them funny. But both men felt bound to acknowledge that there were aspects of the will about which they knew absolutely nothing. When a reporter asked about "this Melvin Du Mar" who was named in the will, Dietrich and his attorney said they had never heard of Melvin Du Mar.

Neither had Will Lummis, or his lawyers, or anyone at Summa, where the will was dismissed as an obvious fraud that would soon wind up in a trash can. Then reporters tracked down a Dummar to a modest filling station in Willard, Utah, where he had moved from Gabbs, Nevada. Dummar told them that he was as surprised as anyone else at the mysterious surfacing of the will at the Mormon headquarters, then related a story about why Hughes had named him in the will. Overnight, The Money elevated Melvin Dummar into national prominence as a unique pop hero—a male Cinderella with a billionaire as his wand-waving fairy godmother, a desert Samaritan whose good deed was about to reap huge rewards on earth.

The new hero was an open-faced, pudgy country boy, with no apparent guile or sophistication. He was thirty-two, twice-married, and had held a series of drudge jobs as a milkman, a door-to-door salesman, and a lathe-and-plaster workman in Gabbs, a tiny village of less than one thousand in northern Nevada. He was a good country singer and unsuccessful songwriter, with an unremitting ambition to make it in the world of entertainment. Among his published songs was "Rockview Blues," written when he was driving a milk truck, "Souped Up Santa's Sleigh," and "A Dream Can Become a Reality." Like an inordinate number of people involved with Howard Hughes, he was a Mormon, and studying for the priesthood.

In January 1968, Dummar told reporters, he was driving alone from Gabbs down to Los Angeles. Around midnight, south of Tonopah, he turned off the highway and up a deserted, rutted little road in order to relieve himself. He had traveled about a hundred yards when his lights picked out the figure of a man sprawled facedown on the road. He walked over to the man, thinking he was dead, and found what he thought was a bum or a wino, wearing only baggy pants, a shirt, and tennis shoes. He had gray, scraggly hair, and over his left ear blood had dripped down onto his collar and dried. Dummar helped him up and asked him if he wanted to go to a hospital or to the police. The man said, "No, I'm all right," and Dummar helped him into his car. When Dummar said he was going to Los Angeles, the man asked if he would drop him off in Las Vegas. He did not initially tell Dummar his name or how he happened to be lying out in the freezing Nevada desert with a bloody head, and Dummar said he didn't ask.

On the long haul down to Las Vegas, the two talked a little. The old man stared a lot at Dummar and asked his name several times over and where he lived and what he did. Dummar told him he worked at a magnesium plant at Gabbs but was looking for a better job. He said he had tried unsuccessfully to get a job at Hughes Aircraft in Los Angeles.

At this point, out of the blue, the stranger said he knew a great deal about Hughes Aircraft because he was Howard Hughes. In Las Vegas, the man asked to be dropped off behind the Sands Hotel. When he got out of the car, he asked Dummar if he had any loose change, and Dummar recalled that he gave him "a coin or two—about a quarter." They parted without further conversation, and Dummar said that at the time he believed he had picked up a derelict with an overactive imagination.

That was the only contact he had had with Hughes or anyone claiming to be Hughes. He insisted that he didn't know who had written the will or how it had turned up at the Mormon headquarters. He disarmingly explained that he sometimes spelled his name as "Du Mar," rather than Dummar, because it seemed more high-class.

PRODDED BY NOAH Dietrich, and lured by the millions in fees Dietrich would collect as executor, Rhoden flew to Las Vegas on April 30, and, with television cameras whirring, petitioned to probate the Mormon will and handed over the necessary seventy-five-dollar check. That evening, watching the 6 P.M. news, he and a legal colleague got their first look at the desert Samaritan who would become a multimillionaire if the will was ruled valid. As they listened to Dummar's story, they both got a sick feeling.

"The will's a goddamn forgery," said the colleague, "and that fat kid we just saw is the forger."

"Hold on," said Rhoden. "Let's reason this out. The kid may be a phony, but does it necessarily follow that the will's a forgery? A forger unconnected with Dummar wouldn't have known about him. So if it's a forgery, Dummar's got to be in on it."

But there was no way, reasoned Rhoden, that Dummar could be the forger. "For someone to pass off a forgery to rip off one of the biggest estates in the world—can you imagine the gall he would have to have? The skill? The knowledge? Does that fit the kid we just saw? I tell you it would be impossible for Melvin Dummar to have been in on a forgery of the will of Howard Hughes. Because Melvin Dummar is too dumb."

This convoluted reasoning—that the Dummar account was probably fiction but that the will itself was valid—sustained Hal Rhoden through the revelations that turned up, one after another, in the next two years. Opposing lawyers termed this logic "the Rhoden doctrine of immaculate conception"—that regardless of dismaying evidence of hanky-panky in the will's creation, it remained an unsullied product of Hughes himself. In Rhoden's mind, the will's obvious weaknesses became virtues, confirming authenticity. Since the handwriting had a close resemblance to that of Hughes, Rhoden reasoned, it would have required considerable study and sophistication to forge it. Such a forger, he argued, would surely have had the elementary wit to look up the spelling of such words as "revoke" and "divide" in a ninety-eight-cent dictionary. Rhoden then researched Hughes's medical history and contrived an alternative explanation that attributed the misspellings to Hughes himself.

On a number of occasions, when investigators ripped holes through Dummar's account, Rhoden teetered on the verge of withdrawing the Mormon will, but, each time, he found new evidence that convinced him that the will was genuine. Some of the evidence, while circumstantial, seemed highly persuasive, at least to a partisan with the will to believe. And Rhoden conceded that he had some collateral motives. "I wanted the fee," he wrote later in a book entitled *High Stakes*. "I wanted the fame. I wanted the fun."

First of all, Rhoden needed up-front expense money. Dietrich could not supply it, but with the scent of a billion dollars or more in the air, the money required to go after The Money began to flow in. A portion came from an offbeat California lawyer and stock speculator named Seymour Lazar, an undersized collector of pre-Columbian art who affected the garb and hairstyle of a hippie and had made a fortune in the market. Lazar agreed to finance a search for handwriting experts and other expenses. "It will cost me $250,000 minimum," he told *New West* magazine, "but I'm hoping for a good chunk of the attorney's fees . . . maybe in the eight-figure category, for my efforts."

Rhoden saw an additional advantage in Lazar's participation. "I'm told Mr. Lazar is very sophisticated financially," Rhoden said. "He could probably be very helpful in the management area if we're successful."

Also into the Rhoden-Dietrich camp came Marvin Mitchelson, the noted Hollywood palimony attorney who had broken new ground with a suit against Lee Marvin on behalf of a live-in lady. "I'd give anything to take some part in all this," Mitchelson told Rhoden. "It's got to be the greatest will contest ever tried . . . I'm fed up with those divorce cases and those nagging bitches. 'I want the house. I want both cars. I want both his balls!' I'd like to do something with class." Several other attorneys offered their services on an if-we-win arrangement, and Rhoden himself put a mortgage on his home to help finance the case.

When the Mormon will refused to evaporate and Rhoden began to move forward in earnest, Will Lummis and the potential heirs also faced money problems. Summa could not finance a contest because Summa was the prize in the will case, not a party to it. On the other hand, the Hughes relatives, as potential heirs, could contest the will because they would lose their intestate status if the Mormon will was found valid. But until a court decision on the heirship—years in the offing—the relatives could not know for certain if they were heirs at all.

That left Will Lummis's former firm, Andrews, Kurth, which represented most of the potential heirs, with a difficult funding decision. A law firm can advance expenses to a client with an agreement that the client will reimburse the firm, and Andrews, Kurth had a reason beyond benevolence to render some assistance. It had been a major Hughes law firm for more than fifty years, and Hughes personally and his Summa Corporation were the foremost Andrews, Kurth clients. If the Mormon will prevailed, Dietrich would replace Will Lummis as administrator, and Andrews, Kurth would almost certainly be out in the cold with him.

In a high-strategy session at Andrews, Kurth, the pluses and minuses of this legal dilemma were debated. An all-out battle against Rhoden would require a major investment of money and legal talent. And victory over Rhoden would not, in itself, yield any immediate return in money to reimburse the law firm for its efforts. A number of senior partners took the view that the risk to the firm was too high.

Bill Miller, among the partners strongly in favor of taking the risk, readily acknowledged that it was indeed a gamble. "It was," he said, "like flipping a coin four times and betting it would come up heads each time. One, we would have to prove the Mormon will was a fraud. Two, a court would have to determine that there was no other will. Three, the relatives would have to be declared legal heirs, against all comers. And four, there would have to be enough money left in the estate, after state and federal taxes, to pay for all this. And in 1976, Summa was in a dreadful state and getting worse."

The odds against a coin coming up heads four straight times are sixteen to one, uninviting even for an enthusiastic gambler. But the alternative, forfeiting control over the estate to Noah Dietrich, was even less inviting. Andrews, Kurth opted for the lesser of two evils and agreed to assist the Hughes relatives in contesting the Mormon will. Relieved at the outcome, Will Lummis commented privately, "If Hughes has written a will, I'll be happy to honor it, but I'm not about to honor a will somebody else has written for him."

Hal Rhoden had his problems, too, not the least of which was old Noah Dietrich himself. While wholly lucid in mind, Dietrich was physically frail and suffering from myasthenia gravis, a terminal ailment. Ten years earlier, in another lawsuit, Rhoden had been granted an early trial because a doctor declared that Dietrich had only one chance in ten of living two years. Dietrich had outlived the doctor, but with a lengthy trial now looming, he conceded that he might not last to its conclusion. He agreed to have a substitute executor named in his place and nominated Rhoden, substantially increasing the height of his attorney's stakes in The Money.

Because Hughes's legal domicile was still unknown, Rhoden offered the Mormon will for probate in California and Texas, in addition to Nevada, following the example Lummis had set earlier in seeking administrator status. Although the California court, after a series of pretrial hearings, decided to sit on the sidelines of the Mormon will, Judge Pat Gregory, in Houston, and Judge Keith Hayes, in Las Vegas, adamantly proceeded with their separate court processes. The litigation was thus at least reduced to a two-ring, rather than three-ring, circus. Many of the pretrial legal moves were made in both courts, with attorneys for both sides wearily ping-ponging between Las Vegas and Houston.

Both sides scrambled to secure handwriting experts to testify about the fakery or authenticity of the writing on the will. Here the ghostly hand of the billionaire reached out from the grave to complicate matters. His handwriting had clearly and, unequivocally, been demonstrated to be susceptible to forgery.

In 1972, Clifford Irving had staged his notorious hoax by faking an "autobiography" of Hughes, which he sold to McGraw-Hill for $750,000. Hughes had even summoned up the energy to denounce the "autobiography" in a telephone call to seven leading newsmen, telecast in a weird nationwide spectacular. But the disembodied voice of Hughes was, for a time, regarded as much less convincing than Irving's handwriting "evidence." Irving had achieved his flimflam by forging letters from Hughes authorizing the publication. McGraw-Hill had submitted them to two leading handwriting experts, and both had firmly, and erroneously, declared that Irving's forgeries were written by Hughes. One expert asserted that the odds were "less than one in a million" that anyone could copy Hughes's handwriting, and the other said that it was "impossible" that the forgeries were forgeries. Before he went off to jail, Irving demonstrated to incredulous prosecutors that he could indeed reproduce Hughes's handwriting. "Irving's lasting accomplishment," said one observer, "was to set back the science of handwriting identification by one hundred years."

Ignoring this sobering history, both sides signed up experts in this less-than-exact discipline. Figuring that his opponents had him outgunned financially and would tie down the top authorities in the United States, Rhoden sent Mitchelson and Lazar to Europe. After considerable difficulty, they lined up two Frenchmen and a Dutchman. "There was a topflight expert in northern Tibet," Rhoden joked, "but I decided to leave him for Andrews, Kurth."

Rhoden moved gingerly into pretrial work with Melvin Dummar's odd tale draped around his neck like a legal albatross. His client was Noah Dietrich, not Dummar, but if Dummar's story collapsed, Dietrich's case could be reduced to worthless rubble. Besieged by hundreds of skeptical newsmen, Dummar stuck by his account. "I was hammered until I almost had a nervous breakdown," he recounted later. "The only good thing about it was that I lost twenty pounds." Now that he was sprayed with the scent of The Money, he became the target of scores of letters from people clamoring for a share of it. "I was even asked to provide school buses for some people in Africa who didn't have school buses," he recalls. In addition, his younger, unmarried sister Savilla got several marriage proposals from strangers attracted by the musk of The Money once removed.

While the prospect of great wealth had its burdens, it also had its rewards. Universal Studios flew Dummar to Los Angeles, installed him in the Beverly Wilshire Hotel—"the fanciest place I ever saw," Dummar said—and signed him up for a movie focused on his desert encounter with the billionaire. A paperback publishing house expressed interest in his life story, music houses suddenly discovered new virtues in his unpublished songs, and he spent a busy summer appearing on national talk shows.

One of the odd circumstances that propelled Rhoden onward was the presence of a Pitney Bowes postal-machine imprint on the envelope containing the Mormon will. Although the envelope had not been addressed for mailing, the machine imprint showed LAS

VEGAS NEV and MAR for March. The day of the month and the year were not visible, nor was the serial number of the Pitney Bowes machine, but the envelope showed a stamp charge of six cents—the price of a first-class stamp in 1968. Rhoden inquired of the Pitney Bowes company and learned that the Desert Inn, where Hughes had been holed up in 1968, had one of their machines. This bolstered his belief in the will's validity; how could Melvin Dummar, up in Utah, have obtained the Las Vegas imprint on the will envelope, and how would he have the sophistication to imprint the proper six-cent stamp charge that prevailed in 1968, but not in 1976, when the price of such a stamp was thirteen cents?

For seven months, Dummar held to his story. Then, in December 1976, the attorneys challenging the will took his sworn deposition in Salt Lake City. The investigation had fine-combed his background and come up with an intriguing piece of evidence. Dummar had taken night classes at Weber State College in Ogden, Utah. A diligent sleuth examined publications there to see if Dummar might have procured samples of Hughes's handwriting. Among them was the book *Hoax,* a detailed account of the Clifford Irving forgery. The book had originally contained an insert of photographs, including a copy of a letter Hughes had written to Chester Davis and Bill Gay—the very letter that Irving had used to copy Hughes's handwriting. But the photographs had been neatly sliced from the college copy. The sleuth had then had the book examined, and Dummar's fingerprints were found on it.

At his deposition, Dummar recounted his familiar story of knowing nothing about the will or its delivery to the Mormon Visitors Center. He said he had never read anything about Irving, including *Hoax,* and had never seen or touched the Weber State copy. Told his fingerprints were on the copy, he changed his story overnight. He suddenly remembered looking at *Hoax* but denied cutting out the Hughes exemplars.

Then Rhoden got wind of a dire discovery. The Nevada attorney general's office received a report back from the FBI laboratory on its examination of the envelope that contained the will delivered to the Mormon headquarters. On one corner of the envelope, the FBI reported the existence of the left thumbprint of Melvin Dummar, directly, and it seemed devastating, tying Dummar in with the will's delivery. Rhoden confronted Dummar, who took refuge in tears. With his composure recovered, Dummar admitted that he had not been telling the truth—and then concocted a new story. He told Rhoden he had got the Mormon will in Las Vegas in 1968 from an unnamed casino manager in a hotel whose name he could not remember. When Rhoden angrily told him to "give up lying and take up bank robbing," Dummar broke into fresh sobs and changed his story again. He said the will had been delivered to his gas station on April 27, 1976, by a stranger driving a blue Mercedes. The stranger had instructed him to take it to the Mormon headquarters and had followed him "bumper-to-bumper" to make sure he followed orders. The man had warned Dummar to tell no one about receiving the will or delivering it or he would be killed.

With three conflicting Dummar stories, even Rhoden began to feel that enough was enough, and a new thought occurred to him. If he could not get the Mormon will probated, he might at least derive public credit by nailing Dummar as a fraud. With this achievement, he could make a reasonable claim for "good faith" fees through the courts to compensate for his substantial costs on the will case if it had to be abandoned. The venue for Dummar's scheduled "confession" was Judge Hayes's courtroom in Las Vegas on January 25, 1977.

Initially, Judge Hayes offered to assist matters by having Dummar join him in his chambers for a prayer session before the proceeding commenced to help clear his mind. Rhoden, however, persuaded the judge that a sterner approach might yield better results. But Dummar conspicuously failed to confess himself a fraud under oath and firmly put another version of the story on the record, his fourth.

In Dummar's final account, the man in the blue Mercedes became a stranger who had showed up and asked him if he was Melvin Dummar. He had said something about a Hughes will being found in 1972 near Joseph Smith's house in Salt Lake City, and wouldn't it be nice to be named in the will. Then, instead of following Melvin bumper-to-bumper to the Mormon headquarters, the stranger had slipped away without saying good-bye. Dummar said he then found the envelope lying on a counter. He steamed it open and discovered to his astonishment that he had been named as a beneficiary.

After reading it several times, Dummar said he resealed the envelope and baked it dry in a small oven. When his wife, Bonnie, returned with their car, he told her nothing about what had happened but drove into Salt Lake City, went to the Visitors Center, and asked where he could find the church president. He was directed to the headquarters across the street and on his way out picked up an envelope and a piece of blank paper. A receptionist on the twenty-fifth floor told him that the president was busy. Dummar went into a nearby rest room and wrote in disguised handwriting the note about the will being found in 1972. He put this, with the will, into the Mormon envelope and addressed it, again in disguised handwriting, to President Spencer Kimball. He walked out, "laid it on a guy's desk, and left."

Dummar was grilled and derided by the attorneys in Judge Hayes's court, but he clung to his fourth version. He conceded that he had lied repeatedly for nine months—in his deposition, to the press, to the public, to Rhoden, to his wife, to his own attorney—but now, he insisted, he was telling the truth. He had told the earlier untruths because he felt that no one would believe what really happened. Judge Hayes—a fellow Mormon—sternly warned him that he would seek criminal prosecution for any perjury and advised him that he had taken an oath "before this court and before God that you will tell the truth."

The courtroom Bible was produced again, and Dummar placed his hand on it.

"Brother Dummar," said the judge, "I want the truth. Where did the will come from?"

"A man brought it to my station . . ." Dummar began once again.

After Dummar's performance in court, Rhoden was approached by a *New York Times* reporter who suggested that Melvin should do a little more work on polishing his story. A more credible version, the reporter thought, could go something like this: "a few weeks after Hughes died, a bi-plane flown in *Hell's Angels* landed in the backyard of Melvin's gas station. Out of the rear seat climbed Jean Harlow, wearing a leather helmet, a white scarf, and nothing else. As she swayed toward Melvin, holding an envelope where decency demanded, she said, 'Mel, honey, Howie wants you to deliver his little ol' will to the Mormon Church in Salt Lake City. Howie has selected you for this errand because there just isn't anyone in the whole world he respects like he does you.' "

Rhoden could see the joke at the time, but only just. With his case in rubble and the press full of stories of Dummar's long-withheld admission that it was he, and not some "mystery woman," who had delivered the will to the Mormon headquarters, Rhoden returned to Los Angeles thoroughly dejected and all but ready to throw in the towel. His legal opponents were insisting that further moves in support of the Mormon will petition would amount to a perversion of justice in the Texas and Nevada courts, and Rhoden was inclined to agree with them. Then the old optimism came flooding back with the emergence of a new player in an unlikely form and from an even unlikelier place.

7

THE BAGMAN COMETH

THE MAN WHO provided Hal Rhoden with fresh inspiration in his bid to legitimize the Mormon will was LeVane Malvison Forsythe, a burly, fifty-three-year-old construction worker, then resident in Anchorage, Alaska, where he ran his own building firm, Arctic Metal Structures. In February 1977—ten months after the will had surfaced—Forsythe came forward to claim that he was the stranger who had delivered the Mormon will to Dummar's gas station. And, what was more, he said he had received the will from Howard Hughes himself.

Forsythe's story was as curious as Dummar's and had a more intricate and longer-running plot. He also had an odd way of recounting it and a Runyonesque style of utterance that was not always easy to decipher. As if to compensate for this fact, the boss of Arctic Metal Structures would finish most of his sentences with a slightly ominous sounding "You know what I mean?"

Forsythe claimed that for thirty years he had been a secret courier for Howard Hughes. He had first met the billionaire in

Ventura County, California, in 1946, when Hughes was shooting a movie on location there. He had tipped off the billionaire that his movie crew was ripping him off in his absence, and Hughes had knighted him as his trusted agent under the code name "Ventura." Over the years, Forsythe said, he had served as a bagman for the billionaire and made some fifty deliveries of cash in envelopes or packages to various politicians. According to Forsythe, he was sometimes assisted by his Uncle Claude, who had been a security guard on the train that brought Hughes to Las Vegas in 1966.

In July or August 1972, Forsythe said, Hughes had telephoned him and asked him to come to Vancouver, where he was then holed up in exile. Forsythe said he went to the Bayshore Inn, to a room number Hughes gave him, and found Hughes alone, seated in a chair and wearing only a bathrobe. There were no guards or aides with him. On the table was a brown envelope.

Hughes said that the envelope "contained instructions in the case of his death" and that he wanted to entrust it to his secret courier. Ventura was not to open it and would probably be retaining it for some time. If Hughes didn't call it back, Ventura was to open it when Hughes died. "I told him I would accept that responsibility," Forsythe said.

He took the envelope home and hid it away. On January 7, 1976—three months before Hughes died—he got a phone call from someone who used his code name Ventura and thus had to be a legitimate Hughes functionary. He gave Forsythe instructions to deliver the contents of the Hughes envelope to Melvin Dummar's gas station in Willard in the event of Hughes's death and to "make sure Melvin is there."

On the day Hughes died, Forsythe said, he opened the brown envelope and found three more inside, one marked "deliver this one," another addressed to Chester Davis, and a third marked "open this one." Inside the third envelope he found $2,800 in hundred-dollar bills, which he took to his bank the same day and deposited. He claimed he later mailed the letter to Chester Davis.

On April 26 or 27, he flew to Salt Lake City, hired a car, and was driven to Willard, where he located the Dummar station and dropped off the will, leaving it on a counter there without identifying himself.

He had said nothing about his role because a secret agent for Hughes never disclosed his identity or what he had done. This was why he had not come forward with his delivery story at an earlier date. But after Dummar finally admitted delivering the will to the Mormon headquarters, Forsythe had received a call from someone named "Ben Harper," who established his bona fides by mentioning Ventura. Harper had told him that the Hughes will was in trouble because Dummar had been caught lying and Forsythe had to help out, and he gave him the name and phone number of Dummar's lawyer. Forsythe initially refused, but Harper had threatened to have Forsythe's son fired from Hughes Aircraft if he did not cooperate. Forsythe was "pissed off" at the threat but decided to perform this last posthumous mission for his old employer.

In his matchup of two improbable tales, Rhoden recognized the possibility that Forsythe and Dummar, despite their geographic separation, could be coconspirators. His opponents would be bound to claim as much, although no connection between the two men was ever established. Rhoden himself, however, was satisfied on this point right from the outset, principally because Forsythe exhibited such contempt for Dummar. In his deposition, Forsythe asserted that "I had him [Dummar] pegged for a dummy when I was down there [at the gas station], and I've got him pegged for a dummy right now. If you think I would get myself tied up with a guy like that, you got to be kidding. If I was going to pick somebody to do anything with, it wouldn't be Melvin Dummar."

At one point, Forsythe took Rhoden aside and told him he had come to a dreadful conclusion. "I made the wrong delivery of the will," Forsythe said. "Somebody gave me the wrong instructions and I delivered the will to the wrong Melvin Dummar. This kid can't be the Melvin Dummar that Hughes knew. He wouldn't have nothing to do with a kid like this, you know what I mean?" Rhoden told him not to worry, there was only one Melvin Dummar, hailing from Gabbs, Nevada, population less than one thousand. He had got his man.

Of somewhat greater concern to Rhoden was the kind of man Forsythe was as a potential witness to the Mormon will's credibility. Investigation revealed Forsythe as someone with a seemingly incurable fascination with Howard Hughes. His appearance front stage in the Mormon will drama was the second time he had injected himself into the billionaire's affairs. In 1970, when Robert Maheu had been ousted in Las Vegas, Maheu had gone to court in the belief that Hughes had been taken out of the country against his will. Forsythe had then popped up with a tale supporting Maheu's suspicions of a kidnapping. He claimed to have been hired by a Hughes aide and paid five hundred dollars to patrol the Desert Inn grounds the night Hughes left. He testified that he had seen Hughes hustled into a limousine between two burly guards and that Hughes had implored someone to "Get Bob Maheu" before he was whisked away. The judge in that case took judicial notice of Forsythe's credibility, terming it "not worthy of belief."

Forsythe told Rhoden this embarrassing episode had all been due to a misunderstanding. Indeed, he had reproached Howard Hughes in Vancouver for "hanging me out to dry" the night of his departure from the Desert Inn. Hughes had explained that he and Forsythe had suffered from a breakdown in communication. Hughes hadn't called out "Get Bob Maheu" to effect his rescue, Forsythe said. Instead, Hughes had explained, he had angrily cried, "Get that son of a bitch Bob Maheu!"

In his second appearance in the Hughes saga, Forsythe again had problems with his script. On his will-delivery mission, he first asserted that he had flown to Seattle and then on to Salt Lake City, and he produced notations, on his 1976 calendar, of flight schedules between those two cities to support his account. Andrews, Kurth investigators, however, established that those flights were accurate for 1977 but not in existence for 1976, when he claimed to have made the flight. Forsythe then remembered that he had flown to Utah not from Seattle but from San Francisco, where he had gone with some friends for a construction conference. They had hired a rental car at the airport, he said, and driven some twenty miles to a hotel in downtown San Francisco. On April 27, he had slipped away, driven back to the airport, flown to Salt Lake City, and on his return had driven the rental car back to the hotel. Investigators then laboriously dug out the car-rental record and found the mileage showed only one round-trip from the airport to the hotel, not two. Undaunted, Forsythe revised his story again to conform with the new facts. He had only started to drive the car to the airport, he said, but had parked in a nearby lot and taken a taxi.

As for his fifty missions as Ventura, the only politicians he would identify as recipients of Hughes cash were all dead. So, investigators found, was Forsythe's Uncle Claude, who had allegedly guarded Hughes on his 1966 train trip to Las Vegas. According to his death certificate, Uncle Claude had died five years before the train's departure. When discrepancies like this arose and were passed on to Forsythe in Anchorage by Rhoden, the boss of Arctic Metal Structures would tell the lawyer to quit nit-picking. "I ain't no fucking memory machine, you know what I mean?" became almost a refrain.

In truth, nobody could fully comprehend Forsythe's meaning, but Rhoden remained impressed by how secure he seemed on the key points in the story. Forsythe readily volunteered for a lie-detector test to elicit his response to three main questions:

1. In Vancouver, in 1972, were you given an envelope by Howard Hughes?
2. On or about January 7, 1976, did you receive telephone instructions to deliver to Melvin Dummar one of the smaller envelopes contained in the larger one given to you by Howard Hughes?
3. Did you deliver the envelope to Melvin Dummar in Utah April 27, 1976?

To each question Forsythe affirmed "yes," and Dr. David Raskin of Salt Lake City, who operated the test, had no doubts about Forsythe's veracity in making his replies. Dr. Raskin regarded a plus-ten reading as a totally reliable indication of a subject's truthfulness. Forsythe had scored plus fourteen.

There was also one oddity that gave some further credence to Forsythe's narrative. Bank records in Vancouver disclosed that Forsythe had, in fact, as he originally stated, deposited twenty-eight old hundred-dollar bills on April 5, 1976, the day Hughes died. If the will had been forged after Hughes's death and Forsythe had concocted his filling-station story after Dummar related it in 1977, how had Ventura had the foresight to deposit the hundred-dollar bills on the day of Hughes's death?

"The answer to that question," said one cynic who followed Forsythe's winding tales, "is that even a broken clock is right twice a day."

RHODEN, MEANWHILE, WAS finding what he regarded as more potent evidence to encourage his pursuit of The Money. He had come across a circumstance that could account for the misspellings and general sloppiness of the Mormon will. This was provided by Hughes's long-term kidney problem, an ailment that could, according to medical experts, often affect handwriting and spelling ability. "Writing performance by uremics will be decreased," one neurologist declared. "Handwriting will be slow and labored. There may be sloppiness and problems with punctuation." This was the kind of testimony that the Mormon will required.

Even more encouraging to Rhoden was the developing evidence on the ink. By a complicated analysis called thin-paper chromatography, it had been established that the Mormon will was written with a Paper Mate pen with an ink formula used in 1968 and discontinued in 1974. This much had been confirmed in tests carried out at the behest of the FBI, though the bureau's handwriting expert maintained that the will was not genuine.

In a deposition from a Hughes aide, Rhoden learned that Hughes had used Paper Mate pens in 1968. There were some three thousand varieties of ink in existence in 1968, but the ink on the Mormon will was identical with that in one of the Paper Mate pens Hughes used. If Dummar, or anyone else, had forged the Mormon will in 1976, Rhoden reasoned, how could the forger possibly have picked out the right kind of pen, with the one-out-of-three-thousand inks in use in 1968 — and no longer on the market? The odds against this were so long, in Rhoden's view, that any jury would be forced to conclude that the document was no forgery. But the prospects for an early trial were clouded by another, unlooked-for development in the Forsythe saga.

Forsythe was reluctant to appear in court, particularly in Las Vegas, where he had been excoriated by a judge back in 1970. In an effort to persuade him to come down from Anchorage, Rhoden made a phone call to Forsythe and in the process got somewhat carried away. Unknown to Rhoden, Forsythe tape-recorded the call. The recording had the following passage:

Rhoden: "We can use a judge in Las Vegas who will protect you, who will see to it nothing bad happens. He's a judge extremely friendly toward us and wants that will to be admitted, and he'd welcome you with open arms, like a savior, because the guy's a Mormon, to save this for his church . . ."

When asked by the opposing attorneys for all the records he had dealing with the case, Forsythe gave them the tape recording. They jubilantly produced it in court and filed a challenge against Judge Hayes, requesting his replacement. Initially, the challenge was upheld, but Judge Hayes appealed to the Nevada Supreme Court and managed to secure his reinstatement. The case of the Mormon will was thus restored to the Mormon judge.

In bewilderment, Rhoden called Forsythe and asked: "Why in hell did you give the lawyers that tape?"

"Why in hell not?" Forsythe responded. "I ain't got nothin' to hide. I'm tellin' everybody the truth, Rhoden, and I'm givin' everybody everything, you know what I mean?"

With a judge he had put through a humiliating ordeal, a prime witness who had told four different stories, a corroborating witness who termed the key witness "a dummy"—not to mention $220,000 already spent—Rhoden went to trial in Las Vegas on November 7, 1977.

WHATEVER THE FLAWS in the will or the chameleon changes in the tales of Dummar the Samaritan and Ventura, the fate of the

Hughes estate would be decided by a jury of eight residents of Las Vegas, a city founded on the whispers of hope and the fantasies of instant riches. Las Vegas was also a city that had been marinated in tales of its eccentric and best-known resident, the invisible billionaire who conventionally acted in the most unconventional way. As Rhoden reminded critics of the Mormon will, "If a Las Vegas jury says it is an authentic will, then it is an authentic will." And nobody doubted the presence of factors that had nothing to do with whether Hughes had written the will but had much to do with The Money.

The press had widely reported that, in the absence of a will, the Internal Revenue Service could gulp down up to 77 percent of the Hughes estate. But under the Mormon will many of the charitable bequests would escape tax. Medical research would benefit, orphans and Boy Scouts and needy students would be helped, the Mormon Church—which had many members in Las Vegas— would get a share, and money would go to four universities, one situated in Las Vegas with an avidly admired basketball team called the Running Rebels. Rhoden saw the tide of local opinion as running in his favor, and his opponents were apprehensive on this score.

At the suggestion of Avis Hughes McIntyre's friend George Dean, newly aboard as a Summa attorney, Andrews, Kurth decided that as part of the preparation for the trial it would be prudent to get a professional appraisal of prevailing attitudes in the town that would supply the jury. In recent years a new ancillary service combining opinion research and psychological insights had been developed for trial lawyers. Dean knew one of the topflight practitioners of this service, an attractive young technician named Kathy Bennett. She was commissioned by Andrews, Kurth to assist in the jury selection and came out to Las Vegas with a colleague, Maureen McLaughlin.

They expected to do the job in two weeks, but when they saw what they faced, they stayed three months. Before the trial they interviewed more than one hundred Las Vegans in depth to get a reliable profile on community attitudes that might bear on the case. Their interviews ran from two to six hours each. They found that everyone knew about Hughes and his eccentricities and that there was a strong tendency to believe stories about his offbeat behavior. There was also a substantial belief that if there was no valid will, "the government will take all the money." Many felt it would be better for the Hughes money to go to worthy, tax-free charities than to the Internal Revenue Service. The researchers also charted the impact of Mormonism on the city and found it was considerable.

On the basis of their jury debriefings in previous cases, they were aware that verdicts are often reached for peculiar reasons that have little to do with courtroom evidence. "The purpose of this research," Ms. Bennett said, "was not to get jurors who favor one's case, but to avoid jurors who may reach a verdict for an unwarranted reason."

In consultation with Dean, they prepared a "jury book" for the trial lawyers to guide them in their jury challenges. "What we wanted," Dean said, "were Missouri mules who had to be shown the facts and would not fantasize about them." They should seek jurors with business experience, knowledge of management, people with a penchant to think things through, who were not likely to be swayed by emotional arguments. They were to avoid, at all costs, prospective jurors who were addicted to television game shows and soap operas with far-out plots and improbable coincidences. The jury selection took two weeks. When its five men and three women were impaneled, Ms. Bennett confidently advised Dean, "We've got a hard-nosed jury with one wobbler on it." For this jury expertise, Ms. Bennett and her colleague were paid $60,000, a substantial fee but a drop in the bucket compared to the size of The Money.

IN HIS OPENING statement, Rhoden sought to defuse the predictable attacks on the credibility of Dummar and Forsythe, to arouse hostility against the Hughes aides, to paint Hughes as a self-centered tyrant—"a spoiled boy who had grown old but not up"—and to steer the jurors to the ink and the medical evidence that gave a measure of credence to a far-out story.

"Members of the jury," Rhoden said, "you'll find that LeVane Forsythe is a crude bagman, sophisticated in the ways of the gutter. A believable witness? No! He'll testify that he received the will from Howard Hughes and was later instructed to deliver it to Melvin Dummar. A believable story? No! No, not until you hear the testimony of witnesses whose credibility you can't question and see the evidence on paper that will compel you to believe Forsythe.

"You'll find that Melvin Dummar is a gentle dunce. He committed perjury when he denied that it was he who had delivered the will to the Mormon Church headquarters in Salt Lake City. Dummar will tell you that on April 27, 1976, a stranger dropped the will off at Dummar's gas station, an unbelievable story told by an unbelievable witness. Unbelievable until you hear and see evidence that proves he's telling the truth—evidence such as the testimony of agents in the scientific labs of the FBI.

"The will itself is bizarre. Bizarre in what it says, in the way it was written, and in the way it was kept for eight years. And bizarre in the way it was delivered to the Mormon Church. But this was the bizarre way of the man who wrote it . . .

"Howard Hughes's brain was poisoned by the waste his diseased kidneys couldn't excrete. This disease causes abnormalities in handwriting and spelling, and those abnormalities will be seen in his will."

Noah Dietrich, then approaching eighty-nine, arrived at the court attired in white slacks and blue blazer and in a jaunty mood. He had been obliged to run the gamut of fast-talking reporters outside the court and had acquitted himself well.

"Mr. Dietrich, do you believe Melvin Dummar and LeVane Forsythe?"

"All I know is, Howard Hughes wrote that will."

"What about the handwriting experts who say it's a fake?"

"What about those who say it isn't?"

"Would you care to comment on the experts who are going to testify that it is a forgery?"

"Only that they might do well to consider another line of work."

"Mr. Dietrich, it's been said that you not only built but ran the Howard Hughes empire for the thirty-two years you were with him."

"Whoever said that is well informed."

As Rhoden's first witness, Dietrich was able to confirm the picture of Hughes as presented in his lawyer's opening statement. He did not personally know LeVane Forsythe, but he was able to outline a possible context for his relationship with Hughes. Rhoden led his witness gently into this area, and the court was rewarded with a rare behind-the-scenes glimpse of Hughes-style politics.

Q: Did Howard Hughes ever make any political contributions?

A: The mayor and almost every councilman, every supervisor in Los Angeles was on Howard's payroll. Congressmen, senators, governors—you name it.

Q: How do you know this?

A: I set it up for him. You see, Howard wanted political influence, but he didn't want to be in politics because that meant talking to people. So he decided to get political influence by buying it. Here's the way he did it. I established a company in Canada and saw to it that in dealing with the Tool Company it made a profit of about four hundred thousand a year. The money then went to the South Hollywood Branch of the Bank of America in an account in the name of Lee Murrin. Murrin would draw out the cash, put it into an envelope, and do what we told him to do with it. Sometimes I'd take the envelope for a delivery, sometimes it would go to whomever we had making the deliveries for us.

Q: Were these deliveries always in cash?

A: Always. And always in one-hundred-dollar bills.

Q: Why a Canadian company?

A: If Howard drew the money out of his own company, he'd have to pay income tax on that money. Howard didn't want to pay income tax on that money. Or on any other money. Next to germs and communists, Howard's bitterest hatred was for the income-tax man.

Q: Did you personally ever deliver cash to politicians?

A: Oh, sure. I delivered several of those envelopes to the Republican House leader to spread among members of Congress as he saw fit.

Q: How much money was in the envelopes?

A: The average was twenty thousand . . .

Q: Were you personally involved in any other payments by Hughes to politicians?

A: Yep. Another one I remember is the one to Dick Nixon.

Ranged against Rhoden, leading attorneys for the prospective heirs were Earl Yoakum, a mountainous Texan, and Phillip Bittle from New York. Yoakum, who tipped the scales at around three hundred pounds, expressed his opinion of LeVane Forsythe by telling Rhoden, "He was a confidential courier from Howard Hughes like ah was the principal ballerina for the Bolshoi."

Yoakum and Bittle called on a series of topflight American handwriting experts to testify that the will was a rank forgery. They also produced the aides who monitored the billionaire constantly at the Desert Inn to testify that he never left his ninth-floor hideout in the four years he was holed up there. Unfortunately, because they had shredded so many papers after Hughes's death, they did not have the logs for the Desert Inn period nor could they pinpoint who was on duty the night that Dummar claimed to have picked Hughes up near Tonopah. But one after another, they swore that they would not accept any money as beneficiaries of the Mormon will if the jury found it valid.

In his cross-examination, Rhoden poured scorn on their stance of selfless rectitude by eliciting their salaries, around $100,000 a year, paid by Summa for doing next to nothing, aside from giving testimony. Rhoden also bored in on their failure to act to save the billionaire in his terminal days. In questioning the chief aide, John Holmes, Rhoden asked:

"During those last two weeks of his life, did anything prevent you from phoning a hospital and saying 'Get an ambulance over here'?"

"Mr. Hughes would not have wanted to go to a hospital."

"Did anybody ask him?"

"No."

"Why not?"

"He wasn't feeling well."

This line of questioning was bitterly resented by Rhoden's opponents. During a recess in the judge's chambers, Bittle declaimed to Judge Hayes, "Your Honor. This has got to stop . . . Mr. Hughes's aides are fine, moral men—decent men with families! Mr. Rhoden's questions are designed to ridicule these witnesses. Why he's actually trying to make it look as though they committed murder!"

"First or second degree?" Rhoden asked demurely, and Judge Hayes allowed his interrogation to proceed.

Nothing that Rhoden could say about the aides, however, rivaled the hostility expressed by Hughes's onetime alter ego, Bob Maheu. Maheu had been called to the stand for the limited purpose of corroborating the testimony of the aides that Hughes never left the Desert Inn. Maheu testified that he had been in daily contact by phone with Hughes at the time of the purported desert encounter between Hughes and Dummar. But he could not say categorically that Hughes had not slipped out of the Desert Inn. Maheu said that he dealt with Hughes only by phone, or through the aides, whom he described, in response to a question by Rhoden, as "zombies."

At this point, Bittle incautiously decided to defuse Maheu's "zombie" reference. "You meant," said Bittle to Maheu, carefully steering his witness, "didn't you, when you called Mr. Hughes's aides 'zombies,' that they didn't get enough sleep and always walked around looking as though they needed some?"

Maheu, who held the Mormon aides, along with Chester Davis and Bill Gay, responsible for poisoning Hughes's mind against him to the extent that Hughes called him "a no-good, dishonest son of a bitch who stole me blind," was not able to contain himself.

"No, counsel, that is not what I meant," Maheu replied. "Those aides were well used by Mr. Frank W. Gay and his gang in the theft and control of an empire from a very sick—psychologically and mentally sick—old man. That theft required the assistance of obedient, mindless men without morals. I call those men zombies. Anyone who would deliver an employer to Houston in that deplorable condition, I call zombies. Howard Hughes slandered me and I had to sue him, and I'm not going to pretend I liked him—I admit I didn't. But I live in a civilized world, and no prisoner in any civilized country in the world would ever be allowed to die like that. And anyone who would follow orders and take part in such an operation, I call a zombie."

Yoakum and Bittle were more comfortable revealing further facets of the character of Melvin Dummar, who was emerging as a country bumpkin with an unusually wide range of accomplishments. He had been a onetime drama student and had appeared, ironically, in an amateur production of *You Can't Take It with You.* He was adept at working his way onto national television game shows and had appeared twice on *Let's Make a Deal* and on *Hollywood Squares* and *The Price Is Right,* winning two autos, a freezer, and a range. He was also capable, the testimony brought out, of bending the truth, appearing on one show that barred repeaters by using a false name.

During the interminable handwriting testimony, Rhoden had been able to demonstrate that Hughes could on occasion reproduce some of the misspellings in the Mormon will. This was done by reference to original memos Hughes wrote in the late sixties and early seventies. Yoakum and Bittle, however, were able to point to more consistent misspellings that more closely paralleled those in the will.

In deposition evidence before the trial commenced, Bittle had asked Dummar's wife, Bonnie, to spell "divide," "companies," and "revoke." In doing so she made mistakes identical to those found in the Mormon will and wrote "devide," "company's," and "revolk."

In court, Bittle did the detailed work of taking Mrs. Dummar through a spelling lesson on the stand, while Yoakum weighed in later with one of his heavier conclusions. "You wanna know who really wrote the will?" he asked the jury. "All the evidence points to Melvin Dummar . . . An' Dummar's wife is involved in it with him. Maybe I cain't prove it, but it's just one of those things you feel. You feel it in your soul!"

While the Las Vegas case ground on, the Texas probate court, profoundly irritated by the long delays in a case that Rhoden had initiated, decided to have its very own Mormon will trial regardless of his convenience. Rhoden asked Wilbur Dobbs, a young Texan on his legal team, if the Texas probate judge, Pat Gregory, comprehended that he was at full stretch in Las Vegas with all the exhibits and witnesses relevant to the case. "He understands," said Dobbs laconically, "but in Texas legalese, he doesn't give a shit. He said that you've had plenty of notice an' he expects you to be ready." Rhoden was formally summoned to the Texas proceeding, but he decided that his only practical course was to let the Texas case go by default, without presenting any evidence. "I could not," he said, "figure out how to be in two places at the same time." On February 15, 1978, in Rhoden's absence, a Houston jury took just ninety minutes to find the Mormon will a forgery on its first ballot. It also found, on a separate issue incorporated into the same case, that Texas-born Howard Hughes was legally domiciled in Texas and that the Lone Star State was entitled to its Texas-sized inheritance taxes.

In Las Vegas, the highest-stakes legal poker game the city had ever seen came to an end on June 8. When the jury began its deliberations, the consensus of the press and courtroom functionaries was that Rhoden had outpointed Yoakum and Bittle and that the jury would rule that the Mormon will was authentic. There seemed to be a very distinct probability of two conflicting decisions on the case by Texas and Nevada and a possibility therefore that it would eventually have to go to the U.S. Supreme Court, which ultimately decides interstate conflicts. Some of the journalists present gloomily contemplated having to stay with the convolutions of the Dummar story for years to come.

Instead, they were out of their misery in less than eleven hours, the time it took for the jury to find that the will was not written by Howard Hughes. The verdict stunned Rhoden, who had already ordered champagne for a victory celebration. Deep in debt, and with another verdict against him on file in Houston, he wearily dismounted his Rocinante and sheathed his legal lance. He announced that he would not appeal the case.

Asked by a reporter if he now conceded that the will was a forgery, he replied: "Hell, no! That verdict doesn't change the writing on the will. That will is genuine. I know it. And some day, perhaps, everyone will know it."

Melvin Dummar received one sixteenth of zero, but he consistently had maintained that he had never asked for anything. "I did a good turn to an old man in the desert," he said recently, "and all I got out of it was grief." He insists that Hughes wrote the will "because either Hughes wrote it or I did, and I know I didn't write it." He did not come out of the affair entirely empty-handed. There was his movie, *Melvin and Howard,* and he was booked, after the trial, for a two-week turn as a country singer at a major Reno gambling resort. The high point of his act was a new song he wrote entitled "Thank You, Howard." It concluded with the line "Thank you, Howard, for leaving me something—you left me frustration." He was also featured in a national television commercial for an ice-cream company with the theme "It's unbelievable." He still gets a trickle of royalty checks from reruns of his movie.

"What hurts me most about this will, worse than having it ruled a forgery, is that I didn't get to play myself in the movie," Melvin says. "I badgered the studio about that every day," he says plaintively, "until they wouldn't take my calls anymore." The studio did give him a bit part as a short-order cook in a coffee-shop scene, which proved prophetic. In 1986 he returned to Gabbs, Nevada, where everything had started, and took over a small coffee shop and hamburger grill.

LeVane Forsythe flew down from Anchorage after the trial seeking a writer for a book about his long career as Ventura, secret agent for billionaire Howard Hughes. Unsuccessful, Forsythe retreated—at least for the moment—to the obscurity from which he had twice emerged.

Rhoden returned to Los Angeles and laboriously hauled himself out of his financial hole by applying his creative legal talents to clients who paid with money rather than dreams of what might be. In seeing the Mormon will through to a verdict, he had sacrificed his beloved twin-engine Cessna 310, but eventually he was able to replace it with a new plane.

At Andrews, Kurth, the partners' jubilation over their court success was tempered when they added up the costs of shielding The Money from those who wanted it. To dispose of the three sheets of yellow paper that Dummar had surreptitiously deposited on a Mormon's desk, Andrews, Kurth expended more than $3 million on lawyers, mounds of depositions, handwriting experts, court fees, and investigators with the patience and know-how required to track Melvin Dummar's fingerprint down to a page on a Utah library book. There was even a moment for alarm during the Mormon will trial when a new dreamer up in Utah informed the Houston court that it was he, not Dummar, who had loaned Howard Hughes a quarter and that he was the proper claimant of Hughes's grateful benefaction. Apparently because he could not find an attorney to put this story into proper legal form, this Samaritan never pursued his claim.

Although the Mormon will was branded a forgery, the identity of the will's writer was never determined or even investigated. Despite the magnitude of the money involved, no government agency undertook to pursue the will's architect. "All those pretrial hearings and an eight-month trial cost Nevada a fortune," said one political commentator. "No one was inclined to waste more money on a long investigation that might go nowhere."

A year and a half after the Mormon will trial, Judge Keith Hayes died of cancer. At a memorial service, a friend related a conversation he had had with the jurist on his deathbed:

"Keith discussed with me the hereafter life he knew he would soon begin. After I named the two souls I most looked forward to meeting in the next world, Keith said that his first was his mother, then Howard Hughes. Keith said something about a question he wanted to ask him."

8

SHOOT-OUT IN THE
BOARDROOM

THE INSPIRATION FOR the Mormon will, and all its close relations, was, of course, the scale of Hughes's fortune. Famous, and
indeed enormously wealthy, people die with great regularity without clogging the probate courts up with phony wills. But Hughes's
wealth seemed to be of a totally different order of magnitude. To
the man in the street, he was the American Croesus, possessed of
assets that seemed incapable of diminution. And this was not just
a popular impression. The specialist business columns would provide ballpark estimates of Hughes's personal wealth that began
around a billion and a half and curved smartly upward.

While not given to public pronouncements about his fortune,
Hughes had certainly cherished the title of billionaire and encouraged its use. In 1968 he had been distressed when a news release
from his own organization had referred to him as a mere "mil-
lionaire." He wrote an angry memo demanding to know who had
so downgraded him and deplored the comfort it would provide to
his legion of unnamed enemies:

"I am sure there is a large army of people waiting in expectant, hushed silence for the first indication of a slide backward in my financial resources . . . There are several hundred millionaires on the horizon now, and since I have been referred to as a Billionaire ever since we became established in Las Vegas, I am fearful some enemy of mine will make a story about it—something like, 'Well, well, has he finally gotten to the bottom of his bankroll?' "

On May 15, 1977, came the deeply shocking news that Hughes, with the help of his business associates, had come close to accomplishing this astonishing feat. In the unsentimental parlance of Las Vegas, the Hughes organization was not that far off from "going flat pocket," at least by any normal billionaire's standards.

The news came in a preliminary report by Merrill Lynch, the nationally known financial company, which had been set the task of valuing the Hughes empire for probate. The figure it came up with was what seemed an almost incredibly picayune $168 million. This, the company claimed, would be what all the Hughes assets would be worth if they were put on the market and sold off as part of a single corporation. Merrill Lynch had spent eleven months working on the valuation and was ready to defend its figure publicly. Privately, a Merrill Lynch executive told Will Lummis, "This is one of the worst-run companies we have ever examined."

It was still true that Hughes was entitled to the rank of billionaire several times over at the time of his death, but this was primarily due to his grip on the Hughes Medical Institute, which wholly owned Hughes Aircraft. The institute and Hughes Aircraft, however, did not formally constitute part of the estate and therefore fell outside the scope of the Merrill Lynch appraisal. As it happened, the Merrill Lynch valuation would prove to be a very substantial underestimate of Summa's true worth, but it did inject a measure of realism into popular fantasies about The Money. It also provided Will Lummis with a useful lever, or so he had thought.

Appalled at Summa's ongoing losses, Lummis had grown hoarse asking his fellow board members where the cash was coming from to sustain the spending. Bill Gay had expensive plans for revival but, as far as Lummis could detect, no clue as to how they should be financed, whereas Chester Davis bluntly suggested that Lummis raise any money required by "hocking Summa's stock." It became clear to Lummis that the popular fantasy about the inexhaustible supply of Hughes money flourished, in its most pernicious form, on the board of Summa itself. With the new valuation report, Lummis felt he had the antidote.

As Lummis saw it, Merrill Lynch provided the clinching evidence of Summa's deep-seated problems, many of which had already been itemized in the pessimistic internal studies conducted by Mickey West and the finance department. It now seemed evident that Summa not only had an acute cash-flow problem but that its overall worth was much less than was first imagined. Lummis had also been informed by one of the estate attorneys that if Summa was suddenly obliged to meet all its projected tax and legal liabilities in one go, "the company would be belly-up in the water." With this compelling background, Lummis felt that he was at last in a position to win over the Summa board to a policy of financial restraint, though he entertained no great hopes for the conversion of the man he had come to call "the impossible person," Chester Davis.

Davis was so wedded to the proposition that a Hughes will deeding his estate to the Medical Institute would either be found or validated as a "lost will" that he saw no real point in planning for other contingencies. Summa, he thought, should not trouble itself with elaborate financial planning to meet death taxes that would only fall due if Hughes had died intestate. Domicile was another nonsense as far as Davis was concerned since it would have no relevance if HHMI absorbed the whole estate. In consequence, Davis did not think that Summa should concern itself overmuch with irritations like the Texas probate court, with its constant demands for Hughes-related papers in order to determine where Hughes lived.

Since many of these papers were under Davis's control, this led to constant embarrassments with the Texas court—for Lummis, the legally responsible person as far as the estate was concerned, rather than Davis, who was supposedly a subordinate. Caught between a rock and a hard place, Lummis's estate attorneys would regularly appear before Judge Gregory asking for more time to meet the court's requirements for documents and information. And the court would grant continuations, but with mounting exasperation. Early in 1977, an estate attorney made specific mention of Lummis's problem with Davis in an attempt to obtain the court's sympathy. This only elicited an unsympathetic growl from Attorney General Hill: "If Lummis can't run the show, let's replace him." This further concentrated Lummis's mind on the Davis problem.

In preparing its financial report on the Hughes empire, Merrill Lynch had worked in close concert with Summa's independent auditors, Haskins & Sells, and it had been agreed that a reserve of $87 million should be established to meet possible litigation costs. In fact, the outstanding claims against Summa at that time came to over $200 million—more than Merrill Lynch's valuation for the entire estate—though many were clearly frivolous. A problem arose when Haskins & Sells said that it could not sign the accounts unless the $87 million figure had formal boardroom approval. Merrill Lynch, in its turn, said that it could not formally submit its appraisal to the Texas probate court without the signed accounts from Haskins & Sells. Meanwhile, the Texas court was pressing impatiently for the appraisal. Something had to be done, and fast.

On April 25, 1977, there was an emergency meeting of the Summa board to resolve the crisis. Lummis explained the problem, and Chester Davis went up the wall. The proposed reserve, Davis claimed, would provide a target for litigants to aim at. There was no way he, as Summa's general counsel, could countenance such a proposal. Lummis finally got the endorsement he wanted for the $87 million reserve from the rest of the board, with Davis and Gay dissenting, but it was a rough ride. "I think," said Lummis's friend Bill Miller, who ran the estate office at Andrews, Kurth, "that's when he really decided Chester just had to go."

The next showdown was not long delayed. On May 18, the Summa board assembled again for what had been earmarked as a financial planning meeting to decide policy over the next eighteen months. Lummis had prepared carefully for the meeting, aware that in any showdown he could wind up the loser. The troika of Gay, Davis, and Henley almost invariably operated in concert. And when issues were pushed to a vote, the two Hughes male nurses, Myler and Holmes, tended to side with them. Mickey West, Lummis's one consistent supporter on the board, called them, with heavy irony, "the business-as-usual party."

Lummis, however, felt there were grounds for encouragement. The emergency vote on the litigation reserve had split his opponents for the first time. Some at least now seemed open to persuasion. This optimism did not outlive the opening minutes of the meeting.

As the board members were taking their seats, Bill Gay quietly moved around distributing an alternate report opposing the document that had been previously circulated by his chairman. Lummis had argued strongly for the employment of outside financial advisers and proposed Merrill Lynch, which had already done $400,000 worth of work for Summa, as the best candidate for this role. The Gay and Davis group asserted that "in-house talent" could easily do the job. The Lummis report called for a brake on all expenditure programs. The Gay report called for a bullish approach to business problems, specifically recommending the expenditure of $49 million on refurbishment of the Desert Inn Hotel and Casino. To Lummis this amounted to adding financial indiscipline to willful ignorance, but he went down on both issues. Those who voted against him in each case were Gay, Davis, Henley, Myler, and Holmes.

Shortly after Hughes's death Lummis had secured recognition in the state of Delaware, where Summa was originally incorporated, as the company's "sole stockholder." Lummis now felt the need to exercise the power inherent in that position. He would later testify in a deposition: "They did not have the foggiest idea of how the company was going to pay for that [the Desert Inn refurbishment] . . . I reached the conclusion that if I was, as administrator and a holder of the Summa stock, going to ultimately receive all of the blame for mistakes being made at Summa Corporation, they were going to be my mistakes. I felt I could not possibly go along with decisions that were being made that I felt were outrageous."

A week after his boardroom defeat, Lummis removed the rug from under the opposition. Davis, Holmes, and Myler were summarily dismissed from the board and replaced by two people who had some proven record of prior acquaintance with balance sheets—Vernon C. Olson, Summa's financial controller, and E. R. Vacchina of the First National Bank of Nevada, which had been named, along with Lummis, as the coadministrator of the Hughes estate in Nevada. Lummis spared President Bill Gay for a period, but not in a particularly merciful way.

In July 1977 Lummis creatively appointed Phil Hannifin, who had previously served as head of the Nevada Gaming Control Board, as the new boss of Summa's Hotels and Casinos group. Gay told Lummis that this appointment effectively left him with nothing to do. Lummis didn't argue the point. A few months later Gay resigned from Summa, and Nadine Henley left soon after.

Chester Davis stayed on as Summa's general counsel—for a while. Lummis would later say in his deposition: "I had hoped to be able to narrow Mr. Davis's area of responsibility to that simply of a counsel, continuing to represent the company in the many lawsuits in which he and his firm had been representing the company. That hope of mine was a forlorn one." In the summer of 1977 the new Lummis-controlled board sacked its turbulent general counsel.

The outbreak of peace in the Summa boardroom did not produce any miraculous relief for Lummis. He had displaced the opposition, but its potency had not been diminished. Indeed, in the short term, Lummis only magnified his problems on the flank occupied by the Howard Hughes Medical Institute, where Davis and Gay enjoyed almost untrammeled authority and where Nadine Henley served as their secretary/treasurer. And the Medical Institute, unlike Lummis's ramshackle Summa empire, was genuinely worth billions.

How the institute and its golden asset, Hughes Aircraft, came to be located outside Hughes's estate is one of the classic tax-evasion stories of all time. Hughes founded HAC in the 1930s as a tiny enterprise to build his private planes when he was breaking major flight records. Hughes Aircraft ceased making planes around the end of World War II and became involved in a far more profitable operation. With a sharp eye for future trends, Hughes converted the company to electronics, so successfully that he almost cornered the nation's supply of electronics experts and engineers, then in scant supply. By 1950 the company was earning serious money with the development of the Falcon, the world's first air-to-air missile. An electronic weapons control system with a combined radar set and computer, Falcon would guide the company into many other applications of electronics to modern warfare. With the outbreak of the Korean War, demand for the company's products hugely increased and HAC became exceptionally prosperous. From $2 million in 1948, HAC's sales shot up to over $200 million in 1953.

But in that year, long-simmering managerial problems boiled over at the headquarters in Culver City, California. They arose out of Hughes's habit of playing one executive against another and his penchant for indecision. He hinted that HAC might be compelled to move operations to Nevada and then disappeared for weeks while his managers seethed. Finally, HAC suffered a mass exodus of talent that almost wrecked the company.

When his general manager, retired air force general Harold George, confronted him with a series of staff requests, including one for stock options, Hughes said that George was seeking to deprive him of the right to manage his own property and that he would "burn down the plant" before letting such a thing happen. "You are accomplishing the same effect without matches," said the general.

George walked out, and so did two of his most creative scientists, Dean Wooldridge and Simon Ramo, who formed what became TRW, Inc. Two other escapees from the shambles, Roy Ash and Charles "Tex" Thornton, founded Litton Industries. Both these enterprises became competitors of Hughes Aircraft, and out of this fractionation grew California's teeming electronics and aerospace industry.

Appalled at the HAC donnybrook, Air Force Secretary Harold Talbott flew to Los Angeles and strafed Hughes for wrecking a company that was vital to U.S. military security. He also delivered an ultimatum: get a competent professional manager, put him in charge, and then leave him alone, "or I will see to it that you never get another dollar of federal funds." He gave Hughes ninety days to put his house in order.

There was no mistaking the seriousness of the ultimatum, but Hughes was able to extract massive tax and public relations advantages from the whole imbroglio. He did this by going into the charity business, though the giving was more apparent than real. Hughes assigned all of his Hughes Aircraft stock to a newly formed Medical Institute—of which he was the sole trustee. Subsequently, he made a complete recovery from this limited act of charity. When he learned that the IRS was, with good reason, questioning the tax-exempt status claimed for his Medical Institute, Hughes tried to take the stock back from his own creation. He was then outraged to learn that his lawyer had drafted an irrevocable grant.

"Of all the goddamn times my planes have crashed," Hughes complained, "why couldn't it have crashed when I was flying in to sign that goddamn stock grant?"

Hughes had no real cause for complaint, however. The IRS would soon back off. This left Hughes with his ostensibly charitable contraption wholly intact and wholly tax-exempt. Meanwhile, on the industrial front, Hughes had shrewdly observed the conditions of Talbott's ultimatum. He appointed Lawrence "Pat" Hyland, the top man from the Bendix Corporation, to run Hughes Aircraft and prudently left him alone. Hyland was as decisive as Hughes was procrastinating. On the rare occasions when he felt the billionaire had a need to know, he would dispatch a memo to Hughes saying what he wanted to do, with the notation that if he received no answer, he would proceed. "Pat had the best of two worlds," said an associate. "Hughes made his money available to HAC but withheld his advice."

Under Hyland's management and that of his successor, Allen Puckett, the company steadily ascended to a position of preeminence in its multiple fields of operations, which extended from navigation equipment to the very latest in "spy satellites." Its many achievements would include construction of the Hughes *Surveyor* spacecraft, the first device to soft-land on the moon and send back pictures via the Hughes Early Bird communications satellite. It pioneered the use of lasers both for manufacturing and directional bombing purposes and, as a sideline, conjured up useful trinkets for espionage purposes like a cigarette case that doubled as a tape recorder and micro radio transmitters capable of being inserted into hollow dentures. By the time of Hughes's death, it was employing over fifty thousand skilled workers, most of them in Southern California, and logging in sales of around $2 billion a year and rising. Most of its lucrative business was with government defense establishments and the CIA.

By the terms of Hughes's original gift of his stock, it was implied that all of Hughes Aircraft's profits would go to the Medical Institute. But Hughes's tax lawyers were able to evolve strategies that ensured this would not happen. As the result of a complicated web of leasing arrangements, HHMI was required to pay interest on a "loan," which had the effect of providing Hughes with far more of the institute's money than ever found its way into medical research. In its first year of operation, the Medical Institute reported an income from Hughes Aircraft of $3,609,785, of which $43,348 was earmarked for research fellowships. The rest went to Hughes and Hughes Tool Company.

The research outlay was, in fact, not even minor-league by established charitable foundation standards. Over the twenty-three years of the institute's existence during Hughes's lifetime, its contribution to medical research barely exceeded an average of a million dollars a year. In the same period Hughes Aircraft chalked up estimated profits of around $2 billion. Hughes would say that the money from HAC's profits contributed to "the benefit of mankind," but, in reality, nearly all the benefits flowed to Hughes, Hughes Tool, and Hughes Aircraft.

Over the years HAC's competitors angrily complained that the Howard Hughes Medical Institute was no more than a tax-dodging device that gave HAC an unfair competitive edge over its rivals by enabling it to feed back undetected, and untaxed, profits into its research and development program. These complaints led to a congressional tax-reform bill in 1969 that contained a passage designed to make life more difficult for Hughes and his institute, but it was loosely drafted and the tax scam survived.

Both Davis and Gay were steeped in the arcane traditions and methods of the Medical Institute. They had been appointed members of its executive committee by Hughes back in 1971, and they ran it on his behalf. Hughes could never bring himself to appoint another sole trustee as his successor. As a result, on his death, the two-man executive committee continued in full control. And after Lummis torpedoed their support in the Summa boardroom, they counterattacked with the HHMI battleship.

The main engagement took place in Delaware, where the Medical Institute, like Summa, had been incorporated. In an action before the New Castle County Court of Chancery in Wilmington, Davis argued that Lummis should be sacked, or have his powers curbed. He contended that his own dismissal, along with that of Myler and Holmes, from the Summa board was improper and that it was never intended that Lummis should exercise such power. Davis recalled that when Lummis was originally invited into the company, it was generally thought that he would be "a mechanic," there to superintend the regular flow of business. But Lummis, according to Davis, had emerged not as a neutral facilitator but as a man of bias who "chose to prefer the possible interests of the intestate heirs over those of HHMI."

The interests of HHMI, of course, were all bound up with the lost will, which would allegedly bequeath Hughes's entire estate to the Medical Institute. All the money would then go to the foundation controlled by Davis and Gay. Tiresome considerations of how to pay death taxes and how to appease the intestate heirs and the overweening Mr. Lummis would be at an end. Moreover, it was conceded by most people who knew Hughes that if a will was found, it would almost certainly feature the Medical Institute as the prime, very likely the only, beneficiary.

Unhappily for Davis, memories were bright of the massive Hughes will search that had just failed. At the direction of the superior court in California, Richard Gano, Will Lummis's cousin and the Hughes administrator in that state, had recently published his investigation into the existence, or otherwise, of a Hughes will. It ran to 274 pages, including detailed search operations in over one hundred banks, and gave evidence of firsthand interviews with scores of people who might have been aware of Hughes's intentions. It was clear that search had been conducted thoroughly and with some zeal, perhaps unsurprisingly, since one of the two law firms assisting Gano with his inquiry was Davis & Cox, Chester Davis's own firm. But at the end of it all, Gano could find no trace of a viable will.

Davis, nonetheless, continued to act like a man with an ace up his sleeve. Summoned to give deposition testimony in relation to the Mormon will case, Davis flummoxed his interviewer by indicating that he had held vital evidence back from his own firm's investigation. As an example of Davis's never-at-a-loss technique, it was something of a gem. It began with Davis asserting that he had in several explicit memos provided evidence of the existence of a Hughes will.

Q: Why weren't these memos included in the Gano report, since they are concerned with the writing of a will?

A: The Gano report, as I understand it, was a description of the result of the investigation activities of the special administrator in California based upon what was found in the papers and documents that fell in the possession and control of Mr. Gano in California.

Q: Well, did you turn these memos over to Mr. Gano?

A: No.

Q: Has Mr. Gano ever seen these memos?

A: Not that I know of. I am sure he did not.

Q: Where are these memos physically located right now?

A: Well, my memos primarily are in—well, as far as I know, they are in my possession and control in my office in New York.

For the action against Lummis in Wilmington, Davis delved into his personal archive and produced one document for the court. This was a Hughes memo that certainly indicated that Hughes was saying he had made a will around 1970. In it Hughes wrote to Davis, "I assured both Bob [Maheu] and Governor [Paul] Laxalt and the Gaming Commission that my will provided the machinery to protect all executives and further to ensure continuity of control." Later in the same memo, Hughes wrote: "Regarding the control of Hughes Tool and the disposition of my estate in the terms of my will . . ." But there also was considerable evidence of Hughes saying he had made wills at much later dates. On its own, Davis's ace-in-the-hole memo did not carry the evidence for a Hughes will forward to any measurable degree.

But Davis did manage to enliven the proceedings by lobbing in an unexpected grenade. Davis asserted that he was advised that either Mr. Lummis or the law firm of Andrews, Kurth had additional documents in the decedent's handwriting, confirming the existence of a will leaving control of Summa to HHMI. This scarcely masked the fact that Davis was accusing Lummis and his law firm of being part of a plot to steal Summa.

Davis could produce no evidence for this allegation, which was promptly denied, but it showed, more than anything, the measure of his antipathy toward Lummis. The chancery court, unmoved by corporate cat fighting, focused on the conspicuous absence of an actual Hughes will. Lummis emerged with his authority over Summa intact, despite everything Davis could throw at him. He had won another significant battle, but he also knew the war was far from over. And there was not much doubt about which side had the better reserves to finance a long struggle.

Lummis's situation as 1977 came to a close was described by a business friend as dire: "The banks were leery of lending Summa any money because what with the Mormon will, the lost will, and the rest, nobody could be sure who owned it or was going to own it. So Summa was hamstrung, the estate was hamstrung, the whole outfit was hamstrung. It was a bad time."

Davis and Gay, in contrast, were absorbed in the problem of how to give money away on an unprecedented scale. This was in large measure due to the long-suppressed generosity of the Medical Institute during Hughes's lifetime. In the final months of his life, the IRS, never comfortable with the charitable status accorded to HHMI, began making seriously menacing noises about having to reclassify the institute as a private foundation. This would have obliged the institute to undergo a much more stringent level of tax scrutiny. At this point HHMI suddenly became very charitable indeed and implemented its "Expanded Medical Research Program." In the year after Hughes's death, Hughes Aircraft thoughtfully upped its contribution to HHMI to $15,750,000, a tenfold increase on the average of previous years.

Gay and Davis presided over this new munificence and pledged that it would continue. In 1978 the contribution was upped again, to $18 million, and the institute's longtime medical director, Dr. George W. Thorn, would write, immodestly but with some reason: "At a time when funds for basic research are becoming more difficult to obtain, at a time when individual freedom by brilliant young scientists is more encumbered and particularly at a time when able scientists in clinical departments are unable to devote adequate time to important clinically related research, the unique policy and program of the Howard Hughes Medical Institute and the opportunities that it offers scientific Investigators constitutes a national medical resource of unusual potential."

Thus, Davis and Gay, through yet another dexterous exercise in tax avoidance, emerged as philanthropists of stature and importance. Their advantage was that in fighting their battles with Lummis, they could portray themselves as the custodians of a real charity for a change. The opportunity for combining public benevolence with private animus could rarely have been more felicitously arranged.

9

—

X RAYS

WILL LUMMIS REALLY liked George Dean despite their disparate personalities. Lummis's standard demeanor, though not unfriendly, was grave, and he tended to inspire a certain gravity in those around him. Dean, on the other hand, preferred the comfort of ongoing jokes and pranks. The one that Andrews, Kurth lawyers in Houston remember most graphically occurred on an evening when several of them, accompanied by Lummis, were going off to a formal dinner together. Lummis was having trouble tying his black tie for the occasion, and Dean solicitously maneuvered round him, lending a hand. As he craned over Lummis's shoulder, intent on the problem, Dean stage-whispered in the ear of the Summa boss: "We're getting awfully close. I hope we won't start any tongue kissing."

Despite such assaults on his dignity, Lummis had enormous respect for Dean's talents as a lawyer, which he had first encountered when they were used against him in pursuit of the heirship claims of Avis and Rush Hughes. And after Dean joined Lummis's legal team, he had proved marvelously adept at teasing out information denied to less exotic citizens. Even so, when Dean ambled into Lummis's office early in 1978 and slipped a king-sized manila envelope onto his desk, Lummis did not know if he was about to be on the receiving end of another leg-pull or whether he was actually going to learn something. It proved to be very much the latter.

The envelope contained the X rays taken at Hughes's autopsy, which had never formed part of the official autopsy report. Dean said he had obtained them from some undisclosed investigative source, but what they showed was clear enough—fragments of broken-off hypodermic needles in both arms, at least six in number. Dean held the X rays up to the light to itemize the needles, and Lummis's reaction was swift: "Could this be why they were so keen to have his body cremated?"

There was more, said Dean. His information was that the codeine level in Hughes's body was substantially, even grossly, understated in the official autopsy report. It was almost impossible to avoid the conclusion that Hughes was an addict and that, given how immobile he had become, that he must have been well assisted in the maintenance of this addiction over an exceptionally long period of time.

Lummis subsequently spoke of this session with Dean as marking a major change in his attitude. He would say: "It tended to confirm many of the published stories about Hughes's incompetence and lifestyle which I had previously doubted to be true. And which I had previously been led to believe were untrue." Among those who had led him to this belief had been Chester Davis and Bill Gay, people to whom Lummis now rendered diminished credence. "As soon as I saw the X rays," said Lummis, "I instructed the Summa attorney, the estate attorney, and the attorneys for any other Hughes entity to begin a thorough investigation of Hughes's condition."

This was in many ways a redundant exercise as both state and federal agencies were already hot on this particular trail. Dean had felt all along that Lummis was conducting his various campaigns in too gentlemanly a fashion, allowing his opponents to make all the initial moves. Dean would advocate a more aggressive approach, designed to surprise his opponents and put them on the back foot for a change. In short, he wanted Lummis to be a shade more like Chester Davis. After the X-ray session, and more specifically after victory in the Mormon will trial in June 1978, Dean got the Lummis he wanted.

The first thing that needed to be done was to launch an attack on Hughes's Medical Institute. Lummis's problems with HHMI in the Delaware court had become almost chronic as Davis and Gay constantly dreamed up new objections to his stewardship of Summa. In June 1978 Lummis deftly gave the problem a new twist by filing his own complaint at the New Castle Chancery Court in Wilmington.

Fastening onto the fact that Hughes had never appointed a successor trustee, Lummis contended that as the administrator of the Hughes estate, and therefore Hughes's legal representative, he should be regarded as the successor trustee and, by direct implication, Gay and Davis should move on. Thus, the court that had the task of appraising HHMI's bid to seize Summa now also had to appraise Summa's bid to seize HHMI. It was a piquant situation, one that would keep the lawyers gainfully employed for a long time. According to Dean, Lummis had no particular interest in ever running HHMI, but he did want to keep the enemy well occupied.

Lummis would also borrow another idea of Dean's that was genuinely original, at least in its legal application. As a technique, psychological autopsy was fairly well known to the courts, most frequently in helping coroners establish the cause of death when it appeared to be uncertain. In those cases psychologists would draw on letters, interviews with friends and associates, and other materials to help determine probabilities. It could hardly claim to be exact science, but coroners would often find it a useful tool when having to discriminate between suicide, accident, and murder. Nobody, however, appears to have thought of using the technique to establish whether a deceased megamillionaire was in his right mind, at least not until George Dean suggested the idea to Will Lummis.

The issue of Hughes's mental competence or the lack of it had reverberations at many levels, from his domicile to what he would have wanted done with the *Spruce Goose*. But the levels of most immediate interest to Summa were legal and administrative. If it could be established that Hughes was not competent when he fell afoul of TWA, Air West, Los Angeles Airways, and all the other seriously vexed litigants, then it might be possible to obtain more merciful treatment by the courts. On the administrative side, if it could be proved that Hughes was not competent when his directors, aides, and doctors were awarded lifelong consultancy contracts, then these contracts might be deemed legally invalid.

The task of preparing Howard Hughes's psychological autopsy was taken on by Raymond D. Fowler, Jr., head of the psychology department at the University of Alabama, where George Dean had once edited the law review and led anti-segregation rallies. Dean gave Fowler a wide brief—"find out as much as possible about the mental condition of Hughes during this life"—and encouraged him to take advantage of the rich flow of authentic Hughes memos that had bubbled up since his death. Fowler did that, and more. He interviewed many of Hughes's intimates from his last years, who apparently found it easier talking to a lone psychologist than to the regiment of lawyers probing Hughes's affairs.

Fowler's final report would run to over sixty pages, and he would circulate the main findings to one hundred other psychologists and psychiatrists. Not all of them agreed with his diagnosis— Fowler thought that Hughes could be classified as "psychotic" in his later years—but all felt that Hughes met the criteria for commitment to a mental hospital. As a work of literature, Fowler's report hardly compares with Oscar Wilde's *Picture of Dorian Gray*, but it has some of the same gruesome fascination. How, the reader asks, could so much gilded promise come to this? Here are some extracts from the report that were translated into affidavit form and used in the courts:

"Hughes rarely knew whether it was night or day, or even what day it was. He had increasingly long periods of unconsciousness, up to one to three days . . . He was mentally inactive, and his speech was sometimes incoherent. He was nude most of the time."

"In his later years, Hughes paid no attention to his personal hygiene . . . as a result of his filthy hair, rotting teeth and unclean body, he had an extremely foul odor as well as an offensive appearance."

"Hughes usually had bowel movements only once or twice a month, and then only after enemas had been administered by aides . . . Sometimes his aides did not know when he had a bowel movement, and they would find him lying in his fecal matter."

"His bizarre ideas and ineffective rituals [designed to combat germs] were so irrational, so strongly adhered to, and so incapacitating that a personality breakdown of psychotic proportions may be assumed . . . Hughes's behavior was clearly regressed to a psychotic degree. Very few mental patients ever show behavior so extremely regressed."

In conclusion, Fowler wrote of Hughes:

"In these last years, his life resembled that of a chronic psychotic patient in the very worst mental hospital. He was incapable of caring for himself or of surviving without the assistance of attendants. He was continuously drugged and his consciousness was clouded. He was ill, emaciated, bedridden and incapable of normal mental and physical activity. He could not have made rational judgments involving complex business and legal affairs; nor could he have given competent assistance to those representing him. Had he been subject to formal questioning not only would he have been unable to respond competently but the prospect of such an encounter would have been so upsetting to him that he would have been emotionally unable to participate.

"Such a person would have met the criteria for commitment to a mental hospital, and a qualified psychiatrist or psychologist would certainly have certified that his condition justified commitment. He was, for all practical purposes, incarcerated in a mental institution of his own making, but he was receiving no treatment for his mental illness and not even adequate care for his basic physical needs."

The Fowler report had some profound effects. In the Air West case, the most expensive outstanding litigation, Judge Zirpoli had awarded a massive $78 million default judgment against Summa. The case had its origins in Hughes's acquisition of Air West back in 1969 when, assisted by Bob Maheu and Chester Davis, he had allegedly engineered a collapse in the company's shares before moving in for the corporate kill. The case dragged on for years, involving the Securities and Exchange Commission as well as outraged stockholders. It ultimately turned, as did so many other things, on Hughes's readiness to testify in some way. Judge Zirpoli warned Chester Davis that Summa would face very severe penalties if Hughes refused to give evidence.

According to Davis he, as Summa's general counsel, had personally apprised Hughes of the threat. According to John Holmes and other aides, the warning never actually reached Hughes. Either way, Hughes never provided the court with so much as a deposition, and a punitive default penalty became inevitable. Until Fowler. After hearing the representations of Dean and other Summa attorneys on the subject of Hughes's incompetence, as evinced in the psychological profile, Judge Zirpoli scaled down the cost of his judgment from $78 million to $41.5 million, a savings to Summa of $36.5 million.

Dean deployed Fowler in other areas. Los Angeles Airways, a commuter company that operated a fleet of helicopters, had taken umbrage against Hughes back in 1970 when Bob Maheu, as Hughes's representative, had made what it regarded as a firm commitment to take over the company. But before things could be finalized, Maheu lost his position, and Hughes thereafter showed no discernible interest in Los Angeles Airways. In 1977 the company filed a $16 million suit as compensation for that episode. Armed with the Fowler report, Dean was able to shave the settlement figure down to $750,000.

Similar, though less spectacular, reductions were achieved in a number of other cases, and the threat posed to Summa and the estate by the backlog of lawsuits began to recede. Originally, it had seemed as if Summa's $87 million litigation reserve would not be adequate to the task, but it proved more than enough. Few of these economies would have been possible if Chester Davis had seen all the cases through. This was not because Davis was an inefficient lawyer; in fact, he could be extraordinarily persuasive in court. It was because he was stuck with a long record of having assured a wide variety of courts, aviation authorities, gaming commissions, and regulatory agencies that Hughes was a man eminently capable of managing his own business affairs. For Davis to start arguing that Hughes was incompetent in court, he would first have to acknowledge perjuries of his own on a near-epic scale.

The persuasive power of the Fowler report was in part due to its timing. Had it been composed shortly after Hughes's death, it would probably have been dismissed as simply unbelievable. But by the time it was completed in the fall of 1978, there had been substantial developments in other areas that made it credible. Long before the X-ray evidence surfaced, two brilliant reporters for *The Philadelphia Inquirer,* Donald Barlett and James Steele, published a story on Hughes's "massive" drug use made possible by "prescriptions issued in names other than Hughes." The story had run on June 27, 1977, and four days later the U.S. Drug Enforcement Administration began to dig into Hughes's drug-supply operation. Knowing that its inquiry could lead to serious criminal charges, the DEA insisted on keeping its cards very close to its chest.

No such constraint, however, afflicted Texas Attorney General John Hill's office in Austin, where the remit to investigate Hughes's domicile was broadly interpreted and included Hughes's mental and physical competence. For a while examination of Hughes's final years was seriously impeded by the reluctance of his palace guard to say anything. Chester Davis had been active and effective in blocking attempts to interview Hughes's personal aides and doctors. But in 1977 the wall of silence began to crumble.

This was largely due to the efforts of Hill and his assistant, Rick Harrison, in assembling a vast collection of Hughes-related documents that needed interpretation by the people who had written them or who were named therein. The most intriguing of these documents, part of a cache that had been left behind when the aides hurriedly decamped from Mexico, were the logs. These were the top-secret reports on the minutiae of Hughes's daily life compiled by his immediate aides. Aside from them, the only people allowed access to the logs were Kay Glenn, who had charge of Hughes's personal staff, Hughes's physicians, and Bill Gay.

The final irony of Hughes's existence was that the fight for his fortune demolished the secrecy The Money had bought for him at enormous cost in his latter years. Philip Marlowe, Raymond Chandler's ace detective, observed that money can buy a great deal of publicity—or a great deal of silence. In Howard Hughes's unique case, it bought both. The armor-plated walls that Hughes had created around himself first cracked and then shattered as the men with him in exile were put under oath and were required to testify. Thousands of his documents, which Hughes described as "the most confidential, almost sacred information as to my innermost activities," were spread out in the public view. Any citizen who could afford the price of a newspaper could obtain a good idea of the drugs Hughes used, the titles of the movies he watched over and over, what he ate or refused to eat each day, when he slept and when he woke, even the precise time he entered and left the bathroom. The man who sought total secrecy and spent millions to secure it became one of the most thoroughly documented human beings in history.

The logs are not complex documents, but the abbreviations they contain require explanation. "BB" stands for Blue Bombers, Valium tablets; 'c' represents the codeine tablets that Hughes dissolved in water and injected; Number '4s' is short for Emperin Compound No. 4, which also contained codeine; and "B/R" means bathroom. Here is a representative extract, a long weekend in the life of Howard Hughes, starting Friday, December 17, 1971, as recorded by his aides:

12:10 AM Chair.
  1:20   "   Screening "WRECKING CREW."
  2:15   "   B/R.
  2:45   "   Chair. Resumed screening "WRECKING CREW."
  3:25   "   Chicken and dessert.
  5:20   "   Finished.
  5:25   "   B/R

5:45   "   Bed and asleep.
7:50   "   B/R and shower.
8:35   "   Chair.
9   "   Screening ARABESQUE.
10:15   "   B/R.
10:40   "   Chair 8c's (23 left)
11:30   "   Chicken
1:00 PM B/R
1:20   "   Chair—"ARABESQUE" reel #3.
2:50   "   B/R—John must, somehow, acquire additional #4s.
3:25   "   Chair—
5:00   "   B/R—called Gordon.
5:50   "   Chair—Resumed screening "DEADLIER THAN
            THE MALE."
6:40   "   Food: chicken only
7:35   "   Finished eating.
8:00   "   B/R
8:20   "   Chair. Screening "DARING GAME."
9:45   "   B/R
10:15   "   Chair. Resumed screening "DARING GAME."
            Reels 1 & 2.
11:10   "   B/R.
11:45   "   Chair. Screening "TENSION AT TABLE ROCK."

Saturday, 18 Dec. 71
12:50 AM B/R.
1:05   "   Chair.
1:30   "   Food: chicken & desert.
3:30   "   Finished.
3:40   "   B/R
4:30   "   Bed and asleep
9:20   "   B/R and awake
11:30   "   Chair
11:45   "   10 #4. 32 left.
5:00 PM Food: chicken only.
6:10   "   B/R

6:30 " Chair. Screening "WRECKING CREW." 5 BB's
7:00 " B/R.
7:20 " Chair. Resumed screening "WRECKING CREW."
7:40 " Food. Dessert only.
8:30 " Finished eating.
8:45 " B/R.
9:00 " Bed. Asleep

Sunday, Dec. 19
3:30 AM B/R
4:50 " Bed
7   " B/R and shower
9:10 " Chair
9:25 " Screening DEADLIER THAN THE MALE
11:25 " B/R
11:50 " Chair
12:30 PM Food—DEADLIER THAN THE MALE finished.
2:00 " Finished complete meal.
2:40 " Asleep
5:20 " Awake. B/R.
5:45 " Chair (12 No. 4's 20 left)
7:10 " B/R
7:30 " Screening "WRECKING CREW."
8:15 " Food: Chicken only.
9:30 " Finished eating. "Wrecking crew" completed.
10:20 " B/R.
         Info: He OK'd the following films to be returned:
         Wrecking Crew, Deadlier Than The Male, Ara-
         besque, Sundowners & Tension at Table Rock.
10:50 " Chair. Screening "NO HIGHWAY IN THE SKY."
         Completed.

Monday, Dec. 20
1:15 AM B/R.
1:35 " Chair. Screening "BULLET FOR A BADMAN."
4   " B/R
4:45 " Chair #2 reel of BULLET again.

5:55	"	B/R
6:25	"	Chair #2 reel of BULLET again.
6:40	"	Chicken
8:25	"	B/R Discontinued eating
9:20	"	Chair #2 reel of BULLET
		About 10 #4's. Maybe ten left.
10:20	"	Chicken
11:10	"	B/R

And so on. In fact, the weekend portrayed above was considerably more varied than most. Hughes often relentlessly viewed the same film over and over. During one three-week period, *Ten Little Indians* was screened no fewer than forty times in whole or in part, though whether this was because he liked the movie or because he was testing it as a potential cure for insomnia is not clear. On the occasion of the thirty-ninth screening, the log reads, with a rare flash of Mormon wit, "Chair: Trying to go to sleep with Indians." At times like this, Hughes's aides, on $80,000 to $110,000 a year, must have thought they were seriously earning their keep.

Of high finance and strategic business dealing, there is little sign, though one aide does record a rather wistful request from the boss: "He wants to know from Chester [Davis] how long this IRS thing will keep us out of the country."

Aside from the litany of pills popped, movies screened, and visits made to the bathroom, the logs featured occasional "Instructions." These illustrated Hughes's immediate concerns and wishes and provided a body of know-how about his care that could be passed on from Mormon attendant to Mormon attendant. Here are some that were issued between November 1971 and January 1973:

Ipcress File reel 3. There is a torture scene about ½ way through that he doesn't want to look at. When he stops at that point, roll the reel to the marker tape before continuing.

Wants to start orange tarts again. Also wants to change the Napoleons so there is cake between custard rather than the flaky pie crust material they now have. The custard and the frosting should remain as is.

HRH says not to get any more Italian westerns.

Do not put the sponge rubber inside any pillow case—in fact he does not want anything whatsoever, put inside the pillow case. He wants the pillow case to be treated as if it were a single layer of material.

His head pillow is to be inserted with the hard blue-green pillow next to his back and the open end of the pillow on his right (not the left as before). Also, carry the pillow by the bottom seam (narrow).

When he goes to the B/R close the door to the hall.

Try to turn the TV off by using remote control. Also turn amplifier off at the same time. Please leave note explaining how set was turned off.

He wanted our flashlight put in the closet on the floor . . . When carrying it to be cleaned he wants double paper towel insulation used.

Please refrain from placing a box containing kleenex on the square table to the left that contains "crew manuals."

When he has designated a time to eat, always notify him 10 minutes prior to the time, especially if he is dozing, so that he can start setting his table.

"He doesn't want to be permitted to sleep in the bathroom" was the instruction on August 10, 1972. This was followed soon after by "Hereafter when he asks for pills, take him the entire bottle (not some on kleenex)." and later by "HRH doesn't want anybody to touch the trash sack, or trash in his bathroom until he instructs."

The logs that survived to be inspected by the various agencies investigating Hughes's physical and mental condition related to the 1971–1973 period. Later logs had been compiled but were never discovered and may have been shredded. But any changes in Hughes's daily lifestyle can only have been much for the worse. After breaking his hip as the result of a bathroom fall in England in August 1973, he would never walk again. Dr. William Young, the English doctor and radiologist who treated Hughes after his fall, was struck by the parchmentlike quality of his patient's skin, the length of his wispy beard, the extreme thinness of his body, and the length of his toenails and fingernails, "resembling those of a Chinese mandarin." Dr. Young would testify later: "During World War II, I had occasion to treat prisoners of war in Japanese prison camps, and I would describe Mr Hughes' physical condition as being in a stage of malnutrition comparable with that of such prisoners as I treated."

After 1973 the only person with any independent insight into Hughes's system of care was Jack Real, a former fighter pilot and Lockheed executive. Hughes had a soft spot for Lockheed—his around-the-world flight had been in a Lockheed 14, and he had subsequently made significant design contributions to the Lockheed Constellation. With Real, Hughes was able to rekindle some aspects of a more ebullient past. This intimacy was resented by most of the aides. Real also, incautiously, made little secret of his low opinion of the way in which Hughes's empire was being run. He was particularly critical of the decision to sell off Hughes Tool at a bargain-basement price, calling it "the financial rape of the twentieth century."

Originally provided with keys that gave him unrestricted access to Hughes's suite, he arrived one day to find the locks changed and that he was not on the list for replacement keys. His access to Hughes thereafter was controlled, as were his communications. The "loose cannon" was firmly tied down. One of the aides would testify that any outgoing messages from Hughes to Real were categorized as "controversial" and automatically referred up for a decision to Kay Glenn or Bill Gay. He also stated that messages between Hughes and Real were sometimes deliberately not delivered. Real, like Bob Maheu before him, represented a threat to the traditional power structures in the Hughes organization, and Hughes did indeed speculate on the possibility of establishing an East Coast division of Summa, headed by Real. But the idea lapsed after the locks were changed on the doors. "Well," Real was asked by one of the aides after the lockout, "what do you think of the eastern division now, Jack?"

Real would testify that his main concern was to bring Hughes more into the world and encourage him to be more active. And before Hughes broke his hip, Real had been spectacularly successful. While in England Real had managed to persuade Hughes to take up flying again on four separate occasions, and these efforts had all been successful, if a shade unnerving for the copilots. But such adventures were criticized by the aides on the grounds that Hughes was "easier to control in his room."

Even after the hip fracture, Real remembered Hughes pleading with him, "Don't let me get in the room and not get out." Discussion on this point was interrupted by an aide arriving with a nannying "Come on, Mr. Hughes, let's go to bed."

In his bedridden state, Hughes's decline was swift, but there would be windows, even as late as 1975, when Real found him "coherent and sharp." For the most part, however, their conversations would be exercises in repetitive reassurance rather than exchanges of ideas. "I recall Mr. Hughes asking me: 'Who is on the board now?' referring to Summa's board of directors. When I told him, he replied, 'Oh. Oh. How many?' I told him 'five.' He would then repeat these questions over and over, never recalling that we had the same conversation shortly before." In mid-1975 Real remembered Hughes expressing a fear that Bill Gay would attempt to have him committed to a mental institution.

Real also remembered trying to tell Chester Davis during a walk on the grounds of the Xanadu Princess Hotel in Freeport that his boss had a disabling drug addiction. Davis swore at him to cut him off and said that Hughes was probably taking a lot of aspirin, that it was none of his business, and that he didn't want to hear about it. For Davis the fiction of Hughes as the powerful, highly aware industrialist was of far greater corporate importance than the truth about Hughes's actual condition, especially when it was a truth that could spoil everything.

Was Hughes then truly mad, or was he the victim of a lunatic situation, originally of his own devising? Even within the Lummis camp, there were different shades of opinion. Mickey West, Hughes's tax attorney for years before he became a Summa director, felt that the picture of Hughes as presented in the logs, though accurate, was incomplete. How so? asked George Dean. West said that whatever the overall damage to Hughes's faculties, he could still spot a good tax loss until close to the end. "This raises a most interesting mental health question," said Dean. "Can a lifelong genius at dodging taxes also be as crazy as a bedbug?"

The other interesting question raised by the logs is how could Hughes, who had not seen the inside of a pharmacy in well over twenty-five years, manage to obtain, and consume, such a majestic quantity of controlled prescription drugs? The answer to this is more clear-cut.

10

CANDYMEN

ON MARCH 16, 1978, a federal grand jury in Las Vegas returned an indictment against John Holmes, Hughes's chief personal aide, and Dr. Norman F. Crane, his leading physician for many years. It charged the two men with illegally supplying Howard Hughes with narcotics over a nineteen-year period. The indictment also suggested that others might be involved.

The Drug Enforcement Agency's investigation that led to these charges had been exceptionally thorough. Their trawl through the medical records had produced evidence of 480 violations of the regulations for controlled substances in the period from 1955 to 1974. This was the number of times Dr. Crane, in consultation with John Holmes, wrote prescriptions for phony patients to ensure a clandestine drug supply for Hughes. Of all the secrets concealed by the Hughes Secrecy Machine, this was the innermost, the most closely guarded, of them all. Now, by degrees, the Hughes drug connection unraveled.

Soon after they were indicted, Holmes and Crane showed a keen interest in plea bargaining. In order to reduce the scale of the penalties they might incur, they indicated a willingness to testify against others in general and against Dr. Wilbur Thain, Hughes's principal physician at the time of his death, in particular.

But there would be another extraordinary development before any of the leading characters could come to trial. The prospect of prosecutions relating to Hughes's drug use naturally led to closer scrutiny of his autopsy to establish whether narcotics had any relevance to his death. In the final autopsy report, signed by Dr. Jack L. Titus, chief of pathology at Methodist Hospital in Houston, it stated that "toxicological studies show only minimum amounts of codeine."

This, it turned out, was both false and highly misleading. A deeply embarrassed Dr. Titus was obliged to tell investigators that he had completely misread the toxicological studies. In transferring the information from the studies to his own report, he had misread milligrams for micrograms, thus underestimating the level of codeine in Hughes's body by a factor of one thousand. Barlett and Steele of *The Philadelphia Inquirer*, who tracked the medical evidence with great zeal, wrote of the existence of "a potentially lethal dose of codeine in Hughes's body."

Dr. Titus would not go so far as to say that, but he did say when describing his mistake in a subsequent interview "that it will probably haunt me forever." His one comfort was that it was "an honest mistake." Had he not made it, he said: "There would have been an additional diagnosis in my final report. It would not have changed the fact that we found chronic renal disease to explain everything, but it would have to be listed as an autopsy finding. There is no question about that."

Nor can there be any question that this mistake, like the curious case of the long-concealed autopsy X rays, very effectively prolonged the life of Hughes's darkest secret. Indeed, the secret might have endured much longer but for the strain on those who had to keep it.

The man who came to shed the most light in this area was the remarkable Dr. Crane, Hughes's long-term supplier, who would inevitably be dubbed "the candyman." Crane was seventy-three years old when the DEA investigators first took an interest in his prescribing habits and, at first, he seemed as grudging with information as most of Hughes's other attendants. But after a while he took to the process of giving deposition evidence, using these sessions as part confessional and part justification for all his works. With his testimony, combined with that of others close to Hughes, the history of Hughes's addiction was laid bare. It began with the 1946 plane crash in which he suffered terrible, near fatal, injuries.

The XF–II twin-engine reconnaissance plane was to have been part of Hughes Aircraft's contribution to the war effort, so Hughes was test-piloting it late, and under pressure. At an altitude of five thousand feet, Hughes suddenly felt "as if someone had tied a barn door broadside to the right hand wing." The right propeller must have changed pitch, and he was never able to regain control before crash-landing into the second floor of 803 North Linden Drive, Beverly Hills. Hughes's charred, unconscious body was retrieved from the blazing wreckage by a marine sergeant who happened to be driving by. An official air force inquiry into the crash ascribed the fault to "pilot error," a verdict that enraged Hughes.

For some days, with his life in the balance, Hughes was given morphine to relieve the pain of the multiple fractures and burns. Hughes would mend physically, but his attachment to morphine became a matter of concern to his physician, Dr. Verne Mason. As soon as he could, Dr. Mason started trying to wean Hughes off morphine by supplying him with Emperin Compound and codeine to help with his withdrawal symptoms. Hughes then developed a fierce attachment to the new drugs and would later show his gratitude to Dr. Mason by appointing him the first head of the Howard Hughes Medical Institute.

Dr. Crane knew Dr. Mason very well. They had once shared premises in Beverly Hills, and some years after the crash Crane was drawn into the task of supplying Hughes with drugs. Crane remembered taking it on with some reluctance.

When he met Hughes to discuss the arrangement, Crane urged him to go back to Good Samaritan Hospital, where his crash injuries had been treated, and undergo a properly supervised detoxification program. Alternatively, Crane said, he could report Hughes to the Narcotics Bureau, and then, with its permission, he could freely prescribe in the suggested amounts.

"My God, Norman," said Hughes, "you wouldn't do that to me. Think of the publicity." Hughes implied that his empire would crash and that his fifty thousand employees would be roaming the streets jobless if news of his drug habits ever became public. Crane, on receiving a pledge from Hughes that he would taper off, consented to supply the drugs.

This pattern of cajolery by Crane and penitential promises by Hughes to get off the drugs would be repeated many times over the years, but Crane kept writing the prescriptions.

Crane did, however, remember his advice being taken on one occasion when Hughes was living in Bel Air. He arrived to find Hughes agitatedly complaining of sensations like electric shocks running down both arms. He also said there were some things crawling around rapidly underneath his skin. Hughes said that if he maintained vigilance at just the right moment, he could sometimes catch one as the head emerged from the skin. Not everybody could see them, said Hughes, but he thought that George Francom, one of his loyal personal aides, had "almost got to the point where he can see them." Crane investigated the matter and ascertained that Hughes had added a strong stimulant to his regular cocktail of drugs. He recommended discontinuation of the stimulant, and the subcutaneous crawling ceased.

Crane never wrote a prescription in the name of Howard Hughes. There had to be some form of cutout between Crane as the supplier and Hughes as the receiver. The medical bureaucracy, cumbrous though it was, insisted on having names.

At various times prescriptions were written in the names of Roy Crawford, John Holmes, George Francom, Levar Myler, Jim Rickard, and Chuck Waldron, all personal aides to Hughes. Howard Eckersley escaped any pressure to join the prescription army, possibly because he had never been resident in California, where the prescriptions were normally filled.

During most of the time Crane prescribed for Hughes, his main contact was with the head of the personal staff, John Holmes. "He was the conduit," said Crane, for all Hughes's requests in this area. Holmes was also the person who ensured that each prescription was filled. The fashionable Roxbury Pharmacy on Olympic Boulevard in Beverly Hills provided the main supply, though its scale, even under a variety of names, did give rise to some apprehension. At one point there was serious talk about getting Hughes to buy a pharmacy business in order to secure fully his source of supply, but this project was dropped.

It was Dr. Crane who taught Hughes how to inject his own drugs. Hughes had complained that oral intake was too slow-acting in its effect. "I taught him," said Crane, "the same as one would teach a person to inject vitamin B_{12} for pernicious anemia, or the same as one would teach a diabetic to take insulin."

Nevertheless, by 1970 Crane had become an exceptionally reluctant prescriber. During his last year in Las Vegas, Hughes had been critically ill, first with anemia and later with pneumonia. A series of blood transfusions had revived him, but he was still in a very weak condition after relocation to the Britannia Beach Hotel in the Bahamas. Crane recalled a conversation with Dr. Lawrence Chaffin in 1971 in which they jointly agreed that Hughes's addiction, which had come to encompass Valium as well as codeine, simply had to end. Crane cannot have anticipated much disagreement on this point as Chaffin, who was rejoining the Hughes medical team as a part-timer after a twenty-five-year absence, had never approved of the drug regime. While in the Bahamas, Chaffin had made it his business to tell everyone, from Chester Davis down to the newest aide, that Hughes's "primary problem" was drugs.

Meanwhile, another prime problem was emerging, quite aside from the state of Hughes's health and welfare. There was news that the U.S. government was about to introduce a new computer-based system for the control of narcotic substances. It was said that it would enable the federal government to determine, at any

time, the number of prescriptions written by any given doctor at
any place in the country. Unusual prescribing practices could
therefore be detected much more easily. There was at least a possibility that new technology would shortly be putting Dr. Crane, and
his retinue of phony patients, on the spot.

This would lead to buck-passing between those involved in the
Hughes drug connection. According to Dr. Chaffin he was approached with a proposal, which he understood was backed by
Bill Gay, that called on the doctors to protect the aides. This, it was
suggested, could be done by writing a brief report stating that the
drugs Hughes used "had been medically indicated and continue to
be medically indicated." Dr. Chaffin, who did not think they were
at all medically indicated, did not warm to this proposal.

The problem for the aides, unlike the doctors, was that they had
very little immunity if they were called to testify in any legal action. In civil actions the doctors could always claim privilege for
the doctor-client relationship and refuse to testify in that area
(though this did not apply in criminal cases). And while the aides,
other than Holmes, knew much less about the drug operation than
Dr. Crane, they still knew more than enough to create a sensation
in any American courtroom. In consequence, they became eager to
know a lot less.

Out of this dilemma evolved a new system of direct delivery of
drug supplies to Hughes. To preserve "deniability" none of the six
aides would actually eyeball the drugs nor would they transmit
messages about his treatment to or from his doctors. Hughes evidently had some difficulty appreciating the benefits of this rather
unsociable new system and had to be reassured as to its merits.
The aides then composed a joint memo for the attention of their
bedridden boss. They explained, with some severity, that in the
event of legal action, they had to be in the position of saying that
he saw his doctors occasionally. But that should be the extent of
their direct knowledge: "what they [the doctors] talk to you about
or administer to you is not known to any of us. This is the reason
that we six [personal aides] should not only not view any medica-

tion you have but not be in the position of handing you any type of medication, even Excedrin."

In other words, the ailing Hughes was essentially on his own with his drugs and his addiction. It was a cruel message, though it would have been kind had it been delivered twenty years earlier.

Crane remembered the early seventies as an agonizing period. He had been adamant in his decision to sign no further drug prescriptions for Hughes back in 1971, but a conversation with Bill Gay and Kay Glenn, who supervised the aides, had weakened his resolve. According to Crane, Gay and Glenn were deeply concerned at the prospect of Hughes going on to harder drugs if he failed to get his regular order. They were worried about the impurities in the harder drugs and the potential, sooner or later, for blackmail. This provided impetus for another series of Crane prescriptions, but by early 1974 the doctor decided it had all become too much.

On April 16, 1974, Crane wrote to Hughes in melodramatic terms:

> I shall hold you to your promise that this be destroyed in my presence immediately after reading.
>
> I want to tell you that I can no longer write prescriptions under the present circumstances, since I do not believe it is in your best interests to do so. We have discussed the possible physical risks to yourself many times of this regime, so I need not go into that again, since my thinking is unchanged. It is the increasing risk, both legally, and to your reputation, which prompts this step now.
>
> As you know, narcotic prescriptions are sent to federal centers in the USA for computer filing. As of this year Valium too is treated more like codeine than ever before. With the increasing and never ending spate of lawsuits, and the Watergate attitude in both the courts and press, I believe my concern is warranted.
>
> In your present organization I can name at least a dozen, possibly more (not including doctors) who have personal knowledge of the medication you presently take or have taken, over the past several years.

Doctors can be forced to testify in criminal cases—otherwise the rule of privileged information prevails. If you wish to know how many doctors have this information, I don't know for sure but I would apply the following rule of thumb:—Any fourth year medical student, given your symptoms and being allowed to examine you, would be "flunked" if he did not come up with the proper diagnosis [i.e., that Hughes was an addict].

To the best of my knowledge the men who have this information are all loyal to your best interests. Suppose an opposition attorney gets one of them on the witness stand and asks if they have personal knowledge re your taking medication. No matter if they tell the truth, perjure themselves or take the 5th [Amendment], a smart attorney would find it easy to ferret out the truth and prove it with factual records. Only you or your legal staff could figure out what financial harm that might cause you in your various law suits. I do not think, however, that it would take an attorney to judge that it would shoot down your present public image forever.

Since I rarely get to communicate with you frankly there is one other public image situation which concerns me during the recent past. Under California law any patient who dies without having seen a doctor within ten days is a coroners case. Even if seen within ten days, unless the cause of death is obvious, it still is a coroners case unless autopsy permission is denied by a close relative. You are no longer married. In the case of a public figure of your stature an autopsy would be mandatory, and your image even after death could depend on only the ability of the pathologist. Sorry to strike such a negative note.

Dr. Crane's positive contribution was to recommend courses of action open to Hughes. These were remarkably similar to the ones proposed almost twenty years before: (1) register as an addict or (2) stick rigidly to a program of reduced dosages. Alternatively, Crane suggested, "you can try to find another doctor to do what I can't justify doing anymore." He concluded, as he began, "glad to see this destroyed when you read it."

Hughes did not destroy the letter, which became a courtroom exhibit, nor did he show much enthusiasm for its content. He may well have recognized that the worries Crane expressed focused on his own situation, not Hughes's.

Crane's anxieties, however, were soon alleviated by the assistance of Dr. Wilbur Thain, a new recruit to the billionaire's medical team. Dr. Thain had started helping out, initially on a part-time basis, while Hughes was in London in 1973. Thain was a family practitioner in Utah, but he came to his new job with a good working knowledge of the exotic practices that characterized the Hughes empire. As a medical student, he had worked for the Hughes organization during his vacations, and he had married Bill Gay's older sister, Mary Elizabeth.

In September 1974 Thain took over from Crane the responsibility for supplying Hughes with his drugs. It was done, according to Crane, on the understanding that the drugs would be tapered off as part of a gradual detoxification program. Hughes was part of this understanding. He gave Thain his word of honor "as a Texas gentleman" that he would be totally off drugs by his birthday—Christmas Eve 1974. In the real world Hughes continued to consume the drugs, and Dr. Thain continued supplying them for the rest of his life.

THE TRIAL OF Dr. Thain opened on September 13, 1978, in Ogden, Utah. A month earlier Dr. Crane and John Holmes had pleaded nolo contendere to the charges against them. In a criminal action such a plea has the same legal effect as a plea of guilty. Both were placed on probation. They agreed to testify against Thain.

The indictment against Thain had none of the close detail that characterized the one returned against Crane and Holmes. It was a simple one-page document that charged the doctor with dispensing a controlled substance, codeine phosphate, "directly or indirectly to Howard R. Hughes, without legitimate medical purpose by a practitioner in the usual course of his professional practice." The drugs were said to have been given to Hughes at approximately six-week intervals between August 1974 and April 1976.

The comparative brevity of the charge was thought to be to Thain's advantage, as was the location of the trial in his home state. Thain was a Mormon and as a family doctor had brought many Mormons into the world. He would estimate the number of babies he had delivered at around three thousand. It was certainly no detriment to his case to find himself on trial in Mormon territory. Even so, the evidence against his plea of "not guilty" looked powerful.

Dr. Crane testified that there was no "medically recognized reason" for giving codeine to Hughes, who had never complained of any injury or pain that would have justified this medication.

Dr. Chaffin testified that there was never any "legitimate medical purpose" for giving Hughes codeine. He took the drugs "because he wanted them," not because he was in pain.

Dr. Titus appeared before the court to acknowledge that the autopsy report on Hughes was "in error" and that the level of codeine in his body was one thousand times greater than he had previously surmised. This was the first time Dr. Titus was obliged to admit his error in public.

Dr. Forest S. Tennant, Jr., assistant professor of public health at UCLA and director of a large drug-treatment program in California, was called as an expert witness. He would say of Hughes: "The autopsy shows his brain and heart in good condition for his age. He could have lived much longer and in better health had he not misused drugs."

Asked if, in his opinion, Howard Hughes was addicted to drugs, Dr. Tennant replied: "I don't think there was any question to that."

The prosecution's evidence also featured a letter from Thain to Hughes, written sometime in 1975, in which the doctor sourly complained about a new drug law enforcement agency "flexing its muscles to justify its existence."

Thain's own direct evidence would also contain some remarkable disclosures. He told the court that he obtained the codeine for his consignments to Hughes direct from a New York pharmaceutical house without ever writing a prescription for the drug. Even more extraordinary was his acknowledgment that, although he would on occasion discuss daily dosages with Hughes and endeavor to lower them, he personally had no knowledge of whether his advice was actually followed. In cross-examination the assistant U.S. attorney explored this point:

Q: You can't tell us precisely what drugs or the quantities that he took on any given day, can you, doctor?

A: On any given day, no, sir.

Q: The only thing you can do and the only thing you have recorded in that record is what you were delivering?

A: That's correct.

Q: As a matter of fact, you weren't even there most of the time those drugs were being administered, were you?

A: I was not there in his presence at any time when he was administering them.

Q: And you gave this quantity to an addict or a person you knew at least had been an addict of the same drug that you were giving him. Is that right?

A: I was not present at the time or had knowledge of the time he was taking these excessive amounts. As to whether he was an addict or not, I don't know, sir.

Q: In your medical judgment, sir, you know that a person cannot take those quantities of codeine without becoming addicted, don't you?

A: I'll have to say yes to avoid getting into an argument with you, but it is an argumentative problem, sir.

Thain never made any attempt to deny that he had supplied the drugs. His defense rested entirely on their medical justification in the circumstances. Contrary to the impressions formed by Dr. Crane and Dr. Chaffin, he thought that Hughes needed the codeine to "control his pain and discomfort." Hughes, he said, had complained to him of specific pains in the neck, teeth, shoulders, back, arms, stomach, and in his bladder when urinating. "I think this gentleman," said Thain, "with his age and his infirmities, had adequate physical problems that could cause his pain, and I gave him the medication to treat him, and I think it was justified throughout my entire course of treatment."

The jury clearly found this argument compelling. After a trial lasting seven days, Dr. Thain was acquitted.

In fact, the trial proceedings posed more questions than answers. One related very directly to the quality of Hughes's health care. During most of the time when Dr. Thain was making his six- to eight-week deliveries of the codeine, Hughes's aides were deliberately taking no note of, or interest in, Hughes's actual drug consumption. Someone (unspecified) would simply deliver to Hughes each week a sealed manila package of drugs from the overall consignment. Yet the evidence provided by the logs kept by the aides in earlier times indicated that Hughes's drug habit did not conform to the daily dosage pattern. He would give himself irregular, but enormous, narcotic belts from time to time. This highly dangerous pattern must have gone completely unmonitored in the last stages of Hughes's life.

Another question raised, but not answered, by the Thain trial concerned the level of codeine in Hughes's body at the time of his death. The final, approved figure of 1.96 micrograms per milliliter of blood was well above the 1.4 microgram level found in the bodies of people known to have died from codeine poisoning. This was an extraordinarily high level, but not necessarily sinister. Hughes's long-term consumption of the drug, often in immense quantities, may have enabled him to build up a high level of tolerance. What was surprising was Dr. Tennant's expert testimony to the effect that the codeine in Hughes's body "was taken within six to eight hours of death." There seems little chance that Hughes administered this final dosage himself, as, according to the testimony of his aides in other cases, Hughes was in a coma for almost twenty-four hours before he died. Someone else must have given him the last shot.

WILL LUMMIS DID not attend the Thain trial, but he was a keen student of its content. When the trial ended, he ordered a transcript, along with copies of Dr. Thain's drug-delivery records, and began his own private analysis. What struck him most strongly was how closely Dr. Thain's tenure as Hughes's sole drug supplier corresponded with the successful efforts by the Summa directors and Hughes aides to secure Hughes's approval of their personal employment and consultancy contracts.

These contracts, first mooted in 1973, were essentially designed to ensure some continuity of employment and/or income in the event of Hughes's death. Given that many Hughes executives, even at the highest level, did not have immediately transferable skills, the contracts assumed an alluring aspect to those who felt they might get one. Hughes, however, was not at all enthusiastic about the idea and would keep putting off making any decision on the subject. This was a major impediment, as the Summa board could not, with any confidence of legality, award contracts to themselves without the approval of the sole stockholder.

As late as the spring of 1975, Hughes was still holding out. He would speak of any such contracts as "a Pandora's box" likely to lead to no end of complications, particularly from the people who did not get contracts. Dr. Thain would play a leading role in dis-abusing Hughes of his concerns. In a letter to his patient, Thain pointed to the highly desirable prohibitions in the contract against divulging any information about Summa or Hughes. "I believe," said Thain, "it is imperative to protect you. This is the only way you can protect yourself from having someone someday writing '*The* story of Howard Hughes.'" He also thought that Hughes would understand that consultancy arrangements are "simply a form of deferred compensation to avoid payment of excessively high taxes during your employees highly productive years."

Dr. Thain also obligingly supplied Hughes with a draft of the wording he might use to ratify the contracts. Hughes was finally persuaded, and in September 1975 the Summa board met at Chester Davis's farm in upstate New York to formally bestow contracts on twelve fortunate recipients: Gay, Henley, Holmes, Glenn, Eckersley, Francom, Myler, Waldron, Rickard, Real, and doctors Crane and Thain. The delicate procedure required each prospective contract winner to leave the room while his merits were discussed by the others and over the telephone with Hughes at "location" in the Bahamas. There were some complications due to Hughes's inability to recall the identity of all those concerned, but no one was disqualified on those grounds. Lummis, when he heard the way the contracts were allocated, would describe it as "an Amos and Andy type of proceeding."

The terms of the contracts varied somewhat according to status, but those with a record of long service could expect to clear $100,000 a year. Dr. Thain's agreement was a shade more modest, but not atypical. His basic contract ran for five years, paying $60,000 a year. Thereafter he would, under its terms, be paid $20,000 a year for consultancy (such consultancy being limited to forty-five days a year). Necessary adjustments for inflation were built in.

To Lummis, Dr. Thain's pivotal role in the contract negotiations with Hughes did not blend gracefully with his role as the physician in a position to give—or withhold—the drugs his patient craved. In fact, the more he learned about the last years of his cousin's life, the more deeply angry he became. He had a long chat with Dr. Chaffin after the Thain trial, and Chaffin described those years as "a terrible, inexcusable tragedy."

Three months after Dr. Thain's acquittal, Lummis threw down the gauntlet. On January 24, 1979, attorneys for the estate, acting on Lummis's instructions, filed a lengthy complaint in the Nevada district court seeking $50 million in damages. Named as defendants in the action were six of Hughes's aides and their supervisor: Holmes, Francom, Eckersley, Myler, Waldron, Rickard, and Glenn; three of Hughes's doctors: Thain, Crane, and Clark; and the two former chieftains at Summa: Bill Gay and Chester Davis. By now Lummis had come to view the old guard's performance at Summa as akin to that of foxes sent to protect a henhouse, and the legal language of the complaint reflected that hostility.

The complaint charged that Davis and Gay, "in concert with the other defendants, took advantage of Hughes's age, poor physical and psychological condition, isolation, and use of drugs to control and manipulate him in furtherance of their personal interests which were inimical to those of Hughes and his companies." The complaint further spoke of "self-dealing schemes and conspiracies" and declared that the doctors "either negligently provided improper medical care or negligently failed to provide proper medical care to Hughes." It also alleged that lavish personal employment and consultancy contracts, benefiting many of the defendants, had been improperly obtained.

A few days after launching this monster lawsuit, Lummis furnished Summa's finance department with a list of a number of personal-contract holders who should no longer be paid.

11

ROAD TO THE
GOLDEN COCK

WILL LUMMIS'S ATTEMPT to crush his opposition with a $50 million lawsuit was one of his least-inspired moves. There was certainly calculation in the idea of running a legal steamroller over Chester Davis and Bill Gay and the members of Hughes's palace guard, but there was also a strong element of personal animus. Lummis had become genuinely angry about the wrongs he felt had been done to his cousin Howard. Indeed, he was outraged. But acting out of rage and anger had never been Lummis's strongest suit. Chester Davis, on the other hand, was rather good at it.

Never more dangerous than when he appeared to be on the ropes, Davis would come back swinging. Under his leadership, the main defendants in the case reacted by filing nine countersuits in New York, California, and Utah. This confronted Lummis and the estate with the expensive possibility of having to litigate essentially the same case in these states, as well as in Nevada. The estate attorneys would thunder on in the Nevada court about the unfairness of this "centrifugal" strategy that, it was claimed, had the undesirable legal effect of "fractionating this controversy and bringing it before courts all over the country." But privately, they would acknowledge its success as a ploy. "Let's face it," said George Dean, "we're being outlawyered by Chester."

Even more worrying for Lummis were the developments in the lost will case, which Chester Davis had initiated in Nevada back in January 1977. For a while it had seemed that case might lose momentum for want of any credible witnesses to a will actually signed by Hughes.

On January 31, 1979, exactly one week after Lummis launched his $50 million action, such a witness emerged and started the process of giving deposition testimony in Los Angeles to lawyers representing the estate, the paternal heirs, and the Medical Institute. The implications of his testimony, it rapidly became apparent, were enormous. If the will in question had been lost, or even destroyed, in the offices of Andrews, Kurth, Lummis and his firm—each standing to gain hugely from Hughes's intestacy— could find themselves accused of perpetrating the legal heist of the century.

The man who raised this specter was John Pettit. The son of a doctor, Pettit had served in the navy during the war and graduated in science before going on to qualify for a Ph.D. in theoretical physics at UCLA. During his college days, he had met Bill Gay and become a close friend. He was a devout Mormon, and one of his many collaborations with Bill Gay involved the production of a handbook for Sunday school superintendents. He had spent most of his working life on the Hughes payroll as a consultant to a wide variety of enterprises. Pettit's specialty was computers, and he advised on their application to everything from corporate plans to the operation of slot machines in Las Vegas. He was fifty-five when he gave his will testimony.

Pettit's story was that he had seen Howard Hughes's will on a visit to Chester Davis's suite of offices in New York in the summer of 1962. The man who showed him the will, however, was not Davis but Raymond Cook, who was occupying an adjoining office. Cook was an Andrews, Kurth attorney, and he, like Pettit, had been summoned to New York to help with the mopping-up operations required after Hughes had successfully taken over Northeast Airlines. Pettit and Cook became friends, primarily through a mutual interest in calculus. One day, as Pettit was passing Cook's door, the lawyer called out: "Come in, Jack. I want to ask you a question."

Pettit anticipated, and got, another question about calculus, but Cook also wanted to show him something very rare and most secret. It was the Hughes will. Pettit's testimony in response to questions on this ran:

> A: My recollection is, first of all, that I was told it was a will. Raymond Cook took deliberate actions to show me that it was signed, and I recognized the signature.
>
> Q: And whose signature did you recognize?
>
> A: It was Howard Hughes'.
>
> Q: Did Mr. Cook say whose signature it was?
>
> A: He said, "This is a signed will. The boss has signed his will" and I saw this.
>
> Now, the recollections that I have are these: Number one, I know very little about wills, but my impression was that a will would be a thick document of fifty or a hundred pages. This was a very thin document. As I recall, it was only a matter of two or three pages. I don't remember how many pages, but it was very thin. That registered on me.
>
> Q: Did you read it?
>
> A: I did read it, at least I glanced through it.
>
> Q: What do you recall?
>
> A: Well, the impression that I have is that everything was left to the Hughes Medical—HHMI, as I have called it. It was totally consistent with everything that the boss had ever told me.

Pettit also recalled that it was a typed document and that it contained "something very vaguely with respect to employees." He could not recall any signatures of witnesses to the document, but he remembered Cook's injunction after showing it to him: "Never mention it to a soul."

Cook was a genial character, and Hughes would consult him on business as well as legal matters. His personal relationship with Hughes had its ups and downs, and on one occasion the billionaire wrote to Cook with the complaint "Raymond! If you would treat me as something other than a cross-breed between an escaped lunatic and a child, you would be surprised at how much better we would get along." But for the most part they did get along, very well.

After Mickey West, the tax wizard, Cook was probably the Andrews, Kurth lawyer Hughes was most inclined to turn to. From the early 1950s Cook was the partner with direct responsibility for nontax matters relating to the Hughes account, and he was chiefly responsible for drafting the certificate of incorporation for Hughes's Medical Institute. Cook also served on the executive committee of HHMI, and years later he and Hughes would have their most serious falling-out over the running of the institute. But back in the early sixties, when the will sighting allegedly took place, Cook would have ranked high in Hughes's confidence and esteem.

The problem was that Cook, the only man who could directly confirm Pettit's story, had died in a car crash in August 1975.

Pettit's story became a deposition marathon—his full testimony would run to over seven hundred pages in four volumes. In the early stages Pettit gave an excellent account of himself, but when his professional record was being probed, he tended to upstage his questioners. An inquiry about some computer work he had done for the Los Angeles police produced the following:

A: It was a proposal for computerizing the police function, giving them a Real Time–On Line system for the police system.

Q: I don't know what you mean by "Real Time–On Line system."

A: Do you know what a CR tube is?

Q: No.

A: Cathode ray tube, terminal.

Q: No, sir.

A: Computer terminal. Well, it's like a television screen. And it has a typewriter keyboard and you can key things in and it's like filling in on a form so that you can call up files.

The best example I can give you of that is a system that I did for Summa Corporation that's in being at the Sands Hotel. It's called the Cosac system. The Cosac system keeps track of all the markers within the casino. Now, we installed that in there, and when a man asks for a marker, they can immediately call up his entire record and have access to it on a screen.

Now, we put the screen in the back room up there and only the markers and the approval, yea or nay, was given to the pits. But that's the same type of system.

Does that answer your question?

Q: I suppose so.

Pettit was particularly specific on his direct relationship with Hughes, which had extended over many months in the latter part of 1954. This was crucial to the point of whether Pettit was in a position to recognize the handwriting on the will as Hughes's own. Pettit said this was no problem. While he was with Hughes in Florida, he had seen many of his memorandums and had often received written instructions from his boss. He was confident on the handwriting issue and equally confident about what Hughes had in mind on the subject of a will.

The Medical Institute had not long been set up, and he and Hughes had many detailed conversations about its future. Hughes had said to him that it would certainly amount to something as he had every intention of leaving his fortune to it. When Pettit inquired whether Hughes intended leaving anything to his relatives, he was told, "Hell, no, not to those so-and-sos."

What was said on these matters, however, was less compelling than Pettit's tales of working close to Hughes. The Florida expedition was supposed to be the prelude to new expansion in that state and naturally covert. Aliases were distributed all around, and young Pettit was relaunched as "Harold Hibbets." Pettit/Hibbets was deployed on many personal tasks, from teaching Jean Peters how to dance to carrying Ava Gardner's suitcases upstairs. He also ran errands. Whatever Hughes wanted under lock and key, Pettit would take down to the George Washington Hotel in West Palm Beach or the Columbus Hotel in Miami and put into safe-deposit boxes. At other times Pettit would be used to buy cars, assess properties, and keep an eye on the climate. Hughes would often ring to discuss the weather, usually around three o'clock in the morning. He was also vitally interested in hearing aids and drew the young scientist into a comparative study of their merits.

Hughes asked Pettit to lay hands on every known variety of hearing aid, and Pettit managed to assemble more than one hundred models. According to Pettit, Hughes was not only interested in the configuration of each model, he also insisted on testing them for ruggedness.

Q: Did you test for ruggedness?
A: Yes, we tested for ruggedness.
Q: How would you test for ruggedness?
A: We would drop them.
Q: At various heights?
A: Yes.
Q: What were some of the heights you tested for ruggedness?
A: I don't recall. They were not really high.
Q: What's the highest?
A: Oh, maybe up to five feet.
Q: And down to as low as what?
A: Down to one foot. We did test at various—we would start at one foot and work up a bit.

When the first stage of Pettit's deposition was concluded in early February 1979, Lummis knew he had a very serious problem. There was no way of testing the validity of Pettit's story by dropping it from varying heights. Indeed, there seemed to be no sure way of testing it at all. At Lummis's request estate attorney Bill

Miller carried out a search of the premises of Andrews, Kurth, especially areas once frequented by Raymond Cook. No Hughes will
could be found.

There were, however, some tests that could be applied to the
ruggedness of Pettit himself. Investigation into this area would
produce some interesting results that at least suggested that Pettit
was more complicated than your average Bible-thumping boffin.
In his testimony Pettit had been asked how many lawsuits he had
been involved in, and he remembered "less than five," including
one related to the Faim Ice Company, a Pettit sideline that sold ice
and rented ice machines. The number of actions brought against
Faim Ice and Pettit's other private enterprises was closer to thirty.

When describing his consultancies with the Hughes organization, Pettit spoke with particular pride of his role in setting up
Hughes Dynamics with the assistance of Bill Gay. This was a little-
known subsidiary of Hughes Tool, established in 1962 to comput-
erize credit rating and management information. Pettit also saw
it having creative applications in the medical field through the development of computer-assisted diagnoses. Pettit's glowing remi-
niscence about Hughes Dynamics was somewhat at odds with that
of Hughes's former alter ego, Bob Maheu. According to Maheu,
Hughes Dynamics was an early example of the imperial growth of
Hughes's empire without the emperor knowing a thing about it.
When he did find out about it—after the subsidiary had gone
through $10.5 million of his money in the space of two years—
Hughes closed it down.

The Hughes Dynamics episode also raised some questions about
Pettit's judgment of people. Among those he recruited was young
Johnny Meier, who subsequently made a name for himself with a
major scam in Nevada. Assigned a role in Hughes's mining division, Meier expended millions of Hughes's money on gold- and sil-
ver-mining claims, almost all of them worthless. It would later
emerge that Meier had close links with the salesmen of these near
useless claims. He also enjoyed close links with the president's
brother, Donald Nixon, who had a patchy record as a business-

man. This intimacy became alarming to the White House, which ordered a wiretap on Donald's phone to monitor his contacts with the resourceful Johnny Meier. During the Watergate revelations this came out, and it was gleefully celebrated in a New York tabloid with the headline: NIXON BUGGED HIS BROTHER.

While Pettit was unfolding his Hughes will story, Meier was being sought by Summa for a court-approved restitution of $7.9 million, the amount he was said to have extracted from Hughes by fraud. He was reportedly in Polynesia.

None of this indicated that Pettit had not seen a Hughes will. But it did suggest that Bill Gay's consistent support was vital to Pettit's employment. And Bill Gay, of course, along with Chester Davis, was the main potential beneficiary of Pettit's will story.

When Pettit resumed his deposition testimony in September 1979, there was a new attorney, Peter Echeverria of Echeverria and Osborne, Reno, Nevada. Echeverria appeared specifically on behalf of Will Lummis, who, given the ominous drift of the earlier testimony, had decided to reach outside Andrews, Kurth, and outside Texas, for representation. It would be Echeverria who asked some pointed questions.

Echeverria was most interested in the narrative of what Pettit did with his secret will knowledge, particularly with Bill Gay, after Hughes's death. According to Pettit, he first told Bill Gay about his will encounter with Cook very shortly after Hughes died, and he remembered being rather put down. Gay had said something like "Don't give me that junk, we have to find a will." Pettit explained that at that time the quest was for "a physical will" and his old sighting did not seem to be of great significance.

At Gay's request Pettit became deeply involved in the hunt for "a physical will." As part of this exercise, he would put in a long series of long-distance calls to Florida to check if there was anything in the safe-deposit boxes he had serviced for Hughes twenty-five years earlier. This turned out to be a dry hole. The Columbus could find nothing, and the George Washington Hotel had been converted into a retirement home. Pettit then sat in on many conferences with Summa executives trying to decide where to look for a will and remembered having a good laugh at some of the phony wills that were surfacing.

Pettit remembered that much later, around July 1978, he told Bill Gay about Cook and the will for a second time. Gay was not so dismissive on this occasion but also did not seem terribly interested.

It seemed to register only when Pettit told Bill Gay, a third time, shortly before Christmas 1978. He and Gay, with their wives, were going out to dine at one of their very favorite restaurants, called The Golden Cock. On the way there in the car, Pettit broached the subject of Cook and the Hughes will. He remembered the decisive conversation going like this:

"I must have said, 'How are they coming?' or 'Are they ever going to find the will?'

"And his comment was 'I don't know.'

"I said, 'Well, Bill, you know, I know this thing existed because I saw it, you know, and I have told you this.'

"And he said, 'What?' He said, 'Jack,' he says, 'I don't recall you ever telling me that.' "

Pettit remembered that Gay on this occasion was like a man "struck by a bolt of lightning." Having finally registered the importance of the information, Gay promptly initiated the process that led to Pettit giving deposition evidence. Gay was the only person Pettit ever entrusted with the will knowledge, apart from his wife.

On the surface, it appeared that it was only Bill Gay's extraordinary slowness on the uptake that prevented the Cook lead from being followed up at a much earlier stage. But Echeverria, evidently a close student of the mystery of why the dog did not bark in the night, did not appear too interested in Gay's alleged delayed reaction. What fascinated him about the account was why Pettit himself did not bark in the broad light of day.

As Echeverria saw it, Hughes's death and that of Raymond Cook, eight months earlier, must have freed Pettit from any residual obligation "not to tell a soul." So why hadn't Pettit himself broadcast his knowledge more widely to the other people he was helping on the will search?

Pettit said his obligation to keep the matter confidential arose because he personally did not learn of Cook's death until as late as July 1978, perhaps even later. Echeverria questioned how Pettit's ignorance on the subject of Cook's death could have been so well preserved.

Pettit had stressed his friendship with Cook. After Hughes died, apparently intestate, and Pettit was helping the will search, Echeverria suggested, surely he would have thought of giving Cook a call since he was the one person who Pettit knew might lead searchers straight to a Hughes will. All those calls to bewildered hoteliers and rest-home keepers in Florida should surely have been preceded by just one call to an old friend in Houston that could have made further investigation and expense totally unnecessary. Yet Pettit, on his evidence, never even tried to contact Cook.

Echeverria posed versions of the question "Why didn't you call Ray Cook during this will search?" no fewer than eight times. The most illuminating answer he got was: "I have no answer. I have no idea. This is like saying: why do you beat your wife."

There were other embarrassments. Paul Freese, representing the paternal heirs, would cause one of them with a seemingly innocuous inquiry about Pettit's original attitude to the Mormon will. Pettit affirmed a strong conviction that it was a hoax. The next exchange ran:

> Q: If the money were to come to your church through a hoax, that would cut through your conscience, wouldn't it?
>
> A: Yes.
>
> Q: Did you at any time make any communication to any church officials to express a view that this document should not be associated with the church for fear that it might sully the church's image?
>
> A: No.
>
> Q: None at all?
>
> Q: Can you say why?

A: What?

Q: Can you explain that in any way?

A: No, I can't explain it.

Pettit was not the only person with a lost will story, but his was the major contender. There was another strongly affirmed sighting of a handwritten Hughes will in the Los Angeles office of Greg Bautzer, another of Hughes's favored attorneys. A bookkeeper was positive she had seen it lodged in the files when she worked there in 1963. But Bautzer, who was convinced that Hughes had made a holographic will, said that no such document had ever been entrusted to him for safekeeping.

The culmination of the Nevada lost will case was the state's supreme court decision of December 29, 1980. By that time the Nevada courts had been obliged to sift through literally hundreds of depositions and statements from all points in the United States, most of them to the effect that Hughes had intended to deed his fortune to HHMI and that he had probably acted on that intention.

In declaring the judgment, Justice Cameron Batjer would acknowledge that there was ample evidence of will-drafting activity by Hughes from 1925 onward. It also appeared that his drafts "benefited medical research." But the provisions of Nevada law were inescapable. For a lost will to succeed, there had to be at least two credible witnesses to its quondam existence. None of those brought to the court's attention qualified on that score.

It was a severe blow to Davis and Gay and their plans for expanding the Medical Institute and cutting down Will Lummis, but not a fatal one. In Texas, unlike Nevada, the law allowed verification of a lost will on the testimony of only one person. And the case could be appealed there, too. The Pettit story would get its opportunity to run and run again.

12

WOMAN WITH A WILL

As soon as a clear picture of the struggle for The Money emerged, somebody could be relied on to throw in the monkey wrench. By early 1981 the contest seemed to have narrowed to a knock-down-and-drag-out struggle between Lummis, the white knight of the heirs, and Chester Davis, the turbulent champion of the dispossessed Hughes retainers. Then along came Martha Jo Graves, a woman with a will and some nerve.

The all-out attack on the Mormon will by the Hughes family had cast a chill on those who contemplated The Money with larceny in their hearts. By expending $3 million on lawyers, expert witnesses, and investigators, Lummis and the other relatives had served notice that anyone turning up with a will would face a formidable obstacle course. Hughes "wills" continued to float in regularly by the mail, but no one showed up to try to convoy them through court. This held true until the summer of 1981, when Martha Jo Graves emerged with a new document, apparently ready to go all the way.

Like Melvin Dummar, who had soared like a rocket across the American scene five years earlier, she, too, said that she had come into possession of the last will and testament of the billionaire.

The five-page document she produced was vastly superior to Dummar's crudely worded Mormon will. The spelling was flawless, and the will was couched in the precise legal language one would expect from a billionaire with platoons of high-priced lawyers at his command. It was dated July 24, 1960, when Hughes had been holed up in a bungalow at the posh Beverly Hills Hotel, and was typewritten on the proper vintage hotel stationery. Unlike the handwritten Mormon will, which legally required no signature but that of Hughes, the Graves document was signed by two witnesses. Both were still alive.

One was a stocky, silver-haired California businessman, Harold W. Mallet, and the other a California physician, Dr. Stanley DuBrin, who headed a clinic in that bastion of Republican conservatism, Orange County. Both subsequently swore they had watched Hughes sign two copies of the will twenty-one years earlier, and Mallet added a colorful Hughesian detail. After the will signing, at three o'clock in the morning, he said, "Hughes never said, 'Hi, good-bye, or kiss my ass.' He was just gone."

Ms. Graves was a plump, brown-haired, forceful woman in her early fifties who resided in an apartment overlooking Sunset Boulevard. She had worked for a number of attorneys and had also founded and promoted several mining and oil-drilling enterprises.

She discovered the will by happenstance, she said, in the effects of a Los Angeles attorney, Earl Hightower, for whom she had worked for more than ten years. Hightower, a onetime FBI agent, had died in a plane crash in Mexico in 1974. She had stored his old files and furniture until 1981, when she sorted through them and threw most away. But she had preserved a blue metal security box with a dial lock with a three-digit combination. "Because it was locked, I thought it might have something valuable in it, maybe some cash," she said. On July 17 she began fiddling with the combination, trying various three-number combinations such as Hightower's street address with no luck. Then she idly dialed ooo, and the lockbox popped open.

Inside were five pages of aging Beverly Hills Hotel stationery headed LAST WILL AND TESTAMENT and bearing the signature "Howard Hughes" and the witness signatures of Dr. DuBrin and Harold Mallet. What she found baffling, she said, was that she knew both of these witnesses—DuBrin had been her doctor—and neither had ever mentioned Howard Hughes or his will. More remarkably, the will left 20 percent of Hughes's fortune to the Acme Mining Company, of which Martha Jo was president and major stockholder.

The will declared that "I, Howard Hughes, a/k/a Howard Robard Hughes, a resident of the County of Los Angeles, State of California, being of sound and disposing mind and memory and not acting under duress, fraud, or the undue influence of any person whomsoever, do hereby make, publish and declare this to be my Last Will and Testament."

It asserted, "I am presently married to Elizabeth Jean Peters Hughes, and that there are no children the issue of this marriage. I declare that I have been married before and have been legally divorced from all prior marriages, and that it is my intention that no present or former wife receive any benefit of whatsoever nature from me or my estate. I declare that I have no children."

It also specifically disinherited "all persons claiming to be, or who may lawfully be determined to be my heirs at law except such as are mentioned under this will." Anyone challenging the will was cut off with a lonesome dollar bill.

Like the Mormon will, which bequeathed one sixteenth of the Hughes estate to "William R. Lommis," the new will also dangled a prize for Lummis and, in addition, spelled his name correctly. It named him, at the death of Hughes, the sole trustee of the Howard Hughes Medical Institute—but only if he refrained from challenging the will.

It left 80 percent of his personal estate to the Medical Institute, thus cutting off the remote relatives with nothing at all. The remaining 20 percent went to "Acme Mining Company, a public California corporation, or to its successor corporation through amalgamation, consolidation or merger."

It directed that Acme Mining be renamed the Howard Hughes Oil Corporation. This, it explained, was "in honor of Howard R. Hughes Sr. and his outstanding contributions to the oil industry and its fraternity. This corporation shall serve as a monument to the memory of my father, Howard R. Hughes Sr. Additionally recent events dictate to me a conscience of compassion with others. Through such vehicle I give of myself to the public."

Martha Jo graphically described her reaction on discovering, in an old lockbox she had tucked away for years, the long-sought will of Howard Hughes. She said she was devastated when she realized, like Melvin Dummar, that she might be fabulously enriched because of a will she had discovered.

"It was like, oh my God!" she said. "I remembered the Melvin Dummar case very well. And this was so incredible, like how can this happen to me? I didn't want any part of it. It seemed incredible. It seemed impossible. I think the best way to describe it would be kind of a state of shock and you don't know what to do. What do you do? I didn't know what to do." She just "cried all day and became very unglued."

But after drying her tears and pulling herself together, she plunged into a frenzy of action. She checked with Dr. DuBrin and Mallet, and they both verified that they had witnessed the will signing twenty-one years ago. They had kept quiet about it, they said, because they had given their solemn word never to mention it.

She consulted a Los Angeles handwriting expert, who declared the Hughes signature genuine. She then telephoned the executor of the Hightower estate, an attorney named Arne Lindgren, and informed him of her discovery. The will had named the Bank of America executor of the Hughes estate, and Lindgren told her to turn the document over to the bank. She telephoned the bank and was told to hold everything while the bank's officers discussed this sensational development. She then telephoned the Nevada attorney for Acme Mining, now known as Acme International Corporation. He told her he would fly to L.A. immediately, take possession of the will, and inform the executives of Summa Corporation. "It will have to be probated in Nevada and Texas," he said excitedly. Martha Jo told him to hold everything and called a lawyer friend in Houston. He advised her to hop on a plane and bring the will on down. Beset with all this advice, Ms. Graves decided to heed the Texas attorney because, she said, "I trusted him like a father."

She packed a suitcase, put the will in a briefcase, and booked a flight to Houston with her live-in companion, a burly ex-Texan named Glenn Bourland. But before she left, she prudently Xeroxed a couple of copies of the will and left them in her apartment.

And then, sure enough, the airline lost her briefcase with the document bearing the original signatures of Hughes and the two witnesses. This mishap, however, was not legally calamitous. There were circumstances, she was told, when a copy of a will, particularly one with living witnesses, could be legally probated.

On her return to Los Angeles, Ms. Graves was served with a court order to produce the will. Instead, she came in with a Xerox copy and bitter complaints about the inefficiency of airline baggage handlers. She was supported by her companion. "It's just an example of Murphy's Law," Bourland said. " 'If anything can go wrong, it will.' "

"Do you mean to say that after the twenty-one years that will reposed in a lockbox," an attorney asked Ms. Graves, "you lost it five days after you found it?"

"That is not correct," Ms. Graves replied. "I didn't lose it. The airline lost it."

WITH A WEARY here-we-go-again, the lawyers addressed the problem of the newfound will. Their immediate and unanimous conclusion was that the will was a fraud, but a more sophisticated one than the Mormon will. "Her story about the airline losing the signed original was a rather clever device," said one attorney. "In the Mormon will case there had been weeks of technical testimony focused on the type and age of the ink and whether it was consistent with the date of the will. The loss of the Beverly Hills original blocked any attempt to date the ink."

One glaring flaw in the will was its skewed time frame. Back in 1960, when Hughes allegedly executed the will, Hughes did not need to create a "monument" to his father. He had an internationally known one in Hughes Tool Company and had pledged as a youth to "continue its development and progress . . . as a permanent monument marking his initiative, judgment and foresight." He had not sold off his patrimony until 1972, when pressed for cash. This indicated that the will was a product of someone who had read current newspapers but not the context of the Hughes chronology.

The clause naming Will Lummis sole trustee of the Hughes Medical Institute had a similar flaw. In 1960 Lummis was a little-known Houston attorney in whom Hughes had evinced no interest. Lummis had come into national prominence only after Hughes's death in 1976. In 1960 he would have been an unlikely choice for the billionaire to nominate as the one-man authority at the institute.

But the Beverly Hills will posed a threat that had nothing to do with its credibility. It had taken the relatives two years and $3 million to persuade a jury to dispose of the Mormon will fraud. In California the court dockets were as clogged as the freeways and a case could take five years to get before a judge. After years of trudging in and out of courts in four states, the lawyers were on the verge of getting an heirship determination in Texas. If the new will were probated in California, the legal battle over The Money might stretch out of sight over the horizon.

Back into the trenches went the lawyers. Two attorneys for the paternal heirs—Paul Freese of Los Angeles and Wayne Fisher of Houston—were designated point men on the new will. Freese employed George Barnes, a seasoned Los Angeles investigator experienced in tracking the tangled byways of seekers after The Money. Barnes had done much effective investigative spadework on the Mormon will. In Yogi Berra's phrase, for George Barnes the Beverly Hills will was "déjà vu all over again."

In January 1982, armed with thick folders of research, the attorneys summoned Martha Jo, her companion Bourland, and the two witnesses for a videotape examination under oath in Los Angeles.

Dr. DuBrin and Mallet gave carbon-copy accounts of how they had come to witness the will of the nation's best-known billionaire. Both conceded that they had never had any other dealings with Hughes. They had been plucked out of nowhere, they said, by attorney Earl Hightower, now long deceased. They had been drafted by Hightower, whom they both knew, for some secret but important project that he did not disclose. He had simply told them that he might need two witnesses on constant standby—day or night. They had agreeably assured Hightower that they would materialize whenever he needed them for this legal whatever.

There had been a couple of false starts that had been scrubbed, and then, sometime after midnight on July 24, 1960, Hightower had aroused them from sleep with separate phone calls and told them that he needed them instantly at the Beverly Hills Hotel. They both sprang up, dressed, and sped to the hotel, where they were told by Hightower to wait in the lobby for instructions. After they had loitered there for about an hour, an emissary led them to a closed door somewhere in the hotel. Neither remembered the number of the room or what floor it was on. The mystery man knocked at the door and a voice inside told the callers to wait a while. After about an hour, during which they grew weary and sat down on the floor, Hightower opened the door but sternly warned them, "Don't come in! Just stand there in the entranceway."

Hightower introduced his two witnesses to Howard Hughes, who was standing about twelve feet inside the room at a table. "You are here to witness my last will and testament," the billionaire told the two strangers who had materialized out of the night. He then signed two copies of the will. Hightower brought the copies out to the witnesses, and they signed them and went home. The entire operation, disposing of one of the great American fortunes, was handled with the casualness and efficiency of a shopper paying for a loaf of bread at a checkout counter. Other than observing that Hughes was tall and thin, neither DuBrin nor Mallet could describe him, the sound of his voice, the length of his hair, the length of his fingernails, or even whether he had a beard, mustache, or was clean-shaven.

After they left neither man expressed any surprise or excitement about the middle-of-the-night encounter with the legendary invisible billionaire. Although they saw Hightower a number of times later, nobody discussed what had happened. When Hughes died and a nationwide search for his will was widely reported, neither man thought to come forward with an account of having witnessed a Hughes will. "I didn't want to get involved," said Dr. DuBrin. "I would have liked to be a thousand or a million miles away."

Martha Jo testified that although she had gone to work for Hightower in 1964, he never said anything about the Hughes will or the fact that he had a signed one in his lockbox. And neither Mallet nor Dr. DuBrin had mentioned the will, even after Hughes died. Only after she had fiddled the lockbox open and found the document did her two friends reluctantly confirm that they had signed it back in 1961. "They just didn't talk much about it," said Martha Jo.

"Now this Acme International Corporation of yours," said an attorney. "That name brings a picture of mines and plants scattered around the world. Tell us about it."

Martha Jo conceded that this "monument" to Hughes's father was an inactive corporate shell, with no employees, no mines, and no bank account and that its sole property was two old filing cabinets in her Los Angeles apartment. She had acquired the company, unaware that Hughes had bequeathed it an estimated $200 million, by purchasing 334,040 shares from the Hightower estate for the bargain price of $5,000, a little more than a penny a share.

Wayne Fisher reviewed the testimony of her witness-friends and asked her what he called "a bothersome question."

"These folks get a call in the middle of the night, and a lawyer they know says, 'I want you to come over to the Beverly Hills

Hotel and do something for me right now because you promised me you would.'

"So these fellows show up at the Beverly Hills Hotel and somebody that they don't know comes up to them and says, 'Follow me, men.' So they get up to the upstairs somewhere that they really don't quite remember, and here they are. It is three or three-fifteen in the morning. One of them is a medical doctor, the other is a businessman.

"And somebody says, 'Wait a while, men. We are not ready for you yet.' So here these men are, not knowing why they are there, what is going on, sitting down in the corridor, if you please, at three-thirty or four o'clock in the morning, just sitting there, not knowing if what is going on inside the room ahead of them is a poker game, whatever, not having any earthly idea.

"And all of a sudden the door opens and somebody says, "Men, you are here to witness the will of Howard Hughes. I want to introduce you to Mr. Howard Hughes. That is what you have been sitting on the floor out there waiting to do.

"Ms. Graves, does it not cause you to be suspicious or alarmed about that recitation of events that neither of those two gentlemen can remember what Mr. Hughes looked like?"

"That is your recitation, not mine," said Martha Jo. "It causes me no concern at all."

MINDFUL OF THE way everyone had walked away from the Mormon will forgery unscathed, Freese and Barnes referred the Beverly Hills will to the fraud division of the Los Angeles district attorney's office, where it was pursued by investigator Jerry Loeb.

Martha Jo and her two witnesses stubbornly stuck to their stories for more than two years. In the interim Martha Jo came up with a bold proposal. She telephoned Will Lummis's mentor at Andrews, Kurth, the venerable Mickey West, and suggested a deal. If Lummis would just promise not to contest the Beverly Hills will in California, she would "consent" to Lummis remaining on as administrator of the Hughes estate, with all the fees and power that position entailed. The incredulous attorney passed the proposal on to Lummis, who declined the opportunity to dump all his relatives for his (and Martha Jo's) personal enrichment.

Dr. DuBrin was the first to break. He obtained a new lawyer and informed the D.A.'s office that he wanted to revise his story "because I consider myself an honest person" and "wanted to do my part as a law-abiding citizen." They put him back under oath, and he admitted that he had never met Hughes at the Beverly Hills Hotel or anywhere else. Martha Jo had typed the will in 1981 and forged Hughes's name, and he had agreed to "witness" it merely as a favor to his old friend Mallet.

"I was very busy in the clinic," he said, "and I signed it just to get rid of them."

Having turned Dr. DuBrin, Loeb used him to turn his old friend. With the doctor's cooperation the investigator was able to obtain a similar series of admissions from Mallet. In return for his belated candor, DuBrin was granted immunity from prosecution. Mallet was then wired up by Loeb and used to trip up Martha Jo.

Meanwhile, she had gotten into fresh and unrelated trouble out in Oklahoma, where she had pledged an oil-drilling well as collateral for a loan. When the rig disappeared, a warrant was issued for her arrest. She became a fugitive, but, before she fled Los Angeles, she got word that Dr. DuBrin was contemplating blabbing to the district attorney. She telephoned DuBrin, he recalled, and "made threats to me that bad things would happen to me if I talked to the D.A. and you'll have problems up to and including murder." But if he did talk to the D.A., she said, "Let me know so I can leave the country."

"I did not tell her," said the good doctor, "that I had already talked to the D.A."

Neither did Mallet, who accompanied her to Houston to talk to a lawyer about her burgeoning troubles. Right behind them went investigator Loeb, with a receiver tuned in to the transmitter strapped to Mallet.

"I picked up a half-dozen Houston cops," said Loeb, "and we staked out the lawyer's office. When Martha Jo and Mallet came out, we tailed them to another office, where they met with Bourland. We stood out in the hall while Martha Jo was reassuring everyone that it would be all right because we were too dumb to track them down.

"So I just knocked on the door, and when she opened it there I was with six armed cops. I said, 'Hi!'

When they went to court in Los Angeles, Martha Jo learned that both her coconspirators had recanted their stories and abandoned her out on a legal limb. She was sentenced to a year in state prison.

Although she did not get a fraction of the press that engulfed Melvin Dummar, nor a movie of her own, she acquired an abiding historical footnote. Of all the scamsters and fake will writers, the president of the Acme International Corporation was the sole person who wound up in jail.

13

WIVES AND WOULD-BES

IN THEIR MARATHON effort to untangle Hughes's affairs, the estate attorneys assumed at the outset that his marital ventures would pose no problem in the determination of who should get The Money. While his business empire resembled an unkempt attic to which only Hughes had the key, his marital history had a seemingly uncluttered simplicity. On the record he had been married twice, divorced twice, and had no children by either marriage. He had settled financially with both his wives, who had later remarried. Neither asserted any claim against the estate. And there had been no paternity suits filed against him in his lifetime.

The attorneys failed to factor in the potency of his image, the mystique with which he surrounded himself and the powerful effect these had on segments of the American imagination. In addition to the musk of The Money, he was marinated in the scents of power, mystery, and sex. This created a kind of glamour that easily outlasted his reclusive years and was in some ways enhanced by them. Into the vacuum of fact there would pour clouds of romantic fantasies that put to shame the pulse-stirring fiction of Barbara Cartland.

His known marriages had taken place when he was nineteen and fifty-one years old. Shortly after the death of his father and his inheritance of the prosperous Hughes Tool Company, he married Ella Rice, a Houston society belle and member of the family that had founded Rice University. His relatives had wanted him to complete his college education at Rice and settle down in Houston, but Hughes had his own agenda. He had become intrigued with moviemaking in several trips with his father to Hollywood, where his uncle, Rupert Hughes, the novelist and screenwriter, had taken him behind the scenes in the studios. A few months after marrying Ella, Hughes took her and his fortune out to Los Angeles, installed her in a suite at the Ambassador Hotel, and plunged into moviemaking. He was fascinated with the Hollywood crowd and left Ella largely to her own devices. She tried to interest herself in the Junior League and made social friends in staid Pasadena.

"Hughes had nothing in common with her new friends and made no effort to hide how he felt," said Noah Dietrich, his longtime financial expert. The marriage never survived the shooting of *Hell's Angels*, during which Hughes first showed the laserlike preoccupation with detail that plagued him throughout his life. Ella, no part of this preoccupation, hardly saw him. One day she packed up and went back to Houston and filed for divorce, charging her husband with "excesses and cruel treatment." Her suit claimed that Hughes had "steadily neglected" her and contended that he "was irritable, cross, critical, fault-finding and inconsiderate." Hughes did not contest the action, and he formally resumed bachelor status on December 9, 1929. Ella received a settlement of $1.2 million, paid in installments, and would later marry James Everton Winston, a commodities and oil broker whom she had nearly married thirteen years earlier, before he was successful.

Self-centeredness also ultimately wrecked Hughes's second marriage. In 1957, when he was already well embarked on the long slide into seclusion, drug abuse, and the bizarre behavior that ended in madness, he married Jean Peters, a major star of such movies as *Captain from Castile* and *Three Coins in the Fountain.* He had met her when she was nineteen, a fresh-faced beauty contest winner from Ohio State University, and had married her after a ten-year on-again, off-again courtship. Jean had wanted her own home and a full-time husband. Hughes preferred hotel living, and he retained several of his young female protégés, whom he stashed in leased houses in Beverly Hills.

That Hughes was fond of Jean Peters cannot be doubted, but his motives for marrying her may well have been more practical than romantic. Hughes was already becoming fearful that senior figures in his empire might seek to have him declared mentally incompetent and committed to an institution. And the recruitment of a wife naturally made this design harder to achieve.

Jean Peters would gamely hang in with Hughes's increasingly weird lifestyle, enduring marathon private movie-watching sessions with her husband at Goldwyn Studios. There would be an abrupt interruption in this routine when Hughes discovered that the rough cut of the musical *Porgy and Bess,* in which all the leading players were black, had been viewed in his favorite screening room. Hughes never set foot in Goldwyn again, but he found another screening room for yet longer sessions. Jean's attendance at these, and indeed most other occasions, became less and less required. The marriage lasted for thirteen years, with the couple living separately for much of the time and totally apart for the final four years. When Hughes acquired his huge cash windfall in 1966 from the sale of his TWA stock, he unilaterally decided to move to Las Vegas, a city Jean detested even more profoundly than Ella had disliked Hollywood.

There ensued a battle of wills, as Hughes huddled hermitlike in a penthouse bedroom at the Desert Inn and Jean in California occupied a leased mansion on a hilltop in Bel Air. Hughes tried to pressure and cajole her into taking up residence in the gambling capital without success. He bought an impressive ranch outside Las Vegas from the widow of one of Germany's arms-making Krupps and leased an expensive town house in Las Vegas for Jean, but she refused even to inspect them. She divorced him in 1971, waiving any claim against his estate in return for a modest settlement of $75,000 a year, adjusted to the cost of living.

After her divorce, she married a Hollywood producer, Stanley Hough, and firmly closed the door on her life with Hughes. She refused all requests for interviews and all offers from publishers for her memoirs. Under California's community property laws, Jean Peters had a claim on a share of The Money, but she preferred a quiet life of her own to a public battle for her ex's billions.

In the long interval between these two marriages, Hughes had burnished his reputation as a compulsive woman chaser. This presented major problems for those assigned the solemn duty of determining who his rightful heirs were. For it was common knowledge that Hughes was not only susceptible to the charms of established movie queens but that he was also an avid collector of teenage Lolitas who never made it onto the screen. Being an unknown did not necessarily mean being unknown to Howard Hughes.

He was seen as a man who had shopped the elite of Hollywood, searching for the perfect woman without ever exclaiming "Eureka!" The idea that such a connoisseur, who had turned away from the likes of Lana Turner and Ginger Rogers, might have chosen and secretly married some obscure Miss Little Old Me was logistically possible. Before he lapsed into seclusion, Hughes had frequently gone gypsying off under assumed names in remote places. He had once worked incognito as an airline mechanic and again in the late forties had vanished for some months, eventually surfacing in jail in Shreveport, Louisiana, as a suspected vagrant. There was no one who could say with certitude that he had not wooed and won Miss Little Old Me in the days before his Mormon aides began logging his every move. And there were many who claimed, with some passion, that this was what had happened.

Under the charge of Probate Judge Gregory to overlook no potential heirs or heiresses, the Texas attorney *ad litem,* Ted Dinkins, and his colleagues diligently examined all such claims. In his five-year, $700,000 assignment, Dinkins and his staff were deluged with telephone calls, letters, and visits from people with wondrous tales. The prize to be won was potentially enormous. The discovery of a previously unsuspected Hughes wife, or child (legitimate or otherwise), or even a brother or sister would totally demolish the intestate line of inheritance assembled by Will Lummis and Andrews, Kurth. Contenders in all these categories pressed their attentions on the *ad litem* team, but Dinkins felt he was on reasonably firm ground in ruling out the possibility of a Hughes sibling.

Since Howard was the only child recognized in the wills of his father and mother, the issue of any brothers or sisters did not come before the court. Judge Gregory was thus spared the postulate of the Hughes Quadruplets, one of the most intricate and creative vagaries to arise out of the misty myths of Howard Hughes. It was formulated, in years of intense research, by a professional woman writer who has produced several international best-sellers and is listed in *Who's Who*. She compiled one of the most extensive collections of Hughes photographs in existence and concluded from a comparative study that they were the photos of four individuals, not one. She then color-coded them, dividing them into four "Hugheses," each of which she triumphantly pointed out had marked differences, such as uniquely shaped ears or hairlines. Other research, too arcane to relate, convinced her that Hughes's mother had given birth to male quadruplets instead of a single son. The quads had been kept secret and conducted a cunning charade that deluded the public into thinking there was only one Hughes.

The Hughes whose dying body was flown from Acapulco was not Howard Hughes, whom she identified as "H.H." or "Eighty-eight," but one of his brothers. "H.H." had slipped out of the Acapulco hotel, she asserted, and still survived in hiding in Anchorage, Alaska. There he was letting the passage of time sort out the good guys from the bad guys in his organization. At the proper time, she affirmed, "H.H." would stride back into public view, expose the scoundrels who had betrayed him, and resume control of The Money.

This outcome might have been something of a relief to Ted Dinkins's *ad litem* team in Houston, which found itself obliged to adopt ever more elaborate security precautions to keep the more tenacious seekers of The Money at bay. In some cases, however, it was possible to discourage hopefuls by pointing out the elementary requirements of the law. A conviction that one was a son or a wife of Howard Hughes, no matter how firmly held, did not meet the definition of evidence. This was a disappointment to the large number of Hughes "children," who had no mother to support their story that Hughes was their father. Among them were two black "sons," untroubled by the fact that the Texas-born billionaire was a bitterly bigoted racist.

There was also a "Queen of Russia, Egypt, and Israel," resident in Alabama, who not only claimed that Hughes was her father but, in a double bid for distinction, asserted that the great female aviator Amelia Earhart was her mother. She was a regular correspondent of both Dinkins and Judge Gregory, inscribing the envelopes of her letters with her royal seal. She interwove her accounts of her noted parents with detailed theories about the assassination of John Kennedy, the kidnapping of Patty Hearst, and the Watergate scandal.

One man filed a will with Judge Hayes in Las Vegas that left the entire estate to himself. The claimant was known as Joseph Brown, but he asserted that he was, in fact, Richard Robard Hughes. He had earlier filed an action in New Mexico seeking to establish that he was the billionaire's illegitimate son. He asserted that he had a radio in his head that enabled him to communicate with his deceased father.

A somewhat similar aspirant in Oregon insisted that she was an illegitimate daughter. She asserted, in numerous phone calls, that she had learned that Hughes was her father "when the FBI hypnotized me." Informed that she was not alone in claiming Hughes as her father, she denounced her rivals as frauds, complaining that "the world is full of greedy people."

Eventually, three purported wives and one daughter persisted past the *ad litem* selection procedures and were heard in court by

Judge Gregory in July 1981. A fiftyish blonde, Alyce Hovsepian Hughes, declared that she had met Hughes in a Philadelphia hospital in March 1946, when he had offered her a screen test. A few months later Hughes had persuaded her to take part in a marriage "rehearsal" and then had disclosed that it was a real, binding ceremony and asked her to adopt the name "Jean Peters." He had subsequently visited her at her family home in Atlantic City but had never disclosed his identity to her relatives. She had seen him for the last time in the fall of 1946, when he had visited her in a New Jersey psychiatric hospital, where she was a patient.

A gray-haired woman named Alma Hughes told Judge Gregory that she originally met Hughes in 1931 in Shreveport, Louisiana. She initially rejected his marriage proposal because she did not want a husband who "would be flying around all the time." They met frequently thereafter in Louisiana, and in 1951 she had borne him an illegitimate daughter. Hughes had disavowed the child because her eyes did not match the color of his own. In 1963 Hughes persuaded her to move to Dallas and frequently met her at a Neiman Marcus store, under the name of "Mr. Conroe." Alma said that Hughes had finally married her in 1973, when she consented to being artificially inseminated, and she had borne him a second child at the age of sixty-four. She volunteered some first-hand, little-known details about Hughes to give credence to her story. He was "rough in bed" and had only one foot, having lost the other in a plane accident. She readily explained why his autopsy had made no mention of a severed foot; the autopsy had been falsified. Those who had done so would someday be punished because "God is a just God" and "Money is one thing and honor is another."

The alleged daughter was Claire Benedict Hudenberg, an ordained minister in an offbeat church and a woman blessed with clairvoyant powers. Like Shirley MacLaine, she had lived many previous lives, in sixteen of which she had royal blood. Her evidence that she was Hughes's daughter was circumstantial. She had discovered her true identity when she saw a newspaper photo of Hughes and was struck by the family resemblance. This was corroborated by a number of people in Las Vegas, one of whom told her that she even "walked like Hughes." There were peculiar happenings that she attributed to her discovery of her paternity. Dozens of men with "great big necks" had trailed her around in Las Vegas and taken pictures of her. Her swimming pool had been laced with arsenic and her roof sprayed with cyanide, deeds she attributed to "the Mormons" or "the Summa people."

Judge Gregory took only a single courtroom session to dispose of all these claims, which were characterized by the estate attorneys as the product of "minds controlled by delusion, fantasy and paranoia." This left the inheritance line clear of brothers, sisters, sons, daughters, and wives—with one spectacular exception.

14

CALL OF THE
LOVELORN ALLIGATOR

AMID THE BLUE-SKY claimants to The Money there swept on-
stage a survivor from the long-gone days of Hughes's manic pursuit of the stars. She was actress Terry Moore, an authentic
participant in a romantic pas de deux with Hughes. She had attracted Hughes's attention when she was eighteen and Hughes was
in his forties and at the height of his long pursuit of whatever he
was seeking. The result was an affair that had dozens of witnesses
and had been abundantly reported in the Hollywood gossip
columns of Louella Parsons and Hedda Hopper.

To the consternation of the estate attorneys, Ms. Moore asserted
that she had been much more than a passing fancy of the billionaire's. She said she had married Hughes twice, never divorced him
even once, and had borne him a child who had died at birth. If her
account survived legal scrutiny, it could establish her as the surviving widow of the billionaire in the inheritance queue, displacing
Lummis, the cousins, and everyone else. The Money—and the
Summa Corporation—would become the property of a middle-
aged actress.

Because of these implications, Terry Moore's case was heard separately from those of Alyce, Alma, and Claire. Before her case's hearing by Probate Judge Gregory, the estate attorneys submitted her account to the full discovery process to uncover whatever legal evidence supported it.

Her story had a number of dizzying plot twists, as if it had been confected by a highly creative movie scriptwriter. She unfolded it in a series of deposition sessions, under oath, in a conference room of the Houston offices of Andrews, Kurth. Suzanne Finstad, the assistant to Ted Dinkins, the *ad litem* attorney, and an observer of the depositions, described the scene:

"Gathered about were the distinguished attorneys, most of them from old-line, socially prestigious law firms, representing interests as diverse as the state of Texas, the unknown heirs, the administrators of Hughes's estate, and, of course, the distant cousins, all vitally interested in the outcome of the heirship determination. At the center of this group sat Terry Moore. Though she was now in her fifties, her era in Hollywood a thing of the past, the old star system still lived in Miss Moore. Trained at a time when actors and actresses were under contract to a major studio and fussed over and pampered from dusk to dawn, she still operated by these rules. Every session found her in full makeup, her strawberry blonde pageboy coif groomed to perfection, every inch the glamour queen.

"For most, deposition testimony is a solemn and nervous undertaking . . . Not so for Moore. Her deposition had the atmosphere of a Mary Kay Cosmetics party. Not in the least daunted by the imposing circle of legal talent that surrounded her, firing questions, she prattled on, happily drawing doodles, relaying inside Hollywood poop during breaks in the interrogation. Without missing a beat, she would occasionally pull out a full-sized makeup mirror, set it up on the conference table, and touch up her face . . . As further proof of her romantic marriage to Hughes, Moore clutched a copy of her unpublished book, then entitled *Howard Be Thy Name*."

Ms. Moore's story follows, as condensed from her deposition and from her memoirs, subsequently published under the title *The Beauty and the Billionaire*.

She had first met Hughes at a bistro in the Beverly Wilshire Hotel in 1949, shortly after Hughes had bought RKO Studios. Hughes, who was four years older than her mother, used a customary intermediary for the introduction. Ms. Moore, born Helen Koford, was a devout Mormon who lived with her parents in Glendale and had successfully preserved her chastity in the hostile environment of Hollywood, where she was already an established starlet. At the outset she found Hughes "utterly repulsive" with "deep brown, penetrating eyes" that she could feel "undressing me." She was put off by the difference in their ages, which also was a sensitive matter with Hughes. "There was a time," she recalled, "when Howard was furious because a young fellow came up to him in a night club and requested his permission 'to dance with your daughter.' "

He pursued her across the generation gap with flowers, phone calls, and displays of his power and money. He impressed her by flying her to a Palm Springs party given by Darryl Zanuck and attended by such stars as Louis Jourdan and Clifton Webb. On their first dinner date, he hired the entire restaurant and its orchestra so they would not be distracted by other guests.

Their first "marriage" took place several months after they had met, Ms. Moore related. Hughes drove her up to a secluded section of Mulholland Drive, which afforded a spectacular view of Hollywood. There, looking down on the lights of the dreamland she yearned to conquer, Hughes had recited a ceremony of his own composition and induced her to repeat it after him. He then switched from the role of groom to minister and solemnly pronounced them man and wife.

"I felt very much married after that," she asserted. "I mean, to me that is when I gave myself to Howard in spirit, although I didn't think I should go to bed with him."

Hughes was not content to acquire only her spirit. He then devised a more convincing ceremony. He telephoned her one morning and invited her on a cruise aboard his yacht out of San Diego. "This time," she quoted him as promising, "we'll get married your way." She eagerly agreed and was flown to the yacht with her mother and a friend named Lillian Barkley, her teacher at the studio school where the young kept up their academic courses. Miss Barkley was "one of the most outstanding people in my life," Ms. Moore asserted, "a niece of Alben Barkley, Truman's vice president," and a woman with "five doctorates in education." With such a witness, and her mother present, Ms. Moore was convinced that Hughes was in earnest in taking her as his wife.

Accompanying Hughes was an older associate, about whose identity Terry was hazy. "It was either Noah Dietrich or one of Howard's lawyers, Loyd Wright. I always thought it was Mr. Dietrich, and so did my mother. I don't know—I used to get Mr. Dietrich and Mr. Wright mixed up all the time." In contrast to her fuzziness about the witness to her marriage, she could vividly recall, after the passage of more than thirty years, what she had worn on the yacht back in 1949. It was a "navy blue off-the-shoulder sweater and a beige linen skirt, embroidered with a tree of life in different shades of blue."

From San Diego the yacht sailed a few hours south into Mexican waters. There, on a shipboard banked with white gardenias and white candles shielded in brandy snifters, the ceremony was performed by a Captain Flynn while the theme from "Meditation" wafted in from a record player. When asked the crucial question by the captain, Hughes responded, "I do—forever." Hughes had neglected to procure either a wedding license or a ring, but they overcame the latter problem by borrowing a ring from "somebody—I don't remember who." With the ritual completed, the yacht made a U-turn and sped back to San Diego, where the others disembarked. The couple spent their nuptial night alone on the docked yacht. There the marriage was finally consummated, with Terry secure in the knowledge that a "sea captain can marry you at sea," a legal fact that she "just knew—from books and motion pictures."

Hughes swore her to secrecy about the marriage on the grounds that the news would adversely affect both of their careers. Her first

major picture, *Mighty Joe Young,* had cast her as the nubile object
of the affection of a huge gorilla, similar to Fay Wray's role in *King
Kong.*

"I made animal pictures," she explained, "and I was the eternal
virgin. Howard had a reputation of being a roué, and it would be
very harmful to my reputation to be married to him." Audiences
might have difficulty accepting her as the vulnerable eighteen-year-
old object of a gorilla's love if they knew that she was, off the
screen, the wife of a middle-aged billionaire.

Late on her wedding night, Moore recalled, she woke and considered the rush of events. "I watched Howard sleeping. I felt so
much like a woman and so much like a wife. I wanted to share my
joy with friends, but I had taken a sacred vow of secrecy with
Howard. I understood the argument concerning the effect of the
marriage news on my career, but something was bothering me. He
had said that a publicized wedding would be detrimental to both
our careers. I couldn't for the life of me see what negative effect it
might have on his career. How a known, rather than a secret wedding could possibly hinder the running of a tool company, a motion picture studio, or an aircraft corporation. I broke out in a
sweat and wanted to be home in my own bed. Did Howard mean
his career of collecting the most beautiful women in the world?"

Their "secret marriage" continued for more than a year, Terry
busy making pictures and Hughes occupied with his many business problems. When their schedules permitted, they had an active
social life as a gossip item but not as a married couple. Hughes
promised future delights that only a man of his wealth could provide—the "biggest yacht in the world" and Terry's very own shopping mall. When they were apart, they conversed on the telephone
as avidly as stricken adolescents. For months Terry was in Florida
making *The Barefoot Mailman,* the high point of which involved
her escape from an alligator-infested river. "I became fascinated
with gators and read Ross Allen's book, *The Sex Life of the Alligator,"* she related. Allen, who ran the alligator farm where the movie
was being shot, "taught me the alligator love call, and I have the
distinction of having the only love call that can equal his . . .

"Howard was as fascinated with the gator as I was. From the first time he heard my sensuous love call, he was hooked. I could never hang up without giving my call of the wild . . . Anyone who happened to be around when I said good night to Howard looked startled when they heard that strange mooning sound coming out of the receiver. It was my alligator, Howard."

Back on the West Coast, Terry's wedding-night suspicions began spoiling their idyll. She became upset by Hughes's increasingly frequent absences. One night Hughes called her and complained that a problem had arisen with his giant flying boat, requiring his present attention at the Long Beach hangar. After exchanging alligator love calls, Terry held the phone dreamily—and heard the operator ask if "the call from Las Vegas" had been completed. Why had he called from Las Vegas when the *Spruce Goose* was in Long Beach?

Terry conferred with her father, who had taken a cynical view of the shipboard marriage. He called a friend, an ex-FBI agent named Leckey, and secured his help. Leckey took Terry to Las Vegas and tracked Hughes to the Desert Inn, where she confronted him and his new playmate.

In sharp contrast to the other Hughes "wives," Terry Moore's saga had verifiable checkpoints embedded in it here and there, like raisins in a pudding. There was indeed a sleuth named A. E. Leckey who had tracked the errant Hughes to Las Vegas; he had subsequently listed this coup on his professional résumé, along with his feats for the FBI. His success in piercing the Hughes wall of secrecy for Ms. Moore landed him another Hughes-hunting job, with the eastern bankers seeking to corner Hughes in the legal battle over control of TWA in the early sixties. Although armed with a generous budget and a staff of trained, trail-sniffing assistants, Leckey was unable to duplicate for the bankers what he had done for Terry.

Infuriated by Hughes's infidelity, Terry briskly rebounded and began publicly dating Glenn Davis, the all-American football star. After a brief courtship, she married Davis on February 9, 1951, without disclosing her shipboard marriage to Hughes. This marriage shortly foundered, and she again took up with Hughes. She asserted in her sworn deposition that in 1952 while making a movie in Germany, she gave birth prematurely to a daughter, who died within a few hours. The delivery was handled by Dr. Verne Mason, Hughes's personal physician, she testified, and she never saw the baby, whose funeral was arranged by Hughes's doctor. By the time she revealed this claim, Dr. Mason was dead, but his son recalled that the doctor had flown to Germany for some unspecified treatment of Ms. Moore.

When her divorce from Davis became final in 1953, Hughes again proposed marriage, this time a public ceremony for all the world to see at the Tucson ranch of Jack Frye, head of TWA. The night before the wedding, Terry had another public brawl with Hughes in Las Vegas when she learned that he had two Hollywood stars stashed on standby and another flying out to meet him. Wedding number three collapsed, although she continued sporadically to see Hughes over her parents' objections.

Her marriage-go-round with Hughes finally came to an end in 1956, when Terry married a wealthy businessman named Eugene McGrath, to whom she was introduced by John Wayne. Meanwhile, Jean Peters had also tired of Hughes's unfaithfulness and had married another wealthy businessman, Stuart Cramer III, only to divorce him after some covert nudges from Hughes. Cramer would later be reported as saying, "If your wife is going to get a divorce, you might as well let her marry someone who can afford to support her. It's the cheapest way out."

In 1957 Hughes also displayed economic wisdom by marrying Jean inexpensively in a secret ceremony in Tonopah, Nevada, in which he concealed the wedding by employing the names of G. A. Johnson and Marian Evans for himself and his bride. Shortly after this marital hugger-muggery, Hughes rendered it meaningless by announcing to the world, via Louella Parsons's column, that he had indeed married Jean Peters.

In a plot twist that would have done credit to a soap opera, Terry then divorced Mr. McGrath and married Jean Peters's discard, Stuart Cramer, by whom she had two sons before divorcing him in the early 1970s. Legally freed from her last husband, she tried again to reunite with Hughes in 1973, when he was in exile in London. Like the process servers and the inquisitive newsmen, she was turned away by his security guards. In 1975, when he shifted from London to Freeport in the Bahamas, she wrote him a letter telling him that "the only marriage I've believed in is ours" and declaring "I'd like to spend eternity with you." The letter was returned to her unopened.

In her deposition, Ms. Moore focused on establishing the authenticity of the shipboard wedding, which was clearly the sine qua non of her case. After the passage of more than thirty years, what had happened on the yacht was difficult to reconstruct. By her own admission, there was no marriage license. Her only surviving witness was her mother. The ship's log, wherein the ceremony might have been recorded by Captain Flynn, had long since vanished. Ms. Moore speculated that the log had been destroyed by Hughes in a fit of rage, or by his associates, eager to retain a grip on his empire.

A number of those who heard her story were convinced that some sort of ceremony had been staged on the yacht, but not necessarily a valid marriage. Hughes was a master at manipulating others to get what he wanted, and he may have staged a charade that would fetch the romantic young girl into what she thought was a marriage bed.

Ms. Moore contended that because she had never divorced Hughes, her subsequent three marriages were bigamous and invalid and that Hughes's marriage to Jean Peters was not binding for the same reason. This would leave her as Hughes's surviving widow and his sole beneficiary.

The attorneys, however, focused on her marriage to Glenn Davis. Although she had married Davis less than two years after her "marriage" to Hughes, Ms. Moore conceded that she had not sought a divorce from the billionaire. She had no choice on this admission: on the Davis marriage license, she had asserted that she had not been previously married.

She blamed her failure to divorce Hughes on her movie studio's "giant publicity machine" and on Howard Hughes. She hadn't

really meant to marry Davis, she said, but the studio publicists in-
flated their relationship into an engagement and things had got out
of hand. "It flew into a crescendo like a snowball," she explained,
"and I was just too scared to stop it." When Hughes read about
the engagement, she said, "He just laughed and said I couldn't
marry Davis because I was already married."

When the wedding day came, "I married him because no one
was there to stop it. I thought Howard would stop it." To an estate attorney who questioned her logic, she replied, "You don't
know what it is like to be a star."

In insisting that she had married Hughes and had then remarried without divorcing him, Ms. Moore put herself in the jaws of
a legal catch-22. If she hadn't married Hughes, she had no standing whatsoever; if she had married him, she was legally required to
divorce him. This derived from a legal doctrine called "estoppel,"
which says in effect that one cannot have things both ways in the
legal system. More long-windedly, estoppel is defined as a "bar or
impediment preventing a party from asserting a fact or claim in-
consistent with a position the party previously took, especially
where a representation has been relied on or acted upon by
others." In marrying her, Glenn Davis had relied and acted on her
declaration that she had no previous marriages. Having taken that
position, Ms. Moore could not back up some thirty years later and
transform herself into the legal wife of Hughes, regardless of the
rewards of such a transformation.

This made what happened on the yacht back in 1949 irrelevant,
and Judge Gregory spared himself the detailed agony and ecstasy
of her stormy May–December romance with the billionaire. In a
brief court session on June 27, 1981, Judge Gregory invoked the
estoppel doctrine and dismissed Ms. Moore's claim as the true
Mrs. Howard Hughes.

Terry Moore, however, had the last word. Her attorney appealed Judge Gregory's decision and a similar estoppel ruling in
Nevada, where her claim had also been filed because there was still
no determination of Hughes's legal residence. Her appeals put the
settlement of the Hughes estate on hold, with Ms. Moore's case

clouding the title to the Hughes properties until the case was disposed of. With the glacial pace of the court system, this could mean a delay of several years.

The Andrews, Kurth firm and Will Lummis turned to George Dean and authorized him to explore a settlement. He settled the claim with remarkable speed with a device employing the Doctrine of Diminishing Returns. He met with Ms. Moore's attorney, Arthur Leeds, and presented him with a settlement figure that would be substantially reduced every twenty-four hours that passed without acceptance. This approach brought an almost instant settlement.

On May 24, 1983, Ms. Moore called a press conference in Los Angeles, her first in many years. When the cameras and the reporters were in place, a press agent announced, "Ladies and gentlemen, Mrs. Howard Hughes." Terry Moore swept in and radiantly announced that the Hughes heirs had finally "acknowledged" that she was the "widow" of the billionaire and had awarded her, as such, a sum of money, amount undisclosed. Under persistent questioning by reporters, she said that the sum was "more than five figures and less than eight figures." This put the settlement between $99,999 and $10 million, a financial ballpark of Brobdingnagian dimensions. Her attorney conceded that it was "closer to the first figure" and referred to her press conference as "her moment in the sun."

The settlement specified that neither side would disclose how much of The Money was involved, but an estate spokesman commented, "I think the lady is counting the zeros after the decimal point." He also insisted that the settlement had not "acknowledged" her marriage to Hughes.

Judge Gregory, who had ruled that she was legally estopped from collecting anything, observed wryly, "What they paid her is called 'go-away-money.' "

Forbes magazine put the settlement at $390,000, a figure later described, independently, by a close friend of Ms. Moore's as "right on the button." And eventually an estate lawyer conceded that this was indeed the actual amount. Asked what he thought the estate had gained from this payout, he responded cheerfully, "Help in moving the ball down the field."

Meanwhile, it was "Mrs. Howard Hughes" who was attracting the most attention for her movement of the ball. Her flamboyant intervention in the heirship struggle had a resuscitative effect on Ms. Moore's career. It brought a clutch of appearances on national talk shows, including *Good Morning America,* an article in *Vanity Fair,* and paperback publication of her memoirs.

It also put Ms. Moore on the cover of *Playboy,* the first woman in her fifties ever featured in that national celebration of the nubile young. Inside was a ten-page spread of nude photographs of what *Playboy* termed "The Merriest Widow." They made abundantly clear why *Playboy*'s Hugh Hefner, who normally operated on the axiom that women over thirty were obsolescent, had devoted the layout to a woman near his own age. It also enabled millions of readers to inspect at their leisure what had induced a billionaire defense contractor to emulate the call of a lovelorn alligator.

15

AND THE WINNERS ARE . . .

AMONG THE CLAIMANTS to The Money were more than five hundred people who could genuinely assert some blood relationship with Howard Hughes. Many were second and third cousins, but they had little prospect of inheriting anything with so many first cousins already identified. Like people with lottery tickets one number short of the winning number, they were prey to disappointment. But unlike most lottery losers, they could, conceivably, change the rules of the game. Too distant to inherit perhaps, but not necessarily so if some fault could be found with the troupe of first cousins and cousins once removed so carefully lined up, and choreographed, by Will Lummis.

Given the stakes involved, the search for some such fault was both assiduous and highly imaginative. Many of the more distant relatives paid fees to freelance "heir-finders," eager to assist them in their quest for The Money. Out of all this activity came some wonderfully gothic tales about a secret drowning, a sterile family man, and the lost girl replaced by a doppelgänger.

Even stranger than the tales themselves was the fact that there was evidence to suggest that they might also be true. All the stories would be obliged to go through the wringer of the Texas *ad litem* process run by Ted Dinkins, and all would emerge, substantially intact, to be adjudicated by Probate Judge Pat Gregory in September 1981.

There was never much scope for creative genealogy on the maternal side of things. Indeed, it would take Judge Gregory less than a day to decide that the parade of relatives on Will Lummis's wing of the family was duly qualified to inherit its share of the estate. But the paternal side provided many sinister avenues for conjecture.

At the center of the speculation was the man who had originally introduced Howard Hughes to the delights of Hollywood, his Uncle Rupert. As far as the five front-running paternal heirs were concerned, there was no more crucial figure. The three sisters— Barbara Lapp Cameron, Elspeth Lapp DePould, and Agnes Lapp Roberts—all derived their claim from being Rupert Hughes's granddaughters. Their mother, Elspeth, long since deceased, was said to have been Rupert Hughes's only natural child. The brother and sister team of Avis Hughes McIntyre and Rush Hughes owed their prominence in the inheritance stakes to their having been equitably adopted by Rupert Hughes.

Thus, if the presumed facts of Rupert Hughes's life could be shaken loose, the whole paternity side of the inheritance could come up for grabs. There was much in Rupert Hughes's life that was unshakable, his talent being one of them. Described in his obituary in *Time* magazine as a "jowly Jack-of-all-literary trades," Rupert Hughes was a prolific writer. He made most of his money writing for Broadway and Hollywood, but he churned out an adequate children's book, many good novels, some able biographies, including a major work on George Washington, a collection of fine short stories, and some excellent polemics. Some of his magazine articles written in the 1920s were regarded as deeply shocking. He would tilt at religion and make mock of the nation's divorce laws. "All this slow hell," he wrote, "could be done away with if the U.S. were civilized enough to permit divorce by mutual consent."

But the solidity of Rupert Hughes's public achievements was not mirrored in other areas. As might be guessed, he was no stranger to the "slow hell" of divorce proceedings. Indeed, his entire private life seemed to have a nightmarish quality. Of his three wives, one hanged herself in the cabin of an around-the-world pleasure steamer berthed in Haiphong, a second died from a massive overdose of sleeping pills, while a third (Elspeth's mother) ended her days in a mental institution.

There was, according to the distant relatives, a further complication in Rupert Hughes's private life—he was not Elspeth's father. This charge, if true, would effectively shut Elspeth's three daughters out of any inheritance on the grounds that they were not blood relatives. And the effect of this could be to open the whole paternal side of the inheritance to other claimants who could prove a blood relationship. All such claimants were, of course, deeply dismissive of the equitable adoption asserted by Avis and Rush Hughes, who made no pretense of being kin.

Those who made the central charge divided into two groups of relatives, called for the sake of convenience "the Iowa group" and "the Alabama group." The case of the Iowa group, more than three hundred strong and consisting mainly of descendants of the siblings of Judge Felix Hughes, the grandfather of Howard Hughes, was simple: Rupert Hughes could not have fathered Elspeth because he was sterile.

It was said to be "common family knowledge" that Rupert had been rendered impotent by a childhood illness that occurred around 1887 when he was attending the St. Charles Military School at St. Charles, Missouri. Several witnesses recalled how this knowledge was passed on down the more homespun ranks of the family in Iowa, Missouri, and Illinois. Rupert was a frequent topic of family conversation, it was said, because "We were real proud of him being a writer."

John Askins, Jr., fifty-eight, a retired Illinois shipping clerk, said he remembered an aunt telling him about his famous Uncle Rupert who could not father children because "the mumps dropped on him and made him sterile." Dorothy Bacon Wilson, sixty-three, of

Missouri, received the same intelligence from her grandfather. Edward W. Hornsby, sixty-nine, had it from his parents that Uncle Rupert was sterile because he "had German measles the same time he had mumps when he was in boarding school." Charles Ireland, seventy-two, was old enough to get the information more directly. He remembered going on an outing with Uncle Rupert as a thirteen-year-old boy. At one point his uncle patted him on the head and said: "I wish I coulda had children." Elspeth, by then, would have been a grown woman.

In making the case for the Iowa group, its lawyer, George Parnham, laid heavy emphasis on Rupert Hughes's failure to acknowledge the existence of a daughter at certain stages of his life. One such occasion had been in 1917, twenty years after Elspeth's recorded birth, when Hughes applied to join the prestigious Sons of the American Revolution. New members were required to fill out a document that had the effect of a sworn statement. In the space allotted for the applicant's children, Hughes had made no entry.

Parnham also indicated another omission that he regarded as significant: in Rupert Hughes's final will, he rather pointedly disinherited all Elspeth's daughters. This seemed to suggest the existence of a troubled family, but as evidence for Elspeth's illegitimacy, it had to be considered at the outer limits of circumstantial. What gave the allegation its credibility was what was known of Hughes's stormy married life.

The answer to what Elspeth's paternity might be if she was not Rupert Hughes's daughter did not require a very high degree of speculation. Hughes's legal separation from Agnes, his first wife and Elspeth's mother, in 1903 made the front page of every newspaper in New York. There were riots outside the courtroom and fisticuffs inside, but what gave the event its sensational edge was the enumeration of the corespondents. Hughes, rather unchivalrously, named eight men as his wife's illicit lovers, raising the possibility that one of them had fathered Elspeth.

The claim advanced by the Alabama group was more complex. They, too, looked back to the generation of Felix Turner Hughes,

Howard Hughes's grandfather, to advance their case. In their submission, however, Felix Turner Hughes was a more complicated individual than had previously been suspected. They claimed that Felix Turner Hughes had actually been born Felix Monar Hughes, a native of Kentucky.

"Monar" Hughes, before he resurfaced in the north as "Turner," was apparently a ruthless character. He sided with the North in the Civil War, which might have been forgiven, but he then organized an ambush that resulted in the elimination of his eight brothers. What remained of Hughes's family in the South, from then on, became naturally vigilant. Part of this vigilance involved monitoring the activities of Felix Monar/Turner Hughes and all his issue. A family historian was appointed to maintain this "surveillance." By the early 1940s the then family historian, Robert C. Hughes, had assembled a trunkful of documents and clippings on this subject. Unfortunately, for the Alabama group's cause, the trunk had been gutted in a house fire shortly after Pearl Harbor.

But Robert C. Hughes's nephew, also called Robert C. Hughes, was around to testify to its relevant contents before Judge Gregory's court in September 1981. In fact, Robert Hughes was the only witness put forward by the 160-odd southern claimants, but his story held the courtroom's attention.

Robert C. Hughes saw no reason to impugn the potency of Rupert Hughes. But, he maintained, the daughter legitimately born to Rupert Hughes and his first wife, Agnes, was not Elspeth. Her real name was "Leila," and she had drowned in a swimming pool at the family home in California. Subsequently, Rupert Hughes substituted another young woman to take the place of his dead natural child. The replacement daughter was allegedly the daughter of Rupert Hughes's third wife, the actress Patterson Dial, conceived in an earlier love affair with another man. She was not a blood relation of Rupert Hughes at all. Her name was indeed Elspeth, and she would go on to have three daughters. But none of them, Robert Hughes contended, could properly be considered in a bloodline of inheritance for Howard Hughes's money. Under cross-examination, Robert Hughes acknowledged that most of his direct evidence for this remarkable story had been incinerated in the trunk.

In trying to rebut this testimony, the lawyers representing Will Lummis's five chosen paternal heirs steered the court in the direction of documentation that could still be found. Paul Freese, on behalf of Elspeth's three children, and Wayne Fisher, representing the two "stepchildren," were able to deploy a mass of paperwork—birth and marriage certificates, letters, church records, and old photographs—to underpin the argument that Elspeth was indeed Rupert Hughes's natural daughter. Fisher would speak contemptuously of the "cock-and-bull stories" presented by his clients' opponents, while Freese radiated lawyer's outrage against "those who would bastardize my clients' mother."

It took the jury less than two hours to find against both groups of distant relatives. But their disappointment would be shared in areas that could not be considered part of a lunatic fringe.

Key staff on Ted Dinkins's *ad litem* team, who had spent almost five years investigating Hughes inheritance claims, were also unhappy with the outcome. Suzanne Finstad and Mrs. Mary Smith Fay, the genealogist, both had strong reservations. They shared a belief, according to Finstad, "based on instinct and fact, that the wrong people may have inherited the estate of Howard Hughes."

Finstad would later argue in her book *Heir Not Apparent* that the stringent rules of evidence in the inheritance case prevented the disclosure of many relevant facts. On the sterility issue, Finstad was inclined to believe that Rupert Hughes could have had children, as he was alleged to have gotten one of his housemaids pregnant. This did not, however, necessarily mean that he was Elspeth's father. Indeed, had Elspeth been the child of one of his wife's lovers, it might, Finstad wrote, "explain Rupert's ambivalent attitude toward his supposed daughter, which was in direct contrast to his exaggerated parental interest in others."

Finstad was more drawn to the weird "substitution" case presented by the Alabama group. Though it was hard to sustain credence in the details of the drowning incident as described by

Robert C. Hughes, it was not, she felt, at all difficult to believe that there had been two Elspeths. In conducting the *ad litem* investigation into Elspeth's early life, she and her assistants had been confronted with inconsistencies and ambiguities about Elspeth's age and inclinations. One Elspeth seemed to be three or four years older than the other, one was fluent in French, the other was not. These tantalizing discrepancies could, she thought, have been the consequence of a substitution. Finstad's book would provide some aid and comfort for the distant relatives, but the Houston probate court's decision remained impervious to all subsequent legal challenges.

The most touching *ad litem* story, never featured in the court hearing, was about an old widow in Joplin, Missouri. There seemed a possibility that she was the daughter of Howard Hughes's father, though she had been brought up and lived her life under another identity. It also seemed that Hughes Sr. might have been fleetingly married to her mother. If this was true, she would qualify as the paternal heir, with precedence over all others. The *ad litem* researchers encouraged the widow to send them family documents, particularly those concerning her birth. The old lady gave the matter some thought, but finally decided she could not "be bothered." If it sometimes seems as if all America was rushing, hands outstretched, for The Money, it needs to be remembered that one of its senior citizens perceived the possibility of becoming a multimillionairess and quietly walked away.

DESPITE THE ENORMOUS publicity accorded to Judge Gregory's heirship trials, the maternal heirs contrived to make almost no impression at all. This was partly because they had been so well schooled by Will Lummis in the discipline of saying nothing. But it also had something to do with the fact that many of them had money and had acquired the ingrained habit of being discreet about it.

The maternal group comprised three interlocking parts of the family—the Lummises, the Houstouns, and the Ganos—and were, with a few exceptions, resident in the Houston area. The Lummises enjoyed the most social prestige and were comfortably wealthy. When Annette Gano Lummis's husband, a leading physician, died in 1969, he left an estate valued at $555,000. Their children, all designated heirs as Hughes's first cousins, had done well or married well: Mrs. Allene Lummis Russell, fifty-six when her heirship was determined, was the wife of a Boston physician; Mrs. Annette Lummis Neff, fifty-five, was married to a banker, while Dr. Frederick Rice Lummis, Jr., fifty, Will Lummis's younger brother, had a prospering medical practice.

Annette Gano Lummis, who played a large role in grooming the family for its potential inheritance, died over a year before Judge Gregory's hearing. Selected portions of her earlier deposition evidence detailing the history and structure of the family were formally read into the record. The only living testimony by a family member was provided by Annette Lummis's second daughter, Mrs. Annette Neff, who gave her evidence in a calm, dispassionate fashion.

A large chart depicting the maternal line told the court nearly all it wanted to know. All Mrs. Neff had to do was supplement the information with photographs, letters, and other family memorabilia. This she did with great composure. No pretense of any great intimacy with Howard Hughes was made, though Mrs. Neff did recall that the great aviator had once offered to take her up in his airplane when she was a young girl but her mother had forbidden it.

The Houstouns' family connection with Hughes derived from another of his maternal aunts, Martha Gano Houstoun, who married a man who prospered in the insurance business. When she died in 1961, she left an estate valued at $712,000.

Martha Houstoun had four children, two sons and two daughters. Both daughters—Mrs. Janet Houstoun Davis, sixty, the wife of the president of a die-casting company, and Mrs. Sara Houstoun Lindsey, fifty-eight, wife of an insurance company executive—became designated heirs. One of the sons, James Patrick Houstoun, Jr., who died in 1976, seven months after Hughes, had a share of the fortune assigned to his estate. The other son, William Gano Houstoun, Sr., died much earlier, leaving an estate of his own of nearly half a million dollars. He also left four children—John, Margot, James, and Richard—who would all qualify for a piece of Hughes's estate as first cousins once removed. When the heirship determination was announced, the oldest, John, was twenty-seven, and the youngest, Richard, was eighteen, which give them a better prospect than most of actually seeing their share of The Money.

The Ganos were another aristocratic clan who could trace their descent back to Richard Montgomery Gano, a Confederate general and renowned Indian fighter who moved to Texas in 1856. By the turn of the century, *The Dallas Morning News* would describe Gano as "perhaps the proudest name in the city's social register." For all that the Ganos seemed to have slipped some way behind the Lummises and the Houstouns, economically at least.

Gano heirs designate were the five children of the late Richard Chilton Gano, Sr., a brother of Hughes's mother. The oldest surviving was Richard C. Gano, Jr., sixty-five, who lived in Anaheim, California, and worked for many years at the Hughes Aircraft plant. The others, all living in the Houston area, were Mrs. Doris Gano Wallace, sixty-three, a schoolteacher; Mrs. Annette Gano Gragg, fifty-five, the wife of an architect; and Howard Hughes Gano, fifty-two, a lawyer. Their oldest brother, William Kent Gano, who worked in a Houston ironworks and suffered long layoffs through ill health, had a glimpse of possible riches to come but died in 1978. Judge Gregory ruled that his estate should be an inheritor.

One attribute shared by all the Lummises, Houstouns, and Ganos was a powerful aversion to the press. On occasion *The Houston Post* would send out its most intrepid reporters to inquire of the nominated heirs what they felt at the prospect of becoming seriously rich. The reporters would return and empty their notebooks of gems like "I'm really not interested in talking about it. I feel that the less exposure I have the better" (from Dr. Frederick Lummis). Or "We would really like to keep as low a profile as possible. I appreciate your position, and I hope you appreciate mine" (from Annette Gano Gragg). The maternal heirs, of course, were under a severe constraint. Their mission, assigned by Will Lummis, was the quiet absorption of The Money, which ruled out any public expressions of delight. The appearance they gave to the process of inheriting riches was that of performing a painful and private duty.

Reporters hunting for real quotes would be obliged to seek out the paternal heirs, who were both less well organized and more outgoing. Avis McIntyre and Rush Hughes, who had to elbow their way into contention with the assistance of George Dean, were good sources. Rush, who weighed in at around 270 pounds, told reporters, "Please, if you must say I look like someone say Papa Hemingway, but not that chicken man." Rush died before the heirship trial, though his estate would inherit. The thrice-married Avis, though almost eighty-one at the time of the trial, continued to fascinate with her deep southern drawl. Most reporters also had a soft spot for the three daughters of the controversial "Elspeth." The general feeling was that Elspeth, whether one woman or two, legitimate or illegitimate, must have been a reasonable mother to have raised such well-balanced offspring.

"I always thought Howard would live to be ninety," said Mrs. Elspeth Lapp DePould on first receiving the news of Hughes's death, "so it is a real surprise to us to be caught up in this." And the surprise never seemed quite to wear off, though the sisters were all of matronly age. By the time of the heirship determination, Elspeth, who lived in Cleveland, Ohio, was fifty-six, Agnes who lived close by, was fifty-seven, while the youngest, Barbara, who lived in Beverly Hills, was fifty-five. Though different in character, none of them had any aristocratic pretension or any stiffness of the upper lip. They were essentially sturdy middle class, leading lives that revolved around husbands and children, doing voluntary work, or, when times were tough, supplementing the family income by working themselves.

Agnes, the oldest, had to undergo eight operations for various cancers. But she also held down a secure position at Branch Park Skateland, where she sold cookies and candy to hungry skaters. She made it clear that the events in Judge Gregory's court would not induce her to give up her day job. On the other hand, she was prepared to commit what the maternal heirs regarded as the cardinal sin—publicly warming to the prospect of The Money like a joyful lottery winner.

The Agnes Roberts plan, she announced, was to go to a health farm for as long as it took to lose fifteen pounds. Then she would get a face-lift. Her next move would be to buy a new Cadillac for her husband and new cars for each of her four children. Finally, she and her husband would go looking for a condo someplace in the sun where they could take extended holidays. She thought Arizona would be really nice.

THE DETERMINATION OF the heirs in Texas represented a major advance in Will Lummis's grand design, but nobody was going to be able to buy a place in the sun in a hurry. The front-running heirs had been around for five years without receiving a cent from the estate, and more such years were in prospect. Terry Moore was still a problem impeding any disbursement, but, more important, the federal and state inheritance tax issues were deeply unresolved. Until it was known what the estate would have to pay out in taxes, there could be no money for the heirs. And perhaps not even then. Some calculations had suggested that the estate might incur an overall tax liability of over 100 percent.

Domicile played a major role in determining the savagery of the tax bite, but that, too, was uncertain. Judge Gregory's court in Houston had asserted that Hughes was Texan through and through. This, however, had not gone down at all well in California.

On top of the tax and domicile headaches, Lummis had to contend with the uncertainties created by the lost will case and pressures from the Medical Institute, which was still in the hands of Chester Davis and Bill Gay, who had not stopped seeking to dislodge him from his command of Summa. Having run into the legal buffers in Nevada, a refreshed lost will case was now plowing through the courts in Texas. There was also the unresolved matter of Lummis's $50 million lawsuit against Davis, Gay, and the Hughes aides and doctors, which was not going well.

What was intended to be the definitive showdown between Lummis and Hughes's ancien régime had turned into an expensive, and inconclusive, legal muddle. Confronted by Chester Davis's adroit tactic of mobilizing counterlitigation in several states, Lummis finally junked the idea of seeking redress through the Nevada court system. Instead, he refiled the same suit in California, where most of the named defendants lived. This had the effect of integrating the case, but it also put Lummis and Summa in the position of playing away from home.

When they were refused a jury trial, they sensed, correctly, that they were on a loser. In a series of judgments handed down between November 1981 and March 1982, U.S. District Judge Manuel Real comprehensively squashed Summa's case. He ruled that the personal contracts, which Lummis had suspended, were valid and that Lummis's many allegations of malpractice and mismanagement were either not proven or simply out of date and therefore beyond remedy.

It was thought that a prompt appeal could produce a better outcome. But the instinct of most of those concerned was for settlement. According to the estate attorney Bill Miller, "The only people getting rich were the lawyers. So Lummis prudently decided to shutter down and cut a deal. He stopped the bleeding."

The precise details of the settlement reached in the summer of 1982 between Lummis and his opponents have never been revealed, though it did involve a transfer of over $2 million, most of which was directed to paying off the personal contracts at a reduced rate. Expressing himself well pleased at the outcome, Dr. Thain announced: "We all agreed not to sue each other anymore."

That is, all except Chester Davis, who, though now a sick man, went litigating furiously on. He figured that Summa owed him $5,225,000 for breach of contract and nonpayment of legal fees, an additional $7 million for the allegedly slanderous statements Lummis made about him, plus a wack of $35 million in punitive damages.

16

"THE 5.2 BILLION-DOLLAR SENTENCE"

THE ARENA FOR the final high-stakes duel between Will Lummis and his tormentors in the Medical Institute was the New Castle County Court of Chancery in Wilmington, Delaware. This was where Chester Davis and Bill Gay had first tried to crush Lummis by having him dismissed from his post at Summa. It was also where Lummis, egged on by George Dean, had counterattacked by asserting his own claim to be the sole trustee of HHMI.

In 1983 it was the court that stripped the Davis and Gay regime bare of any authority.

Although this was the truly decisive court battle, at the time it passed virtually unnoticed. There were several good reasons. In May 1983, nine weeks before the trial was due to begin, Chester Davis died from a stroke. Nadine Henley, the other key scheduled witness, had also suffered a stroke some months earlier and was unable to speak or write.

With the main witnesses dead or disabled, the court decided that its only recourse was to hold a paper trial. Its deliberations would be based on the deposition evidence previously supplied by Davis,

Henley, Gay, and many others and a stack of documents, some six feet in height, that had been assembled over the years. There would be long written arguments and submissions by the lawyers, but no witnesses would be called. This made for a dry and unexciting proceeding, but one of enormous consequences.

The case originated in Lummis's dramatic counterattack in June 1978, though Lummis himself would be little more than a spear-carrier in the final act. In making his original bid, Lummis had persuaded the Delaware attorney general, Richard R. Wier, Jr., to join him as coplaintiff in his application to the court to appoint him "or some other appropriate person" as the new HHMI trustee. Lummis had never been much interested in taking on HHMI, but he wanted what he described as a "neutral" institute, that is, one not dominated by Davis and Gay.

Davis and Gay, who now described themselves as vice presidents of HHMI, responded to the new threat by voting for the abolition of the office of trustee. Subsequently, in October 1979, they successfully applied to the court to have Lummis dismissed from the action, and, as a result, the Delaware attorney general became the sole plaintiff. This would work much to Lummis's advantage.

Lummis's exit effectively removed any suggestion of personal animus from the case. This meant that it no longer turned on who the perceived good guys and bad guys were in the legal wrestling match for Hughes's billions but on what the state of Delaware conceived as being in the public good. The attorney general's sole interest was in whether the legal provisions governing the trusteeship of HHMI had been abused.

Already deeply fascinated by the power struggles that characterized life at the top of the state's wealthiest charitable foundation, the Delaware lawyers began to pare down the issues for trial. This, ultimately, led them to focus on one solitary sentence. Conceived by Chester Davis, and carefully handwritten into the 1971 bylaws of the Medical Institute by Nadine Henley, the full sentence read: "In the absence of a trustee, the executive committee shall also have and may exercise the powers of the trustee."

The "Davis sentence," which would subsequently become known as "the 5.2 billion-dollar sentence" after HHMI sold Hughes Aircraft to General Motors, could hardly be faulted on the grounds of imprecision. It was the clear mandate for the stewardship of Davis and Bill Gay, the sole executive committee members at HHMI at the time of Howard Hughes's death. It was also the legal underpinning for their actions in the costly wars against Will Lummis, and, after their ejection from Summa, a claim on entitlement to income. From 1978 through 1982 Davis and Gay had drawn aggregate salaries in excess of $500,000 each from HHMI, while Davis's law firm did $1.5 million worth of new legal business with HHMI and Hughes Aircraft.

Though the sentence was clear enough in its wording, the attorney general's office found two problems with it, problems that only seemed to intensify as more deposition evidence was developed: (1) there seemed to be no evidence that Hughes had agreed to it, and (2) there seemed to be powerful evidence that if Hughes had known about it, he would have vetoed it.

DESPITE ITS BREVITY the Davis sentence had quite a long prehistory. As sole trustee of the Medical Institute, Hughes enjoyed absolute power, which he rarely exercised but never ceded. His employees knew that Hughes was opposed to diluting his authority in any area. In addition, the Medical Institute was crucial to the tax-avoidance strategy of his whole empire. Under the institute's original charter, a successor trustee could only be named by "the original trustee [Hughes himself] or in such a manner as the original trustee may designate." Hughes showed no inclination to designate his successor.

Even so, through the 1960s, as Hughes became more sickly and more remote, the problem of how to ensure the future—the euphemism for what would happen to HHMI after Hughes's death—of this huge, largely untapped asset came to exercise many capable minds. Among those who took a keen interest was Raymond Cook, the Andrews, Kurth attorney who became the alleged custodian of Hughes's lost will.

Cook had served on the institute's executive committee in its earliest days, but this body had effectively lapsed after a few years. The actual work of HHMI, relatively modest throughout Hughes's life, was done by the Medical Advisory Committee. Cook, however, persuaded Hughes that it would be a good idea to revive the idea of a properly functioning executive committee to steer its activities.

At the time both Congress and the IRS were in the process of mounting inquiries into the activities of tax-exempt foundations. Cook argued in a memo to Hughes that the time had come for the institute to "regularize" itself, if only to protect itself from any possible outside threat. Accordingly, by a resolution dated July 3, 1968, Hughes sanctioned the creation of a new HHMI committee composed of Cook, James R. Drury, another partner in Andrews, Kurth, and Raymond Holliday, who ran the Hughes Tool Company.

Shortly afterward, without Hughes's knowledge, the new committee regularized itself still further by equipping itself with a set of bylaws. These contained what would be called "the Cook sentence," which ran: "If the original Trustee shall fail to name successor Trustees or to designate the manner in which they are to be selected, then the Executive Committee shall name the successor Trustees."

The effect of the Cook sentence was to place Cook, along with the two other committee members, in a position to control the institute on Hughes's death. Also, if Cook had indeed seen a Hughes will bequeathing everything to HHMI, he would have known that it put him in a position to control Hughes's entire empire. This glamorous prospect lasted only a short time.

It was Bob Maheu, no great fan of Ray Cook's, who brought the bylaws to Hughes's attention. Hughes was outraged. He called Cook's action "an obvious misuse of authority" and told Chester Davis that he intended to dissolve the committee and have the bylaws revoked.

On Davis's advice Hughes held off for a spell. Davis was then involved in hearings before the Civil Aeronautics Board where the issue of continuity of control of Hughes's interests had come up. Davis thought the CAB would be disturbed if the institute suddenly junked its committee and its bylaws. Hughes acquiesced on this advice, but only until the end of the hearings, at which point, still enraged, he looked to Ray Holliday to undo the evil deed.

Holliday, who was away on business in Belfast, Northern Ireland, received a message from Hughes ordering his immediate return to the United States. He was told to ensure the revocation of the detested bylaws and to secure Cook's resignation. Hughes, Holliday remembered, was like someone who had "blown a fuse." He was "terribly angered" by the provision saying "that the Executive Committee could, if he failed to act, name a successor trustee. He was very upset about that, extremely upset, and that message came through loud and clear."

On his way back, Holliday stopped off in New York to discuss the situation with Chester Davis, who "already knew what the hoorah was about." Holliday remembered Davis confirming that "the old man was on the warpath" and "extremely angry" about the Cook sentence.

On May 20, 1970, Holliday completed his mission by getting the bylaws revoked and by ensuring the departure of both Cook and Drury, who resigned "due to pressure of other matters." Hughes let it be known that Cook should have nothing further to do with the institute.

Hughes's absolutism was preserved but only at the risk of another peril. Without any bylaws, the Medical Institute became vulnerable to the attentions of the tax man. Brand-new federal Treasury regulations required a charitable organization—which HHMI earnestly claimed to be—to make specific provision within its internal structures to ensure that contributions coming in were actually distributed. Without this they would lose their tax-exempt status. This awful prospect obliged Hughes to revise his attitude to bylaws. He would put up with them, provided they were written right.

Holliday was set to work on a crash course of bylaw writing with the assistance of Seymour S. Mintz, a partner in Hogan &

Hartson, a Washington, D.C., firm that had acted as counsel to the institute since 1953. Throughout they kept two supreme objectives in mind. The first was the achievement of a phrasing that would effectively neutralize any threat from the tax man. The second, and even more important, was the avoidance of any hint, or hint of a hint, that Hughes might interpret as an encroachment on his own power by the executive committee.

There were large gaps that needed filling on the committee if HHMI was to exhibit any kind of regular appearance for the federal authorities. As things were, Holliday was the only man on the executive bridge in what had become IRS-infested waters. And there were question marks over Holliday.

By this time Bob Maheu was no longer on the scene, having been ousted by Gay and Davis with a proxy signed by Hughes. Holliday had done his bit by making heavy complaints to Hughes about Maheu's alleged profligacy. In a memo to Hughes dated June 1970, Holliday had gone on about Maheu's expenses and the need to provide any "right or left hand ass wiping machine he [Maheu] may require." With Maheu gone Holliday, as the long-time boss of Hughes's oldest and most consistently profitable business, saw himself emerging as Hughes's new right-hand man. But his cowarriors in the victory over Maheu had other plans.

Holliday was a drinker, and Hughes's primly abstemious aides suddenly appeared to feel alarm on this score. Responding to Bill Gay's leadership, the aides became keen lobbyists for new men on the Medical Institute's executive committee. Howard Eckersley, when pressing Hughes to act on HHMI, silkily informed his boss that Holliday liked to drink, which left responsibility for the institute "in sometimes shaky hands."

Holliday, like Maheu before him, was rapidly moving into the Mormon-managed exclusion zone. When Hughes Tool was sold off a year later, Holliday would go with the company, leaving Hughes's employ. On February 21, 1971, Hughes finally made his decision and sent in the cavalry, appointing Chester Davis and Bill Gay to serve on the institute's executive committee alongside Holliday until he moved on.

Although neither could claim to have seen a Hughes will, both Davis and Gay—like all his entourage—would have assumed that the institute would one day control the whole Hughes empire. There was no reason, however, to suppose that the institute's executive committee would exercise that control. The revised bylaws specifically pared the executive committee's powers to a minimum. There was no provision for an executive committee role in what was called "the future"; in fact, if Hughes himself decided not to appoint a successor trustee, it seemed more than likely that the disposition of the institute on his death would be decided by the state of Delaware, where it was incorporated.

Out of this dilemma was born the Davis sentence, which closely resembled the Cook sentence in that it conferred the same powers on the executive committee in every important respect. The Cook sentence had caused Hughes to go on the rampage and dismantle the institute's administration, while the Davis sentence entered the bylaws without any hint of a demur from Hughes. It would first appear, neatly handwritten in blue ink by Nadine Henley, interlineated between two paragraphs in the bylaws fashioned by Holliday and Mintz.

The Delaware attorney general's office became convinced that the reason Hughes never kicked up a fuss about the Davis sentence was because he had no idea that it was going into the bylaws. All the evidence, as they saw it, pointed to the fact that the destiny of his $5 billion institute had been determined without his knowledge or consent.

In deposition testimony on this point, memories failed people. Bill Gay, for example, had no recollection whatsoever of the bylaw change that had ensured his governance of HHMI for seven years after Hughes's death. Taxed on the question of how he learned of the bylaws incorporating the Davis sentence, he was flummoxed. When told that Nadine Henley had probably sent them to him, nothing came back to him, as this exchange demonstrates:

Q: In any event, Mr. Gay, do you have any memory of ever having received a copy of that letter from Miss Henley?

A: No, sir, I do not.

Q: Do you have a memory of receiving at some point in 1971 a copy of the institute's bylaws from Miss Henley?

A: No, sir, I do not.

Q: Do you have a memory—let me ask you this: Do you deny receiving Plaintiff's Exhibit 1 [the bylaws incorporating the Davis sentence]?

A: No, no. That doesn't mean I did not receive it. It just means I don't have a memory of having received it.

Q: Do you have any memory at all of ever receiving a copy or seeing a copy of the institute bylaws in 1971?

A: No, sir, I do not.

Chester Davis's recall had been slightly better, but deeply puzzling. He remembered calling Hughes at the Britannia Beach Hotel in the Bahamas in the spring of 1971. It was a rather chaotic conversation, initially conducted through an aide. Hughes eventually came to the phone in a slightly grumpy condition. They had some talk about the bylaws and the trustee's succession, and Davis more or less "off the cuff" elaborated his sentence. Soon afterward, in a memo dated April 5, 1971, Davis sent Hughes the precise wording of his sentence. After that his involvement came to an abrupt end. He received no direct reply from Hughes to indicate whether or not his sentence had been approved. He just assumed it had been because, months later, he saw the "In the absence of" sentence incorporated into the bylaws.

So Davis, while readily acknowledging authorship, could shed no light whatsoever on how Hughes came to approve this momentous addition to the bylaws.

The person who should have known was Nadine Henley, who had originally achieved prominence as Hughes's personal secretary at the Romaine Street operations center in Los Angeles and who had a history of loyalty to both Hughes and the institute. Holliday called her "the mother superior" of the institute, though she preferred to be known as its "godmother." Henley was also known as Hughes's "eyes and ears" at the institute and since 1955 had regularly attended meetings of its Medical Advisory Committee. Apart from being the most knowledgeable of Hughes's executives on the past and present of the institute, she was also well versed in all the arguments about its "future."

Holliday relied heavily on Henley during his lone stewardship of HHMI, and she played the central role in the preparation and dissemination of the Holliday/Mintz bylaws into which she inserted the Davis sentence. She sent them out to the members of the executive committee—Holliday, Davis, and Gay—on July 16, 1971, with this note: "Attached is the signed Resolution of the Trustee of Howard Hughes Medical Institute adopting the By-laws of the Corporation, dated March 18, 1971, to which is attached the By-Laws consisting of 13 pages."

The attached bylaws included the "In the absence of" provision as part of the text, without any explanation. Another oddity in this communication was the date mentioned, March 18, when Hughes signed the resolution giving legal effect to the bylaws. There was no possibility of Hughes's having giving assent to the Davis sentence by that date, nor was there the possibility of Henley herself writing it by that date. Davis himself did not write it down until April 5, almost three weeks later. Henley's testimony of the subject of the "In the absence of" sentence was that it had been dictated to her by a lawyer and she "assumed" the lawyer was Chester Davis. But she was clear on the fact that she did not have it in hand before April.

Hughes had indeed signed the resolution on March 18 and for a very good reason. He was right up against the IRS deadline that required foundations that wished to remain tax exempt to make bylaw provisions guaranteeing the expenditure of contributions made. Accordingly, the IRS was assured in March that HHMI had the requisite bylaws in existence and in effect.

But no signature by Hughes on March 18 could conceivably ratify the "In the absence of" sentence, which had yet to come into existence. If the sentence was to have legal force, there would have to be some evidence of its adoption by Hughes after April 5. At this point the attorney general's lawyers, trying to piece together what went on, ran full-tilt into a void.

Despite Hughes's ill health and remoteness, there had been plentiful direct evidence of personal initiatives by him in relation to the Cook sentence, the Holliday/Mintz bylaws, and the Davis and Gay executive committee appointments. It was clear that institute affairs could still engage his attention. But on the subject of the Davis sentence there was nothing: the sound of silence.

Initially, it seemed as if Nadine Henley might fill the void. She was alleged to have prodigious powers of memory, and she would even commend herself on her own competence, volunteering that one of her nicknames was "Madame Nitpick." Henley was absolutely sure that she would not have sent out the bylaws with the "In the absence of" sentence without being assured that Hughes approved of them. This approval would necessarily have come through a third party. Henley, still based in California, had ceased having direct personal communication with Hughes years earlier, but she knew all those with the authority to pass on Hughes's directions. One of them had given her the go-ahead.

This emerged strongly in her deposition evidence:

Q: Do you have a recollection, as vague as it may be, that the problem with the bylaws was ultimately solved?

A: Well, it obviously was because we put them into effect. I mean I sent them to Holliday and put them into effect in July.

Q: You would not have done that unless someone who you believed knew what Mr. Hughes had authorized and told you he had authorized it; is that correct?

A: That's correct. That's correct.

The identity of the person who had transmitted Hughes's approval to Henley was naturally a matter of curiosity. But on this subject Henley's mind was an almost total blank.

Q: Do you remember from whom you learned that Mr. Hughes had approved the bylaws [containing the Davis sentence]?

A: I wish I did, but I don't.

This, of course, was the 5.2 billion-dollar question, and it would be put forth time and time again in slightly different forms. Henley remained firm in her position of nonrecall. But the constant repetition threw light on what probably happened as Henley was pressed to comment. Thus:

Q: At some point prior to your sending out your letter in July 1971, do you recall being informed by somebody that the by-laws had been approved by Mr. Hughes?

A: No, but I would have had to, to have sent that letter.

Q: And that would be by somebody who was in a position to know Mr. Hughes's directions; is that correct?

A: Yes, Chester or Holliday.

Q: Or one of the aides?

A: I would think the way he [Hughes] was working this with Chester that it would have been Chester or Holliday.

This would be refined slightly in another exchange on essentially the same question:

Q: I believe I asked before if you believed when you sent [the July letter] that the bylaws had been approved by Mr. Hughes, the bylaws which are part of that exhibit.

A: I am sure I did.

Q: And what was the source of your belief to that effect?

A: That I do not know.

Q: Do you have any recollection as to the source of that belief?

A: I am sorry I do not recall.

Q: Do you recall who asked you to send [the July letter, enclosing the bylaws with the Davis sentence] to Mr. Holliday, with copies to Mr. Gay and Mr. Davis, copies of these bylaws?

A: I would assume that Mr. Davis did.

Q: Do you have any recollection that Mr. Davis did?

A: No, sir.

Though more disjointed, this last exchange was perhaps the most revelatory:

> Q: Although you have no memory, you believe that you would not have mailed the July letter including the final bylaws had you not been told—
> A: I am sure I would not have.
> Q: —that Mr.—
> A: That is exactly what I'm saying.
> Q: —that Mr. Davis had notified Mr. Holliday that it was approved?
> A: Or me.

There could be no real doubt that Henley thought she received Hughes's okay to the Davis sentence from Davis himself, though her convoluted testimony did not preclude other possibilities. Of the possibilities Holliday and Gay, the two other institute committeemen, both testified that they had no knowledge of any approval given by Hughes. Mintz, the principal architect of the new bylaws, did not learn of how his draft had been topped up with the Davis sentence until months later. Most of Hughes's messages by this time would have been transmitted by aides, but no aide could be found who could remember transmitting his approval to the bylaws after April 5, 1971.

Davis, as one of the very few people able to talk directly to Hughes on the telephone, could have secured Hughes's assent without going through the aides. But Davis, on his own deposition testimony, never did this or indeed anything else to establish that Hughes approved his "In the absence of" sentence. This, in evidential terms, was what left the unfortunate Nadine Henley revolving slowly in the wind.

Had Davis lived long enough to occupy the witness box, his cross-examination would have been quite something to behold. Knowing that Howard Hughes detested the Cook sentence, how did Davis come to evolve the Davis sentence, which made essentially the same provision? Was it not true that the Davis sentence put Davis in the position to reap lifelong employment, enhanced law fees, and other fringe benefits, among them the control of a $5 billion foundation? And was it not true that Davis did so reap? Was it not a fact that in relation to the Davis sentence, Davis himself acted in much the same manner as a lawyer who writes a will for a client including himself as the main beneficiary? Was it not the case that Davis led Nadine Henley to believe that Howard Hughes had given his assent to the Davis sentence when no such assent had ever been given?

No one can know what Davis would have said, but the Delaware court would deal with many of these questions. In his long written judgment, delivered in December 1983, Chancellor Grover C. Brown said of Henley's evidence, "In all probability someone gave her the go-ahead to include the [Davis] sentence in the bylaws, but it does not necessarily go on to establish that Hughes gave his word of approval to whoever it was who gave the word to her." Brown refrained from direct speculation on the identity of the "whoever," but elsewhere in his judgment he laid heavy emphasis on that fact that in the early stages of bylaw preparation Henley was "apparently seeking approval at that time from Davis, not Hughes."

On the main issue before the court, Chancellor Brown simply concluded: "Hughes never adopted the 'In the absence of' sentence."

The immediate consequence of this decision was a hunt for new trustees who had to be approved by the Delaware court. The court recognized that a "caretaker" role had been previously played by the Davis and Gay executive committee but its authority was now at an end. Another casualty of the decision was the Davis and Gay vote abolishing the office of Trustee, part of the strategy to fight off Will Lummis. This was deemed to be an infringement of the Institute's original certificate of incorporation. It was therefore declared void.

The Delaware court would later seek safety in numbers by appointing nine trustees to run the Medical Institute. Seven of them were leading figures in the worlds of medicine, business, and academic administration. The court would also, perhaps with a touch of humor, anoint two further trustees with some grounding in the institute's storm-tossed past. Their names were Will Lummis and Bill Gay.

According to one of his Houston lawyer friends, Lummis planned to have Gay made the trustee "responsible for emptying the wastepaper baskets." But Lummis could afford to be magnanimous.

For Lummis the Delaware court decision represented the culmination of a year of achievement. Terry Moore had been bought off; the last embers of the lost will case had been stamped out in the Texas appeal court, and the heirs had actually got some money from the Hughes estate—$16 million split in twenty-two directions.

After seven years of waiting, this was enough to appease, though scarcely enough to excite. The vast bulk of The Money was still held back. But the mere fact that there had been any distribution at all showed that Lummis was beginning to feel confident about the outcome of the final battle with his cousin Howard's oldest enemy—the tax man.

17

TAX MAN

ONE OF THE main problems with Howard Hughes's highly per-
sonalized, deeply unstructured business empire was that nobody
really knew overall what was going on. Only Hughes knew and, as
he got deeper into drugs, he didn't know either.

After his death this created a legacy of uncertainty, not only for
Lummis and the estate but also for the teams of hovering tax men,
both state and federal. And the level of trust that existed between
the various parties was not spectacularly high.

Around the time that Merrill Lynch produced its $168 million
valuation of the Hughes empire for probate, the California inheritance tax referee did some figuring on his own. The sum he came
up with as the correct valuation for the Hughes assets was seven
times as much—$1,106,345,516.

A very small part of this discrepancy could be attributed to the
late discovery of some assets. It was some months before the estate
realized that Hughes had stashed well over $60 million in various
bank accounts. Pinning down the exact location of all of Hughes's

real estate took years, and it was almost a decade before Lummis realized the estate had a functioning oil well tucked away in Louisiana. But even with a generous allowance for such items, the gap was still huge. In fact, neither estimate bore much resemblance to any final assessment, but the gap between them was a yardstick of the extent of suspicion at the time.

Anything to do with Howard Hughes was suspect in a tax man's eyes. His tax phobia was legendary. When a journalist reported that a major Nevada nuclear test had prompted the billionaire to dive under his bed, Nadine Henley scoffed, "The only thing that could send Mr. Hughes into hiding under his bed is the approach of a tax collector." Lummis was no Hughes in this respect, but he did have a powerful motive to minimize tax impact on the estate.

When Lummis applied his calculator to the California estimate, he came up with a minimum death tax bill of around $763 million. This, he thought, was a tallish order for an estate that he had been told was worth less than $170 million. If this was the situation, Lummis perceived that his best course of action as administrator would be to wind everything up promptly, close the office, and go fly-fishing.

But it was not the situation, as was well known to all parties. What was taking place was an exercise in which bluff and counterbluff were as important as ostensibly objective calculations. The whole tax-gathering enterprise was like a marathon game of poker, played with vigor and even some finesse.

The original hand dealt to Lummis was an intriguing one. If he could get Nevada accepted as Hughes's domicile, the estate would not be obliged to pay any state inheritance tax at all, though it would still be subject to federal inheritance taxes, which could go as high as 77 percent. If the courts held that Texas was Hughes's domicile, however, it would have to pay a 16 percent death tax in that state. And if California successfully asserted that Hughes had been domiciled there, it would ask for 24 percent of the estate.

Thus, if both Texas and California stuck rigidly to their domicile claims, Hughes's estate could face a combined federal and state tax assessment of around 117 percent. There would be a 16 percent federal tax credit in the event of full payment of state taxes, but even with this concession the total tax would come to 101 percent.

The prospect of Hughes's estate being totally obliterated by tax with no money for the heirs and no business left worth speaking of was in no way illusory. Nevada domicile and the clement Merrill Lynch valuation were basically Lummis's opening bids in the game, a mark of what he wanted rather than what he expected to get. He would play the Nevada card for all it was worth, even to the extent of recruiting Dr. Thain as one of his key supporting witnesses. Dr. Thain was ready to testify that Hughes had asked him to take out a Nevada medical license so that "I can take care of him when he goes home to Nevada." His impression on his patient's final choice of domicile was that "Nevada was Hughes's first choice, Houston was the second choice, Canada was his third choice—he never mentioned California at all."

Even so, it became evident that Nevada was not going to deflect the other states from asserting their claims. Since Nevada would not gain anything in taxes, whatever the outcome, it was not highly motivated. Texas and California, on the other hand, were. State officials who had observed Hughes trying, usually successfully, to live in a tax-free nowhere for most of his existence were reluctant to be denied now that he could be defined, albeit posthumously, as a regular taxpayer.

The definition necessarily turned on what was meant by domicile, a concept hard to apply to a man who lived much of his life in hotel rooms. Legal domicile indicated a deeper attachment to a place than the simple fact of residence. It implied a physical presence in a place with the idea of remaining there permanently. Domicile could be changed, but only by establishing the same intention in another place. If no such intention could be discerned in a person's life, then he or she remained controlled by their domicile of origin. According to Texas judge Gregory's reading of the law: "An individual is born with a domicile, and they keep that domicile by never intending to formulate a new one."

This formula created wonderful conflicts when applied to the life of Howard Hughes. In Texas, Attorney General Hill's office had no problem establishing that Hughes had been born and raised in the state. But had he maintained that domicile of origin? Great, even prodigious, ingenuity was devoted to providing an affirmative answer to this question for the benefit of the probate court. The massive research effort carried out by Rick Harrison, Hill's energetic assistant, was almost all directed to proving that Hughes could not—voluntarily at least—have intended to reside permanently anywhere but in his home state.

Much emphasis was laid on the "Texanness" that Hughes exhibited after he left the state. Perhaps the most potent evidence to this effect was the speech he made in 1938 on a brief visit to Houston to attend the celebration of his record-breaking around-the-world flight. Brief, laconic, and quintessentially Texan, it went:

"If you don't believe I wrote this myself, just try to read the handwriting. Coming from Texas, particularly if it's a person flying around the world, there is nothing you can see anywhere that you can't see in Texas. After you have flown across Texas two or three times the distance around the world doesn't seem so great. We didn't see any mountains on our trip that were any steeper than the mountains in West Texas. We didn't see any plains that were any broader than the plains of central Texas, and we didn't see any swamps that were any wetter than the swamps of Southeast Texas."

It also seemed that many years spent in California had not rendered him any less Texan. In evidence of this the court was asked to review testimony given in the rather unsavory 1952 case involving Paul Jarrico, a left-wing screenwriter who had been sacked by Hughes for not cooperating with the House Committee on Un-American Activities. Hughes had been asked, "Where do you live?" by Jarrico's attorney, Edward Mosk. This turned out to be a rather complicated question.

A: Do you mean my domicile or present location?
Q: Where do you live?
A: Well, I still ask you, do you mean my legal domicile or where I am living at present?
Q: Where are you living at the present time?

A: Well, I spent last night at the Beverly Hills Hotel.
Q: Do you consider that to be your home, Mr. Hughes?
A: Not my legal domicile, no.
Q: What is your legal domicile?
A: Well, I consider that to be Houston, Texas.

Hughes had no home in Texas at the time and had not maintained one there for twenty-five years. He had kept his parents'
home on Houston's Yoakum Boulevard for a while, but he had
given the house, with all its effects, to his Aunt Annette soon after
he effectively left Texas in 1927. He did, however, maintain one
connection with his home state throughout his life. His uninfor-
mative personal income-tax returns were filed regularly as clock-
work in Austin, Texas. Even in the years when his companies were
raking in megamillions, Hughes would submit personal income
statements in the region of $20,000 a year. Hughes, of course,
never required his companies to pay him very much. His identity
was bound up with their prestige and growth, and his peripatetic
needs were supplied as a business expense and were deductible.
But it was clear that Hughes's attachment to his home state went
deeper than a tax return. Indeed, its cultural imprint would mark
his last promise to Dr. Thain to give up drugs on his word as "a
Texas gentleman."

Yet it was hard to conceive of Hughes being domiciled in Texas
in any real sense. After the 1938 visit, which lasted less than two
days, he was not seen in Texas again until 1949, when he flew in
to deliver an airplane and stayed for a few hours. He was back
again in 1956 when his plane, en route from Florida to California,
stopped to refuel. Hughes never left the plane. For the last twenty
years of his life, Hughes never set foot in Texas.

As far as California was concerned, the Texas domiciliary hearings amounted to a gigantic bluff. They were a route to the tax
dollars in the Hughes estate, tax dollars that could logically all
come to California.

By California's calculation Hughes had spent less than one week
in Texas in the last fifty years of his life. Against that, Hughes had

spent almost forty of those years in California. For twenty of them, he had even disciplined himself to the extent of keeping a home on Muirfield Road, Los Angeles, where he had lived something resembling family life with the first Mrs. Hughes and subsequently with Katharine Hepburn.

California was where Hughes had made his money in movies, aviation, and electronics. California was where Hughes had lived relatively openly throughout the most creative period of his life. There could indeed be uncertainty about Hughes having had any credible domicile after he left California—flitting from one darkened hotel room to another in Las Vegas, the Bahamas, London, Vancouver, Managua, and Acapulco—but California certainly became Hughes's domicile after he left Texas.

When all efforts to delay the Texas domiciliary hearings failed, California decided to take its aggravation to the Supreme Court of the United States in a complaint simply entitled *State of California* v. *State of Texas*. The California controller, Kenneth Cory, who prepared the action, announced that the two states were on a "collision course."

For Lummis the falling-out between the two states offered what seemed to be a matchless opportunity. For one thing it was bound to create delay, giving him much more time to repair the ravaged fortunes of Summa before the really big tax bills came in. The other advantage was more specific. California had originally seemed to be the more belligerent state on the tax issue, but in a legal fight with Texas it needed effective allies. In point of fact, it needed Lummis.

Before the action was publicly launched, Lummis and Cory met in secret session to work out a formula that would give a measure of security to both parties. Cory was disturbed by the apparent "rush to judgment" in the Texas domiciliary hearings and firm in his opinion that "Howard Hughes was domiciled in California and that the division of his estate ought to reflect that fact." With Lummis's cooperation he perceived a way of heading Texas off at the pass.

The agreement devised by Cory and Lummis was conditional upon a judgment in the Supreme Court that Hughes was not domiciliary in Texas at the time of his death. This was something that

California meant to prove to the court's satisfaction with the wealth of depositions and other testimony previously assembled by Lummis and the estate's lawyers.

The deal was that California would drop its inheritance-tax claim from the standard 24 percent to 18 percent in the event of California or indeed anywhere other than Texas being established as the domicile, but it would still get 2 percent even if Texas was upheld. From Cory's point of view, this guarded against the possibility of California coming up empty-handed. Whatever the court decided, all his bets were covered.

From Lummis's standpoint he was losing out on the highly unlikely Nevada option but gaining hugely in other directions. The proposed reduction in California's tax demand was significant, but much more important was the prospect of the Supreme Court nominating a single domicile, thereby finally eliminating the threat of double taxation. It was a sinuous maneuver of which Howard Hughes himself might have been proud.

When the deal became public with the commencement of the action, Lummis said: "The administrators of the estate have consented by the agreement to incur a maximum tax against the estate of 79 percent, to avoid the specter of a tax of 101 percent. It's just that simple."

Simple it may have been, but the Texans were much more impressed by the fact that it seemed to be an arrangement essentially designed to benefit California and "disbenefit" Texas. On this interpretation Lummis was simply cooperating with the enemy. Relations between Lummis and Attorney General Hill's office, which had taken a turn for the better after Chester Davis had been booted out of Summa, went back into the freezer.

Things might have deteriorated even further but for the shrewd inaction of the Supreme Court. After the opening salvos had been fired, the court backed off sharply from any notion of trying the case, at least in the short term. In its advisory opinion the Supreme Court counseled that the interests of all the parties might be better served by an "interpleader action," a conciliatory legal proceeding designed to consolidate conflicting claims. Basically, the court was telling California and Texas to go away and have a good talk about it all and to try, if at all possible, not to come back.

While Texas and California were wrangling with each other, the men from the IRS were quietly going about their business. The IRS's job was not merely to collect the federal tax but also to provide, for legal and tax purposes, the official gross determination of the value of the Hughes estate at the time of his death. And it took this part of its responsibilities very seriously indeed.

Within the Hughes estate, inheritance-tax issues were handled principally by Bill Miller, with help from Charles McMillan, a Summa accountant, and a small team of assistants. They would all become widely traveled. From the outset the IRS made it clear that it was not interested in a Merrill Lynch–type valuation that involved making a general judgment of what the Hughes empire could fetch, as a single entity, on the market. It wanted to inspect each and every asset (and liability) in the empire's far-flung sixteen divisions and appraise it piece by piece. With Bill Miller or one of his team acting as travel guides, this was precisely what the IRS did.

It was a slow process, but by 1981 the IRS had arrived at an estimated gross value of $460 million, almost three times the Merrill Lynch valuation but less than half the figure conjectured by California. This implied a minimum federal inheritance tax of $275 million. Lummis felt this was still far too high, and the estate formally contested the IRS figures. Lummis by now had given up all hope of engendering any official enthusiasm for the Merrill Lynch valuation, but the IRS might still be persuaded to chip away at many of the individual items in its valuation package.

The estate had developed its own itemized estimates to set beside those of the IRS, and most of them certainly gave the appearance of being open to further negotiation and compromise. In fact, the distance between the estimates was sometimes so great as to be almost laughable.

The Silver Slipper Casino in Las Vegas, beset with legal problems, was valued by the estate at one dollar; the IRS reckoned it was worth $5.5 million. The Air West airline, also saddled with legal difficulties, was valued by the estate at $842,000. The IRS said $7 million.

The seventy-five thousand shares in Summa, all of which were owned by the estate, were valued by the estate at $108 million. The IRS thought that $396 million was a more realistic figure. A cardboard box full of old gambling chips, no longer any use for live action, was, the estate reckoned, worth $64. The IRS said $320. The closest the two sides came was over the value of three of Hughes's old movies—*Jet Pilot, The Outlaw,* and *The Conqueror.* The estate said they were worth $225,000; the IRS said they were worth twice as much.

The final session in this game would not be played until three years later when Bill Miller and his team went up against Rocky Venden, the IRS chief of appeals, and his men in Houston's federal courthouse on July 24, 1984. By this time there had been a lot of give (mainly by the estate) and a lot of take (mainly by the IRS) in valuation terms, and both sides were keen to secure an agreed settlement.

According to one of Miller's team, an interesting procedural method was evolved in an effort to surmount the final hurdle. Both sides wanted to avoid another tedious session of haggling over the value of individual assets that could, if unleashed, put everybody back to square one. After a morning of polite exchanges, it was therefore resolved that each side should spend its lunch hour figuring out the gross valuation each could live with—the upper limit in the case of the estate, the lowest as far as the IRS was concerned. Each would write this figure on an index card and keep it to themselves until after lunch. The theory was that the idea could work only if the figures were disclosed as close to the same time as possible. Without this feature the IRS was almost bound to try to leapfrog any initial proposal by the estate, while the estate was just as likely to try to undercut any original figure the IRS put up.

The afternoon session formally commenced with the synchronized slapping down of index cards. There was just $6 million between the two figures, which did not leave a whole lot that needed to be talked about. And when one representative of the IRS growled, "No way are we splitting the difference," there was literally nothing more to be said. For the IRS at least, the poker game was at an end. It left the estate with an official gross valuation of $361,704,267—higher than Lummis had hoped for but a lot lower than he had feared.

On August 29, 1984, just over a month later, California and Texas announced the outbreak of peace on the death-tax issue. The parties had been back to the Supreme Court on three separate occasions for guidance and interpretation on procedural matters, but both sides had balked at forcing the issue there. There was always the nagging worry about the consequences, for one or the other, of a winner-take-all decision by the court. This kept the two states on speaking terms—just. Finally, the court assigned University of Michigan law professor Wade McCree to the task of overseeing the dispute, and with his help the two states reached an accord. The final document recording their agreement was three inches thick, but its content could be briefly summarized—basically, Texas got the glory and California got the money.

Hughes's Texas domicile was mutually recognized, and Texas was awarded $50 million in inheritance tax to go with it. California contented itself with the lion's share of the inheritance-tax allocation—some $119 million. Included in this figure was $7 million for attorney costs in the long controversy over domicile and tax.

At the press conference in Austin, announcing the deal, it was revealed that the breakthrough had come when the two states had decided to stop bickering about domicile and simply address themselves to the fairest way of chopping up the money between them. The new Texas attorney general, Jim Mattox, declared himself well pleased with the way his state had come out of it: "To get fifty million dollars out of a case when the old boy hadn't been here but for forty-eight hours in the last fifty years of his life, hell, that ain't a bad deal. Our theory was 'Once a Texan, always a Texan.' "

Will Lummis, the other Texan on the platform, wore a slightly pained expression through it all, but he did manage to express himself "content" on behalf of the estate. He also said: "It's hard to say you are elated, but it's a good compromise."

In fact, this was almost precisely the outcome that Lummis had maneuvered to avoid, a double tax bite by two of America's largest and most powerful states. But there were compensations. Originally, Texas and California had envisaged a combined tax levy in the region of $250 million, but the estate had been able to reduce this, partly as a result of the IRS scaling down its determination of value. Moreover, it was agreed that the state taxes could be paid gradually over three years, and, in the case of California, over half the amount owed was paid off not with money but with real estate. In addition, Bill Miller had alertly ensured that almost 80 percent of the state tax bill could be classified as interest. Such interest was conveniently deductible against federal tax.

Meanwhile, Lummis had already ensured that the estate stayed on the side of the IRS by making substantial payments even before full liability was determined. Though the estate would not make its final IRS payment until some years later, this, in outline, was the inheritance-tax picture at the end of 1984:

Total estate value for federal tax purposes	$361,704,267
Federal government taxes prepaid	$147 million
Texas tax including interest	$50 million
California tax including interest	$119 million
Total inheritance taxes	$316 million

On the face of it, it looks as if the estate was not that far from obliteration by tax. But appearances in this case are wholly deceptive. This is mainly because the Hughes estate of 1984 was radically different from the eccentric enterprise of 1976 that provided the basis for inheritance-tax assessment. By the mid-1980s the estate was worth not $361 million but close to a billion dollars. Not only could it face what looked like enormous tax bills with equanimity, it could stay in business and make the heirs rich beyond any normal dream of avarice.

This remarkable transformation was effected by Will Lummis with the help of Howard Hughes, as his abiding exemplar on how not to run a modern business corporation.

18

THE MONEY REBORN

WILL LUMMIS HIMSELF was never particularly illuminating on the subject of how he turned the derelict Hughes empire into a money-spinner. When asked by rock-ribbed Republican acquaintances how it was done, he was inclined to tease them by saying how useful the inflation under Jimmy Carter had been.

Inflation, undoubtedly, did play a part by helping to distend the apparent value of the estate under Lummis and by helping to reduce the value, in real terms, of the tax dollars paid out. But it was never a major factor. The key to Lummis's success was the fact that he was able to give a sense of direction to a business empire that had existed without one for years. This would be something that even his sternest critics in the Texas attorney general's office came to admire. "Lummis has done a very good job," said Assistant Attorney General Rick Harrison as early as 1980. "He's flat turned that company around."

Chester Davis had said that Lummis would rapidly damage Summa's interests by selling off its main assets on the cheap. This proved wide of the mark. In the long term Lummis certainly intended selling off as much as was necessary to satisfy the tax men and appease the heirs but not in a way that gave the appearance of a fire sale of assets. His aim was to sell the ones that could be developed at the very top of the market, and this he almost invariably achieved.

In pursuit of this strategy, Lummis was to some degree assisted by the tax laws. One of these allowed inheritance taxes to be paid over a ten-year period when a closely held corporation constituted a major part of the estate. Its purpose was to give such entities a chance to pay the tax out of profits without being forced into liquidation. Lummis would exploit this useful regulation to the limit and beyond. The estate would not settle its final inheritance-tax bill until August 1989, over thirteen years after Hughes's death.

The other clemency in the tax laws was that once the value of an estate was determined, it could not be frivolously revised as a result of subsequent good fortune. Thus, if a man inherited a cabbage patch and had its value assessed by the IRS at normal cabbage-patch rates, the IRS could not come back and reassess it if the man subsequently struck oil under the cabbages. In terms of the Hughes estate, this meant that if it could metaphorically strike oil with some of its disparate assets, it could enrich the estate without imperiling its inheritance-tax position. Lummis became adept at prospecting in this area.

Lummis viewed the estate as dynamic, using its money to make money, as opposed to a static entity, simply doling funds out to creditors. Another Houston lawyer, who also did estate administration work, said: "If they'd given the administration to a bank, they would have cleared it all up in a couple of years. Taxes paid, liabilities settled, and maybe a few peanuts for the heirs. But Lummis hung in and really appreciated the value. He made an adventure out of it."

The adventure began with the trashing of many interests that Hughes once held dear. His Summa legacy of sixteen ill-fitting business lines, operating on an unplanned and generally unprofitable basis, never made much corporate sense, nor were they designed to. They were the organizational consequences of Hughes's fancies, sometimes abiding but more often fitful. There were some that even Bill Gay and Chester Davis could not defend as being in any way businesslike.

Lummis quietly bulldozed Summa's chaos—killing or selling off assets that seemed incapable of being groomed. These included an ocean-mining division that had provided a front for the CIA's *Glomar Explorer* sublifting mission, a Las Vegas TV station (bought to provide Hughes himself with a diet of all-night movies), a tabloid football newspaper, a sports telecasting network, three thousand inactive mining claims, a few ranches, a warehouse, and a sign-rental firm. While freely acknowledging that many of these things "reflected the personal interests of Mr. Hughes," Lummis saw no reason to apologize for getting rid of them.

After Davis and Gay had also been bulldozed, Lummis believed that Summa could reap rich rewards simply by behaving more like any other business corporation. This implied reducing it to the core of enterprises with profit potential and furnishing new managers with clear lines of communication and authority. Into the welcome void created by Davis's and Gay's departures, Lummis introduced James A. Cox, an experienced accountant who also happened to be the brother of Archibald Cox, the Watergate special prosecutor. Lummis and Cox reorganized Summa into three main baronies—hotels and casinos, aviation and aircraft construction, and real estate—and it promptly began to make money.

In 1978 Summa registered a profit, the first since its creation, earning $30.9 million on sales of $763 million. Sales went up sharply again in 1979, but a strike at Hughes Air West reduced the scale of the profits. Lummis was not taking the risk of having that happen again, so he sold Air West (valued by the IRS at $7 million on Hughes's death) to Republic Airlines, Inc. for $38.5 million.

Lummis's great aerial coup, however, came through his management of Hughes's helicopter division, one of the great loss makers of all time and one of the few defense establishments that could claim to have been actually impoverished by the Vietnam War. Eager to get back into aircraft construction after his failures in World War II, Hughes had deliberately authorized below-cost

pricing for his OH–6 reconnaissance helicopter in negotiations
with the federal government. This gave him a competitive edge
over close rivals and the contract. Hughes's thinking was that once
the machine was in production, he would be able to jack up the
price. But serious production delays, at a time when the war was
at its bloodiest, hardened the government's attitude. No price rise
was allowed, and Hughes Helicopters found itself obliged to churn
out hundreds of machines at a loss of $62,000 apiece. In the space
of three years, from 1967 to the end of 1969, the company lost
over $100 million. Since then it had limped along, managing to
stay in business by supplementing its military work with the man-
ufacture of small machines for the police and for agricultural uses.
Meanwhile, employment at the factory plummeted—from fifty-
five hundred in 1969 to a little over a thousand.

When Lummis assumed responsibility for the company, he was
advised by Jack Real, Hughes's old Lockheed pal, to do himself a
serious favor and sell Hughes Helicopters before it nose-dived any
further. The value put on Hughes Helicopters at that time was $17
million, one of the few figures not seriously contested by the IRS.

The conventional wisdom was that Hughes Helicopters, with its
proven record of being able to lose money at record-breaking
speed, could eat up the rest of the estate. This aspect came into
even sharper focus in late 1976 when, against all the odds, a
Hughes Helicopter Company prototype won out in competition
with Textron Inc.'s Bell Helicopters to become the front-runner for
the biggest helicopter contract in the Pentagon's gift since the Vietnam War.

The Hughes AH–64 tank-destroying helicopter, which would
later become more familiarly known as the Apache helicopter in
the Gulf War, immediately put Lummis on the spot. He could take
the immediately profitable low-risk option of selling off Hughes
Helicopters for a good deal more than $17 million. On the other
hand, if it could actually land the Pentagon's final production contract, he could think in terms of selling it for hundreds of millions.
But the process of getting the run-down company up to scratch,
producing the three more prototypes required and getting it into a

full production mode, would take a hundred or more million of Summa's cash, which Summa didn't have.

Lummis was not a gambling man, but as one of the estate lawyers put it, "He blew on his fist and rolled the dice on this one." Lummis resolved the liquidity crisis by creating a potential debt crisis, opening up a $125 million line of credit with the Bank of America, with Summa acting as its guarantor. He also prevailed upon the originally skeptical Jack Real to take on the job as Hughes Helicopter's new chief executive, with felicitous consequences. The final production order came through in 1982, and Lummis later confessed his relief: "If that contract had been canceled, I'd have got on a plane and headed west, and never come back."

Lummis never went in for much in the way of public rejoicing, rarely granting interviews and, when he did, he tended to deliberately underplay his abilities. He was inclined to emphasize that he was no more than an amateur at business and lament his lack of training "as a corporate administrator" which, he said, made it all a bit of a strain. One of his closest friends, however, was of the opinion that "Will had a lot more fun out of all this than he liked to admit." And, as the worry drained out of the helicopter venture, Lummis did begin to exhibit modest symptoms of exuberance.

A stern critic of wastefully expensive business trips, Lummis nonetheless thought that it was his duty to attend the early gyrations of his helicopter at the Paris Air Show, although there was not much he could profitably do there. After being taken aloft by one of the pilots, he was asked to give his considered opinion of the AH–64's performance. "It's a great machine," said Lummis, "but right now I need a drink."

Ultimately, of course, it was the helicopter's financial performance that counted, and this, too, proved quite intoxicating. In 1984 Hughes Helicopters was sold to McDonnell Douglas for $470 million, which, allowing for the funds Lummis put into it, gave the estate a return of almost $300 million.

The helicopter story would be described by Bill Miller as "Lummis's home run," but his performance in other areas, though less spectacular, was impressive. His idea of turning a gamekeeper into a game-runner by appointing Phil Hannifin, former chairman of the Nevada Gaming Control Board, as Summa's hotels and casinos boss soon produced more attractive balance sheets. By 1979 the hotel casino division had reemerged as the group's largest moneymaker, earning $38.7 million.

To achieve this some staff changes had proved necessary, but these were almost all at the top. Some of Bill Gay's men were eased out to give elbowroom for Hannifin's recruits, who included two hard-nosed executives from Caesars Palace and a professor of casino management from the University of Nevada. Each was assigned a casino. For the first time in many years, Hughes's gaming operation was actually being run by people who were as smart as the smartest punters.

The casinos-hotels strategy combined the dumping of ineffective parts with a general program of nursing the rest of the operation back to health. The Landmark Hotel and Casino, an uncompleted hulk that had not turned a profit since Hughes acquired it back in 1969, was the first to go. Hughes had parted with $17 million for it in his money-is-no-object Las Vegas buying binge, but Lummis was thankful to get $12.5 million for it from a Kansas-based investment group. It took another surefire loser off his books.

Other properties eventually deemed surplus to requirements were the Xanadu Princess Hotel in the Bahamas, the Castaways in Las Vegas, which yielded almost $50 million, and the Silver Slipper, which Summa had valued for probate at one dollar. Eventually, the legal controversies over the Silver Slipper's lease would be resolved making it a useful earner and, when it was sold off in 1983, it brought in $11.5 million.

In other areas Lummis was, to some extent, beholden to Bill Gay and Chester Davis. Their last boardroom hurrah at Summa had committed Lummis to the investment of almost $50 million in the Desert Inn, Hughes's ailing flagship. Though enraged by this original decision, Lummis did see most of the renovation program through and, as the casinos became profitable, he would even extend its range. Harold's Club in Reno, and Summa's two other Las

Vegas casinos—the Sands and the Frontier—would have their appearance enhanced by development funds.

Lummis, nonetheless, was never entirely at home with his reputation as a gaming supremo. Though he had come to recognize gambling as one of Summa's core profit-making activities, his attention was more strongly engaged by something in which Hughes had taken almost no interest at all, namely, his land. The estate owned vast undeveloped swatches of it in California, Nevada, and Arizona. Hughes had bought it in manic phases of acquisition and left it neglected.

The twelve-thousand-acre tract in Tucson, Arizona, had originally been purchased when Hughes had a mind to move Hughes Aircraft out of California. He had even ordered Bob Maheu to purchase three houses in the Tucson area as suitable personal residences for himself. This would come to nothing but would provide a sizable windfall for the estate. When the IRS began to exert pressure for early payment, Lummis sold the Arizona holdings for $75 million.

In most cases, however, Lummis recognized that the land was not readily transferable into cash and that the way to release its enormous potential value was to put things on it. With John L. Goolsby, a lanky, soft-spoken Texan with an intimate knowledge of the property market who had joined Summa in 1980, Lummis began to put together some creative projects. To finance their ideas Lummis and Goolsby had no hesitation in going against Hughes's aversion to business partnerships. Indeed, joint ventures were central in much of what they did.

By inviting others to do the developing while retaining title to the land itself, Summa became more of a landlord than an entrepreneur. "What we are doing," said Goolsby, "is creating an investment base for the company."

It proved to be a wide base. In Nevada Goolsby had twenty-five thousand acres to play with extending from the foothills of the Red Rock Mountains to the western edge of Las Vegas. Hughes had acquired most of the land in a swap deal with the federal government back in the late 1940s. His original plan had been to make it the site of a laboratory for Hughes Aircraft, but he abandoned this idea. The land—which became known as Husite—remained much as it had been when the Paiute Indians roamed across it.

Goolsby developed Husite as a planned community called Summerlin (named for Hughes's grandmother). It combined office space, homes, a golf course, and schools. It was a long-term program, but realization of its early stages, at a cost to Summa of some $40 million, had a magical effect on the land's cash value. According to local developers, a one-acre parcel of prime Husite, worth perhaps $20,000 when Hughes died, would achieve a value of almost $90,000 as part of Summerlin. Goolsby also made extensive developments on valuable Hughes sites in the Las Vegas city center and out by the city's McCarran airport. These also extended the investment base.

In Los Angeles there would be scope for the Howard Hughes Center, an office and hotel development on a seventy-acre tract bordering the San Diego Freeway. But the prime project involved the nearby 1,200-acre Playa Vista site in the affluent Playa del Rey section. For years the land had sat there, visible from LAX-bound planes as a great green oasis near the Pacific, a verdant anomaly in a hectic metropolis. Like the *Spruce Goose,* which had been manufactured nearby, it was impressive but without any immediately discernible logic.

Potentially the most valuable of all Hughes's properties, Playa Vista would prove the most difficult to develop. The city authorities, initially welcoming, began to fret about the potential for traffic gridlock created by a fresh clump of office blocks and nine thousand new homes, while a vigorous environmental group sprang to the defense of the Ballona wetlands, a seawater marsh that was part of the site. It was a frustration for Lummis, but Goolsby was confident that they would soon find a way.

As the tenth anniversary of Howard Hughes's death—April 5, 1986—approached, Lummis had many grounds for self-congratulation. He had outmaneuvered all his corporate enemies. Though Chester Davis, the fiercest of them all, had died in 1983, his law firm litigated aggressively on, but Lummis finally laid even this to rest with an inexpensive settlement. He had wrestled the threat of cataclysmic tax demands down to a proportion that the estate could comfortably digest. He had turned a money-guzzling business into a confident money-maker. And, as a direct consequence, he had more than doubled the value of the estate.

As the lineaments of this financial miracle became apparent, national magazines from *Business Week* to *Time* would write articles lauding Summa's achievement, saying things about Lummis that the diffident man would not dream of saying about himself.

At this high point in his public esteem, Lummis's life was reentered by George Dean, his old comrade in arms in Summa's greatest corporate battles. And Dean blew his old friend a loud raspberry.

19

THE FALL AND RISE OF HUMPTY DUMPTY

WHEN GEORGE DEAN retired from the legal fray at the age of fifty-four, he had two excellent reasons for never working again. For one thing his health was uncertain, and an artificial heart valve combined with a pacemaker provided a constant reminder of this fact. For another he knew that if he could live long enough, there was no way he could avoid becoming a multimillionaire.

Dean's original arrangement to represent Mrs. Avis Hughes McIntyre and her brother Rush Hughes, who had become legally approved heirs on the strength of their equitable adoption by Howard Hughes's Uncle Rupert, was on a contingency basis. With such an arrangement, a lawyer agrees to forgo regular fees in exchange for a proportion—commonly between a half and a third— of the client's ultimate cash award. The predicted final payout for the Hughes heirs was in the region of $500 million, and the terms of the agreement between the heirs accorded 9.5 percent to Mrs. McIntyre and her recently deceased brother's estate—around $48 million. The exact percentage of Dean's contingency was probably the only subject Dean was ever coy about. But even if the figure was at the lower end of the scale, Dean's legal team would wind up with $16 million.

In the meantime, he was not at all short of money of his own. His five years as Will Lummis's adviser, court jester, and friend during the fiercest battles for Summa had provided a lucrative finale to a busy career. And in 1983, when Dean put all the sound and the fury behind him to start a new life in Chestertown, a peaceful colonial town on the banks of Maryland's Chester River, Lummis was among his warmest well-wishers. It was generally agreed among the estate's lawyers that no man was more deserving of a quiet and restful retirement.

It was not long before news started filtering back to Houston and Las Vegas that Dean was again causing trouble, and in a totally unexpected way. Instead of quietly blending into the restrained, academic surroundings—Chestertown is best known as the home of Washington College—he rapidly earned himself a reputation as an aggressive, insensitive nouveau riche. One conservative inhabitant was quoted in the local press as saying: "Damn George Dean! If I had a cannon, I'd blast him out of town."

Much of the specific resentment could be traced to the Imperial Hotel, an exquisite turn-of-the-century building that Dean acquired, refurbished, and ran in distinctive style. The cuisine excited some favorable comment, but Dean himself had little of the obsequiousness expected of a trained hotelier. One offended lady customer told Dean that she was writing to all her friends advising them to take their business elsewhere. Dean offered to supply the stamps for this operation.

People were also upset by Dean's noisy involvement in renovation projects in the run-down areas of town. "We have our roots here," sniffed one of the town's father figures. "He is trying to buy his." Though not without allies among what might be termed Chestertown's progressive element, it was certainly true that Dean was laying out a great deal of money and that not a lot was coming back.

The restoration of the Imperial Hotel alone had absorbed $2.5 million, of which $750,000 was put up by Dean personally. In

1985 it registered a loss of $198,000. Though still affluent, Dean wearied of being a multimillionaire-in-waiting and wanted to become one in the immediate present. He reached for the Hughes money tree and gave it a vigorous shake.

Until the spring of 1986, there had been no public criticism of Will Lummis's administration of the estate by the heirs; indeed, showing any impatience was frowned upon for tactical as well as social reasons. Patience about The Money had served them well down a long road littered with the burned-out cases of noisier claimants. But the journey had not been without stress. As the estate's value edged up toward the magic billion-dollar figure, it was obvious that the heirs' expectations were still a long way short of fulfillment. After the initial distribution of $16 million in 1983, there had been another in 1984 of $75 million, carefully divided, in accordance with the agreed Lummis formula, of 71½ percent to the maternal heirs and 28½ percent to the paternals.

But there had been no distribution in 1985 and nothing in the early months of 1986. The estate was digesting the consequences of the big tax decisions, and Lummis, as ever, was advising patience.

On the tenth anniversary of Hughes's death, Dean broke ranks in dramatic fashion by filing a court petition in Houston asking the court to order the final distribution of the Hughes estate. Dean was quoted in the newspapers as saying that Lummis had prolonged full distribution of the estate "beyond all reason." And he would give a lively populist twist to his actions by distributing T-shirts printed with the slogans TEN YEARS IS ENOUGH and FREE THE HUGHES HEIRS. His court application was formally filed on behalf of Avis McIntyre, then eighty-six years old, and he was joined in the action by Norton Bond, representing the estate of the deceased Rush Hughes. As far as Lummis and the estate were concerned, it was clear that Dean had resumed his old position outside the tent.

To be sure that Lummis grasped the point, Dean and Bond coauthored a remarkable letter to him in which they maintained that "you have no responsibility to invest and reinvest estate property in an effort to increase its values." This led on to the charge that "attempting to perpetuate your control over the estate's investments represents an affirmative breach of your duty as an administrator to distribute the estate without delay. . . . After ten years 'if and when' can no longer govern the administration of the Howard Hughes estate."

Their concluding thought was "We do not think you have administered the Howard Hughes estate with a correct view of what is required of an administrator. Ten years is long enough for the heirs to wait to receive what belongs to them. Rush Hughes died waiting for his inheritance. Avis Hughes McIntyre is in her 80s and in failing health. These facts make the prolonged delay in distribution tragic."

The level of chutzpah in this letter was quite enthralling. Dean knew far better than most that Lummis's investment and reinvestment tactics were the very things that provided the estate with its funds and that, had such tactics not been used, the heirs could have wound up with nothing. On the other hand, he did have a strong, simple point to make, that struck a chord with many of the silent heirs. There had to come a time when Lummis's creative endeavors on behalf of the collective interest had to stop and the heirs could know for certain what they, as individuals, would get.

Lummis responded to the crisis with some skill. He sent out copies of the Dean/Bond letter to all the heirs with a cover letter of his own that blended sympathy with censure. Lummis said that he could understand the frustration vented by Dean and Bond but that its public articulation could only be counterproductive and would inevitably undermine the strategy pursued by the estate.

He argued that a perception in the market place that the Hughes estate was under pressure to sell its assets in a limited time could work against them all. The success of its operation thus far depended to a very large degree on a public perception that no "fire sale" of Hughes assets could ever be counted upon. Any threat to this perception could, in Lummis's view, wreak havoc on the ultimate prospects of the heirs. Lummis made it clear that George Dean's resort to the media constituted such a threat.

The heirs, of course, had heard much of this before. But Lummis, under real pressure from Dean, concluded on an uncharacteristically populist note. The large rewards, he inferred, would not be long delayed, if they were patient. Together the heirs had carried the ball 95 yards down the field and were now very close to what he called "a winning touchdown." All the more reason, as he put it, not to fumble the ball at this late stage of the game.

On April 14, 1986, Lummis and Dean met in Houston to discuss their respective "winning touchdown" strategies. With the assistance of other estate attorneys, they would try to achieve a new accord. Lummis felt that Dean should know that the estate was very eager to dispose of the gambling casinos but did not want, for price reasons, to advertise the fact. And they still hadn't seen the last of the legal problems. The TWA litigation, a still-lingering consequence of Hughes's alleged mismanagement of the company back in the 1950s, was dragging interminably on, and it could still cost the estate $50 million to make it finally go away. They were very close, Lummis maintained, to a final distribution, but not close enough to abandon all discretion. No details of this occasion were released to the media, but Lummis would refer to it as the estate's "putting Humpty Dumpty back together again" meeting. Soon afterward Lummis and Dean were reported to be the "best of friends, yet again."

Dean's petition for an immediate winding up of the estate was allowed to lapse, mainly because there was no need for it. After the "Humpty Dumpty" accord, the disposition of the estate's assets went into a higher gear. When Lummis became Summa's boss, he had thirteen thousand employees on the payroll. This had gradually been reduced to a little under seven thousand by the summer of 1986. Within two more years it was down to two hundred.

Most of this reduction had been brought about by concluding the sales of the Desert Inn and the Sands and Frontier hotels in Las Vegas and of Harold's Club in Reno. In the end the total extracted from Hughes's casino operations came close to $500 million.

By 1989 the heirs had collectively received almost $400 million from the estate, and there was more to come. This consisted principally of share allocations in the real estate empire built up by Lummis and John Goolsby. Though there was some suggestion

that this should also be liquidated, the 1988 slump in property values convinced even the likes of George Dean that it was no time to
unload good real estate with good prospects. And in the case of
Nevada's Summerlin, with its phase plan to create a 200,000-
person community over twenty-five years, the prospects seemed
almost limitless. Valuations of the privately held Howard Hughes
Company, which controlled the heirs' property interests, would
run into the hundreds of millions. A conservative estimate of the
value of the "winning touchdown" to the heirs in money and
property shares would be $500 million and rising.

With his mission effectively at an end, Lummis retired in January
1990, having, in the words of the faithful Bill Miller, "turned a sow's
ear into a silk purse." Over subsequent years the heirs were able to
take advantage of an inheritance-tax reform that extended advantages to those leaving money to their grandchildren. Consequently,
the numbers of assigned interests in the estate swelled from 22 to
over 150. Regular checks, deriving from profits from the rents and
sales of Hughes's property, would arrive every three months.

It was an orderly flow of money to, for the most part, orderly
people. Of all the beneficiaries of the flow, only George Dean, the
late-running hotelier, restaurateur, and property developer, exhibited much flamboyance. And example was sadly cut short in 1992
by the fatal heart attack he had long been expecting. Of the heirs
only Agnes Roberts, the cancer sufferer who worked behind the
snack-bar counter of a Cleveland skating rink, did much to excite
the imagination. She eventually quit her day job and moved with
her husband to a pleasant spread in Arizona, finally achieving her
place in the sun.

What Howard Hughes, the weirdest, wackiest, and in some
ways the most spendthrift billionaire of them all, would have
thought of the careful husbandry of his money by his heirs would
probably have been much the same as what he would have
thought of a Hughes empire devoted exclusively to maximizing the
value of his long-neglected real estate. Not a lot, one imagines.
Nor can Hughes have been enamored with what happened to the
extraordinary airplane forever associated with his name.

20

THE PLANE THAT FLEW

"OH MY GOD," exclaimed the matronly lady tourist from Ohio. "I just can't believe it!"

Head tilted back, she gazed up at the largest plane ever built, the plywood monument to the genius, folly, and intransigency of the late Howard Hughes. It was 1983, and she had joined the throngs flocking to Long Beach, California, to marvel at one of the wonders of the times, nicknamed the *Spruce Goose,* a levity Hughes had detested. It had just emerged from thirty-six years of baffling concealment imposed by Hughes, and it was something to see.

Its tail was as high as an eight-story building. Its wingspan was longer than a football field and twice the distance of the Wright brothers' first flight. For the tourists' convenience there was a flight of stairs one could toil up and have one's photo taken alongside a life-sized dummy of Hughes, in his customary snap-brimmed fedora, seated at the plane's controls. A single ticket of a few dollars granted entry to the *Goose*'s giant hangar and the boarding of another attraction, the old British liner *Queen Mary,* permanently anchored alongside.

Hughes, who never catered to crowds, wouldn't have liked any of this. He had hidden away the giant plane back in 1947, when he had been keelhauled by an angry Senate committee for grossly overrunning his budget and failing to complete the plane until two years after World War II. "That big lumberyard will never fly" one critic had jeered. Hughes had responded by pledging to leave the U.S. and never return if he couldn't get the plane in the air.

On November 2, 1947, he had taken it out in the Long Beach harbor for some taxiing practice. On the third pass, he had suddenly strained against the heavy controls and taken the plane up seventy feet for a scant mile. The feat effectively ended the congressional investigation and caught the public's fancy, stirring the brief flowering of Hughes-for-president clubs.

Hughes had then hidden the *Goose* away in a windowless dry dock on nearby Terminal Island, just west of downtown Long Beach, and surrounded it with barbed wire, overlooked by a gun tower and patrolled by armed guards. There it remained until his death, while a tight-mouthed crew of a dozen or more mechanics worked away, week after week, year after year, doing who knew what. Like the myth-encrusted Hughes, the plane became encrusted with its own myths. A favorite one was that Hughes was replacing the plane's eight massive piston engines with huge new jets that could lift the two-hundred-ton plane higher than seventy feet for a distance greater than a mile. The plane remained in its pristine state and never flew again.

Because of wartime metal shortages, Hughes had been forced to build the plane with plywood sheets—mainly birch, not spruce—bonded together by a complex, arcane technique. The wood survived the passage of time like polished metal, without a warp or crack. The workmen, like guests in a Japanese home, had preserved the plane's cosmetics by removing their shoes and padding about in special socks.

Since he had to account to no one but himself, there was no record of how much money Hughes poured into the *Spruce Goose*. He had exhausted his defense grant of $18 million, intended for three giant planes, on only one and had then poured

$7.2 million of his own money into it. He had to lease the plane from the government, which had title to it, lease the Terminal Island dry dock from Long Beach, and pay the salaries of all the guards and workmen for all those years. He also had to pay a public relations expert to respond to all the questions about the project with "No comment."

There were three motives behind concealing the plane. One, which he confided to Noah Dietrich after his solitary flight, was that the controls were so heavy they were hardly manageable and that he would never fly the plane again. "It scared the hell out of me," he admitted.

Another was that he was humiliated by the fiasco and that if he turned the *Goose* back to the government, it would be stripped down and the plywood would be burned in a shameful public bonfire.

The third emerged the year before his death, in a harsh complaint from a usually admiring colleague, his longtime personal secretary, Nadine Henley. She told him that his attorneys thought he should donate the giant plane to the Smithsonian museum to give it "a dignified place in history" instead of continuing it as "a laughingstock" and a "plaything for a billionaire." She asked, "How can you possibly keep the interest and respect of your employees under such circumstances? How can we get them to watch the dollars for you when all these millions are being thrown away on something we will never live down in our lifetime? . . . We implore you for your sake and your name in history . . . to take the ghost out of the hangar and allow the Smithsonian to make a shrine forever."

The letter also disclosed that tax exemption for maintenance of the plane for seven years was "still open" with the IRS and might result in about "six million dollars which otherwise will be charged to you personally" plus "a possible forty-two million dollars" charged against his Hughes Tool Company.

The spacious Smithsonian did not have room for the giant plane but was willing to take a slice of one wing. Hughes preferred that the plane go to some organization that would build a museum that could house the whole plane, and it remained intact at Hughes's death.

Will Lummis had more pressing financial problems when he took over at Summa in 1976, and whatever Hughes had lavished on the *Spruce Goose* was already long gone. Washington had released title to the plane, and the city wanted to convert the Terminal Island dry dock into an oil-tanker facility. Having trailed red ink for almost half a century, the plane had no ready market and was sold to the Aero Club of Southern California for a dollar and wound up next to the *Queen Mary,* leased by the Walt Disney firm. It lasted there for nine years until Disney exercised an escape clause because of mounting losses.

Homeless again, the plane was auctioned off in 1992 and acquired by an aviation buff and industrialist, Del Smith, for a proposed aerial museum in McMinnville, Oregon, a small town near Portland. Smith had a collection of twenty-five classic old planes and contemplated a $40 million museum with the Hughes giant as centerpiece.

Just moving the plane out of Long Beach proved enormously difficult and expensive. It couldn't fly and was too large for any ocean tanker, so it had to be disassembled and moved in pieces. A sixty-foot window was cut in the hangar and removal of thirty-eight sections of the plane required six weeks. The 1,055-mile journey to McMinnville, by land and tugged barges, took another 138 days. All this cost Smith $4 million. The pieces of plane, shrink-wrapped with plastic for protection from the weather, were stored in a temporary structure with a plastic roof. The eight engines were housed by a builder in a nearby town.

Smith downsized the museum to a smaller one at one fourth the cost, with completion expected in 1996, four years after the fragmented plane was unloaded in McMinnville. The reduction in size ruled out reassembly of the huge craft, which would be displayed in sections. Construction of the museum had not begun as of 1996, but Smith insists it will be built despite serious setbacks in his international air cargo business. The Portland *Oregonian* reported that his Evergreen Aviation Company defaulted on $125 million of its bonds but avoided bankruptcy. The museum project has been transferred to a newly formed organization. It is non-profit.

The flying boat can only wait for what will happen next. It is accustomed to waiting. It missed action in World War II and was hidden from the busy fifties, sixties, and seventies. But it has one achievement that is not likely ever to be surpassed. It enjoyed the most memorable, publicized, and expensive one-minute flight in aviation history.

Hughes's great plane may yet rise again Phoenixlike in McMinnville, but the Hughes legend has now moved on to an even more ethereal realm of incongruity by way of a place called Bethesda.

21

BETHESDA

THE DOUBTS ABOUT the Howard Hughes Medical Institute were not interred with the bones of its founder. They lived on not only in the tax man's mind but also in the appreciation of the medical research community that it was, in theory at least, supposed to benefit. Two years after Hughes's death, the influential *New England Journal of Medicine* took HHMI to task for operating behind "a veil of secrecy that has engendered legends, criticism and misunderstanding throughout the academic medical establishment."

Under Chester Davis and Bill Gay, fitful efforts were made to retouch the institute's reputation, but the bitter controversy over their stewardship effectively preserved its old, shoddy image. The path-breaking Delaware court decisions of 1984 that ruled "the Davis Sentence" invalid and imposed a new board of trustees on HHMI were designed to change all that. Even so, the institute's more deep-rooted problems remained resolutely intact.

HHMI was still obliged to go cap in hand for its money to Hughes Aircraft, and the priorities of that giant corporation had not much changed since Hughes was alive—investment in advanced weaponry and space research first, medical research a long-distance second. The money had flowed less sluggishly since Hughes's death, but once the institute's running costs had been covered there was never much left over for a rainy day, and a veritable monsoon was on the way. The IRS, ever more exasperated about a record of tax evasion going back almost twenty years, began issuing back-tax demands that were, in the words of one of the new trustees, "capable of making your hair turn white." The new masters of the institute perceived that they were on course for the financial rocks.

There was also uncertainty about their capacity to chart a new course. While the new board exhibited an impressive range of achievement—from Irving Shapiro, onetime boss of du Pont, to Donald Fredrickson, a former director of the National Institutes for Health—it was hard to feel total confidence in the unity of purpose of a group that included Will Lummis and Bill Gay. They had split the Summa board asunder ten years earlier and had battled over the control of HHMI ever since. Now here they were, wounds barely healed, being asked to work constructively together. Surprisingly, this was what they did as they helped to evolve a remarkable rescue policy. The only sure way to save the Howard Hughes Medical Institute, the trustees collectively realized, was to expunge all traces of the influence of Howard Hughes himself.

The first symbolic indication of the Howard Hughes tradition being jettisoned was a change of headquarters, from Florida, which Hughes had always favored, to Bethesda, Maryland, in the heartland of the American medical research establishment. This was followed soon after by a sacrilegious act—Hughes Aircraft sold off to General Motors for $5.2 billion in June 1985. For the first time in its history, the institute had control of its own money, which it then proceeded to use in a most un-Hugheslike way, by suing for peace with the tax man. In March 1987 the IRS extracted $35 million in back taxes and a firm promise from the institute that it would direct $500 million to medical education over the next ten years; this was to be in addition to its research activities.

With this deal HHMI was at last free from the taint of its founder's policies.

Donald Fredrickson, the institute's director, publicly rejoiced in "the exorcism of hobgoblins from the institute's ghostly past." And once exorcised, the new HHMI focused on its own course.

By 1993, when the institute moved from Bethesda to even more exalted headquarters in Chevy Chase, just outside Washington, D.C., its activities were inspiring comparison with those of the Medici family in fifteenth-century Florence, the main difference being that the Medicis patronized great art while the Hughes Institute fostered excellence in science. The extent to which the academic community had come to accept the new HHMI could be measured by the fact that more than fifty Hughes laboratories now graced the country's leading universities and teaching hospitals. Its front-line investigators included five Nobel laureates and forty-one National Academy of Science members, all bent on unlocking the body's biochemical secrets. At the same time the institute was creating a new generation of emergent young research stars in genetics, immunology, cell and structural biology, and in specialized branches of neuroscience. All of this was achieved without in any way imperiling the institute's economic base. Quite the reverse. With the freedom to invest its own funds, the institute's assets climbed to $8 billion, making it the wealthiest philanthropy in the world, comfortably ahead of Ford ($7 billion) and the W. K. Kellogg Foundation ($5 billion).

Under the leadership of Dr. Purnell Choppin, an eminent virologist who succeeded Fredrickson as director, the institute also assumed a more general philanthropic character. Curators of many zoos, aquaria, and botanical gardens were both stunned and delighted to find their enterprises irrigated by Hughes funds. Multimillion-dollar grants for science education were made to leading historically black colleges, a benefaction that could not conceivably have occurred in the founder's lifetime. Hughes funds were also funneled into "hands-on science opportunities" for children on Indian reservations. Indeed, it was hard to detect any level of American science education that was not benefiting to some extent from HHMI's money. And beyond America there was the world.

By the mid-1990s Choppin was directing grant-in-aids to scientists in Mexico, Canada, New Zealand, Australia, and Britain. By 1996 a new offshoot, HHMI Moscow, based at the Shemyakin Institute of Bioorganic Chemistry, was helping with the supervision of Hughes research programs in Hungary, Poland, the Ukraine, Estonia, Belarus, Latvia, the Czech Republic, and Slovakia. The grants, directed to the support of scientists in their own institutions, were described by *Science* magazine as "a lifeline" for East European science. Meanwhile, HHMI was preparing to extend a similar "lifeline" in the direction of Latin America.

HHMI stands out as the most towering of all triumphs for The Money. It is also a monument to Hughes himself, a bizarre one perhaps for a man who variously humiliated his own medical advisers by ignoring them or turning them into drug suppliers who pursued his bizarre health rituals to a point that devastated and laid waste his own body, and who viewed medical research as a useful cover for fiddling his tax. But it is, nonetheless, a monument built to last.

WHETHER WHAT HAPPENED to Hughes's fortune after his death was in any way in accord with his living intentions is not easy to gauge. Certainly, most commentators since his death incline to the view that Hughes would have been bitterly disappointed by the evolution of a Hughes empire completely denuded of casinos and airplanes. No doubt he would have been delighted by the distinction achieved by the Medical Institute, but the form of it was not shaped by his actions or ideas. In the wake of the Delaware court decisions that helped in the transformation of HHMI from a tax dodge to a genuine philanthropy, the state's then attorney general, Charles M. Oberly III, expressed the view that "Howard Hughes, whatever he may have been, has left something of value to all American people. But I just don't think that was ever his intention." And there must be similar question marks over all the main beneficiaries. Were they people Hughes seriously wanted to enrich and reward?

We know, or think we know, that among the people Hughes held in least regard were doctors, relatives, and those who collected tax on behalf of the state and its citizens. We certainly know that these three groups of people got the lion's share of The Money, with lawyers coming a very close fourth. Hughes didn't like lawyers either, though he kept many in employment if only for the pleasure of giving them grief. The phenomenon of a man who leaves enormous wealth to those he doesn't much care for is so astounding that there lingers a feeling that somewhere, someplace, there could be a genuine Hughes will or perhaps the indecipherable ashes of one that once illustrated his clear and true intentions. But this may be falling into the trap of measuring Hughes by the yardstick of other men.

Unlike most of the very rich, Hughes was not attracted to money per se but to its inherent power. He was not given to personal ostentation even in his public years, and one of the extra expenses incurred at his burial was caused by the need to buy him a suit. He did not collect art, like the Mellons and the Gettys, or erect great mansions, like William Randolph Hearst. Hughes valued money because it enhanced his will and helped him to impose it on a stubbornly unruly world. And since what he treasured about money was the personal power it gave him, he may have found it intolerably hard to hand such power on to anyone else by executing a will. To Hughes it must have seemed like a surrender of himself.

The ultimate Hughes legacy may be the example he provides of self-driven, unpredictable personality in a full range of human circumstance, from supreme achievement and exaltation to degradation. He was a one-man show that is never likely to come around again. In life he entertained the world by being so extraordinarily different and by keeping all guessing as to what he was really about. By dying intestate, he ensured that this guessing game would continue.

And that, very likely, is the way he would have wanted it.

BIBLIOGRAPHY

BOOKS

Anderson, Jack, with James Boyd. *Confessions of a Muckraker: The Inside Story of Life in Washington During the Truman, Eisenhower, Kennedy and Johnson Years.* New York: Random House, 1979.

Barlett, Donald L., and James B. Steele. *Empire: The Life, Legend, and Madness of Howard Hughes.* New York: W. W. Norton, 1979.

Barton, Charles. *Howard Hughes and His Flying Boat.* Fallbrook, Calif.: Aero Publishers, 1982.

Bell, Jerry, with Gay Burk. *Howard Hughes: His Silence, Secrets and Success.* Utah: Hawkes, 1976.

Brown, Peter Harry, and Pat H. Broeske. *Howard Hughes: The Untold Story.* Boston: Little, Brown, 1996.

Burleson, Clyde W. *The Jennifer Project.* Englewood Cliffs, N.J.: Prentice Hall, 1977.

Burnham, Davis. *A Law Unto Itself: Power, Politics and the IRS.* New York: Random House, 1989.

Ceplair, Larry, and Steven Englund. *The Inquisition in Hollywood: Politics in the Film Industry, 1930–1980.* New York: Anchor Press, 1980.

Colby, William, and Peter Forbath. *Honorable Mention: My Life in the CIA.* New York: Simon & Schuster, 1978.

Dale, Peter. *Crime and Cover-Up: The CIA, the Mafia and the Dallas Watergate Connection.* Berkeley, Calif.: Westworks, 1977.

Davenport, Elaine, and Paul Eddy, with Mark Hurwitz. *The Hughes Papers.* New York: Ballantine Books, 1977.

Dean, John. *Blind Ambition: The White House Years.* New York: Simon & Schuster, 1976.

Dietrich, Noah, and Bob Thomas. *Howard: The Amazing Mr. Hughes.* Greenwich, Conn.: Fawcett, 1972.

Drosnin, Michael. *Citizen Hughes.* New York: Holt, Rinehart and Winston, 1985.

Fay, Stephen, with Lewis Chester and Magnus Linklater. *Hoax: The Inside Story of the Howard Hughes–Clifford Irving Affair.* New York: Viking, 1972.

French, Philip. *The Movie Moguls: An Informal History of the Hollywood Tycoons.* Chicago: Henry Regnery, 1971.

Finstad, Suzanne. *Heir Not Apparent.* Austin, Tex.: Texas Monthly Press, 1984.

Gardner, Ava. *Ava: My Story.* New York: Bantam, 1990.

Garrison, Omar. *Howard Hughes in Las Vegas.* New York: Lyle Stuart, 1970.

Genevoix, Sylvie, and Marianne Gosset. *H.R.H., ou Une Amérique.* Paris: Plon, 1972.

Gerber, Albert B. *Bashful Billionaire: The Story of Howard Hughes.* New York: Lyle Stuart, 1967.

Haldeman, H. R. *The Haldeman Diaries: Inside the Nixon White House.* New York: Putnam, 1994.

————, with Joseph DiMona. *The Ends of Power.* New York: Times Books, 1978.

Harris, Warren G. *Cary Grant: A Touch of Elegance.* New York: Doubleday, 1987.

Hecht, Ben. *A Child of the Century.* New York: New American Library, 1955.

Hepburn, Katharine. *Me: Stories of My Life.* New York: Knopf, 1992.

Higham, Charles. *Howard Hughes: The Secret Life.* New York: Putnam Berkeley, 1993.

Irving, Clifford, with Richard Suskind. *What Really Happened: His Untold Story of the Hughes Affair.* New York: Grove Press, 1972.

Jewell, Richard B., with Vernon Harbin. *The RKO Story.* New York: Arlington House, 1982.

Kaminsky, Stuart M. *The Howard Hughes Affair.* New York: St. Martin's, 1979.

Keats, John. *Howard Hughes.* New York: Random House, 1966.

Kistler, Ron. *I Caught Flies for Howard Hughes.* Chicago: Playboy Press, 1976.

Koppes, Clayton R. *JPL and the American Space Program: A History of the Jet Propulsion Laboratory.* New Haven: Yale University Press, 1982.

————, and Gregory D. Black. *Hollywood Goes to War: How Politics, Profits and Propaganda Shaped World War II Movies.* London: Collier Macmillan, 1987.

Lacey, Robert. *Little Man: Meyer Lansky and the Gangster Life.* Boston: Little, Brown, 1991.

Laytner, Ron. *Up Against Hughes: The Maheu Story.* New York: Quadrangle, 1972.

Leaming, Barbara. *If This Was Happiness: A Biography of Rita Hayworth.* New York: Viking, 1989.

————. *Bette Davis: A Biography.* New York: Simon & Schuster, 1992.

————. *Katharine Hepburn.* New York: Crown, 1995.

Liddy, G. Gordon. *Will: The Autobiography.* New York: St. Martin's, 1980.

Lukas, J. Anthony. *Nightmare: The Underside of the Nixon Years.* New York: Viking, 1976.

McClelland, Doug. *Susan Hayward: The Divine Bitch.* New York: Pinnacle, 1973.

McCrystal, Cal, with Lewis Chester, Stephen Aris, and William Shawcross. *Watergate: The Full Inside Story.* New York, Ballantine, 1973.

MacDonald, John J. *Howard Hughes and the Spruce Goose.* Blue Ridge Summit, Penn.: Tab Books, 1981.

Magruder, Jeb. *An American Life: One Man's Road to Watergate.* New York: Atheneum, 1974.

Maheu, Bob, and Richard Hack. *Next to Hughes: Behind the Power and Tragic Downfall of Howard Hughes.* New York: HarperCollins, 1992.

Mankiewicz, Frank. *Perfectly Clear: Nixon from Whittier to Watergate.* New York: Quadrangle, 1973.

————. *U.S. v. Richard M. Nixon: The Final Crisis.* New York: Quadrangle, 1975.

Marchetti, Victor, and John D. Marks. *The CIA and the Cult of Intelligence.* New York: Knopf, 1974.

Mary, Arthur. *The Nine Lives of Mickey Rooney.* New York: Stein and Day, 1990.

Mathison, Richard. *His Weird and Wanton Ways, The Secret Life of Howard Hughes.* New York: Morrow, 1977.

Moore, Terry. *The Beauty and the Billionaire.* New York: Pocket Books, 1984.

————, with Jerry Rivers, *The Passions of Howard Hughes.* Los Angeles: Los Angeles Publishing Group, 1996.

Norman, Barry. *The Story of Hollywood.* New York: New American Library, 1987.

Odekirk, Glenn E. *Spruce Goose: HK–1 Hercules: A Pictorial History of the Fantastic Hughes Flying Boat.* USA: Frank Alcanter, Inc., 1982.

O'Brien, Larry. *No Final Victories.* New York: Doubleday, 1974.

Parrish, James Robert, and Michael R. Pitts. *The Great Gangster Pictures.* Metuchen, N.J.: Scarecrow, 1976.

Parsons, Louella. *Tell It to Louella.* New York: Putnam, 1961.

Phelan, James. *Howard Hughes: The Hidden Years.* New York: Random House, 1976.

———. *Scandals, Scamps and Scoundrels: The Casebook of an Investigative Reporter.* New York: Random House, 1982.

Quirk, Lawrence J. *Fasten Your Seat Belts: The Passionate Life of Bette Davis.* New York: Signet, 1990.

Rhoden, Harold. *High Stakes: The Gamble for the Howard Hughes Will.* New York: Crown, 1980.

Rogers, Ginger. *Ginger: My Story.* New York: HarperCollins, 1991.

Rummel, Robert W. *Howard Hughes and TWA.* Washington: Smithsonian Institute Press, 1981.

Russell, Jane. *An Autobiography: My Path and Detours.* New York: Franklin Watts, 1985.

Sampson, Anthony. *Empires of the Sky: The Politics Contests and Cartels of World Airlines.* New York: Random House, 1984.

Schary, Dore. *Heyday: An Autobiography.* Boston: Little, Brown, 1979.

Solberg, Carl. *Conquest of the Skies: A History of Commercial Aviation in America.* Boston: Little, Brown, 1979.

Thomas, Tony. *Howard Hughes in Hollywood.* Secaucus, N.J.: Citadel Press, 1985.

Tinnin, David B. *Just About Everybody vs. Howard Hughes: The Inside Story of the Hughes-TWA Trial.* New York: Doubleday, 1973.

Varner, Roy, and Wayne Collier. *A Matter of Risk: The Incredible Inside Story of the CIA's Hughes Glomar Explorer Mission to Raise a Russian Submarine.* New York: Random House, 1978.

Wayne, Jane Ellen. *Ava's Men: The Private Life of Ava Gardner.* New York: St. Martin's, 1990.

NEWSPAPERS, MAGAZINES, AND PERIODICALS

For many years Howard Hughes was able to deploy his Secrecy Machine to defy the publishing industry and prevent books from being written about his life. Television was also never in a position to provide much in the way of insight. As this most potent medium was emerging, Hughes was in the process of disappearing and his most abiding televisual legacy is as a disembodied voice denouncing an "Autobiography" manufactured in his name but without his knowledge. As a result the burden of scrutinizing this least-accountable of men fell heavily on the working press. Not all of the reporting was of Pulitzer Prize standards in terms of accuracy, but a lot of it was diverting and entertaining. Among the publications we found most instructive and/or enjoyable while tracking The Money were:

Albuquerque Journal
American Medical News (Chicago)
Arizona Daily Wildcat
Aviation Week and Space Technology
Billboard
The Boston Globe
Boxoffice
BusinessWeek
Chicago *Daily News*
Chicago Sun-Times
Chicago Tribune
The Chronicle of Philanthropy
Cleveland *Plain Dealer*
Commerce Business Daily
The Commercial and Financial Chronicle
Dallas *Times Herald*
The Denver Post
The Des Moines Register
Detroit Free Press
The Detroit News
Esquire
Forbes
Fortune
The Hollywood Reporter
Honolulu Star-Bulletin
Houston Chronicle
The Houston Post
La Jolla University City Sentinel
Las Vegas Review-Journal
Las Vegas *Sun*
Little Rock Gazette
Long Beach *Press-Telegram*

Los Angeles Herald-Examiner
Los Angeles Times
The Miami Herald
The Montgomery Advertiser
The Nation
National Enquirer
The National Law Journal
The New Republic
New York *Daily News*
The New York Times
New York Post
Newsweek
North Las Vegas Valley-Times News
Orange County Register
The Philadelphia Inquirer
Psychology Today
The Quincy Patriot Ledger (Massachusetts)
Reno Gazette
The Sacramento Bee
St. Louis Post-Dispatch
The Salt Lake City Tribune
The San Diego Union
San Francisco Chronicle
San Francisco Examiner
Science
The Sun (Baltimore)
Time
The Times-Picayune (New Orleans)
The Wall Street Journal
The Washington Post
Whittier Daily News (California)
Waxahachie Daily Light (Texas)

INDEX

ABOUT THE AUTHORS

JAMES R. PHELAN has been described by *The New York Times*'s Pulitzer Prize–winner Wallace Turner as "one of the best investigative reporters of his generation." Mr. Phelan's track record for the big story is a long one. Former governor Edmund (Pat) Brown credits his re-election in 1962, when he defeated Richard Nixon, to Phelan's article in *The Reporter* magazine on the Hughes-Nixon loan. Reporting for the *Saturday Evening Post,* Phelan was the first journalist to show that former district attorney James Garrison had no case against Clay Shaw when Garrison accused Shaw of conspiring to kill President Kennedy.

For over twenty years, James R. Phelan has been following the career of Howard Hughes and has written about him in numerous publications, including the *Saturday Evening Post, Paris Match, Playboy,* and *The New York Times*. His previous books include *Howard Hughes: The Hidden Years* and *Scandals, Scamps and Scoundrels*. He lives in Temacula, California.

LEWIS CHESTER was born in the East End of London and graduated from Oxford University with a first-class honors degree in history before studying American politics at Harvard as an associate Nieman Fellow. He learned his trade on *The Sunday Times* (London) where he was chief reporter, feature writer, and editor of the paper's celebrated investigative team, Insight. He has co-authored many books on current-affairs topics, among them *An American Melodrama: The Presidential Campaign of 1968* and *Watergate: The Full Inside Story*. He is the author of *Hoax,* about the fake Howard Hughes autobiography. He now works freelance and lives in North London.

ABOUT THE TYPE

This book was set in Sabon, a typeface designed by the well-known German typographer Jan Tschichold (1902–74). Sabon's design is based on the original letterforms of Claude Garamond and was created specifically to be used for three sources: foundry type for hand composition, Linotype, and Monotype. Tschichold named his typeface for the famous Frankfurt typefounder Jacques Sabon, who died in 1580.